JEWISH POLEMICS

JEWISH POLEMICS

Arthur Hertzberg

Columbia University Press
New York

Columbia University Press
New York   Oxford
Copyright © 1992 Arthur Hertzberg
All rights reserved

Library of Congress Cataloging-in-Publication Data
Hertzberg, Arthur
   Jewish polemics / Arthur Hertzberg.
      p.   cm.
   Includes bibliographical references.
   ISBN 0-231-07842-0 (alk. paper)
   1. Jews—Politics and government—1948– 2. Israel—Politics and
government. 3. Zionism 4. Jews—United States. 5. United States—
Ethnic relations.   I. Title
DS143.H37   1992
956.9405—dc20   91-46615
                                                        CIP

Casebound editions of
Columbia University Press books are
Smyth-sewn and printed on permanent
and durable acid-free paper.

Book design by Teresa Bonner
Printed in the United States of America
c 10 9 8 7 6 5 4 3 2 1

For
Robert Silvers and Barbara Epstein
with affection and admiration

CONTENTS

PREFACE: A BIT OF AUTOBIOGRAPHY

ACKNOWLEDGMENTS

I.
In Debate with Menachem Begin

1. An Open Letter to Menachem Begin   5
2. The View from Cairo   9
3. Begin and the Jews   15
4. Begin Must Go   24

II.
In Debate with Israel

5. The Tragedy of Victory   29
6. The Uprising   43
7. An Open Letter to Elie Wiesel   52

III.
In Defense of Political Zionism

8. In Debate with the Arabs, and Their Friends: "Zionism Is Racism"—
A Counterattack   63
9. In Debate with Jewish and Palestinian Extremists   70
10. Zionism Revisited   82

IV.
In Defense of Cultural Zionism

11. Ahad Ha'am, 100 Years Later   86
12. In Debate About the Diaspora: Gershom Scholem as Zionist
and Believer   96

V.
Contemplating America, Without Illusions

13. Why Did the East European Jews Come to America?   114
14. The Graying of American Jewry   120
15. "The Triumph of the Jews": A Critique of Charles
Silberman's Optimism   136
16. Sharing Culture: Learning to Talk Together as Jews   149

VI.
In Debate with American Jews

17. In Support of Affirmative Action   162
18. Reagan and the Jews   164
19. The Illusion of Jewish Unity   175

VII.
In Debate with Christianity and Christians

20. Synagogue and Church in the Age of Revolution   189
21. Disagreeing with Friendly Catholics   198
22. John Paul II's Theology of Judaism   201
23. The Case for Untidiness: Another View of Church and State   204

VIII.
The Jewishness of Modern Jews

24. The Return of Maimonides   212
25. The Emancipation: A Reassessment After Two Centuries   226

IX.
The Holocaust: In Debate with Man and God

26. Who Looked Away?   236
27. A Lifelong Quarrel with God   241

X.
Concluding Reflections

ENDNOTES   257

PREFACE:
A BIT OF AUTOBIOGRAPHY

In recent years I have wanted, several times, to write down a connected account of my views on the range of problems which concern American Jews, in relationship to themselves, to other Americans, and to Israel. When I turned to this task in the spring of 1990, I began by rereading the many essays I had written in the last decade on the vexed questions Jews were facing. As I read, it became apparent that I could best explain myself if I preserved the verve and passion of the original polemics. I decided to attempt a coherent statement of views in the rhetoric in which they were first expressed. The result of that decision is this book.

The essays chosen for inclusion are arranged by topic. Repetitions are removed, and some of the essays are shortened, but no judgment or assertion has been changed. On all the important issues, the views I first expressed in these essays are those I still hold.

I remain in opposition to many of the policies of the dominant elements of the American Jewish establishment. National and local Jewish organizations are zealous in protecting the Jewish interest, but their leaders, almost without exception, operate with little knowledge of the complex history of the Jewish people, and of the classic texts in which its moral responsibilities were defined. For many American Jews, Jewish history begins with the immigration of their immediate ancestors to America; Jewish suffering is experienced by remembering the murder of six million Jews by the Nazis; and the central religious and moral fact for Jews is the state of Israel. I share all these emotions. I am myself an immigrant, having arrived in this country as a Yiddish-speaking child of five in 1926; all my mother's family—her father, her siblings, and all their children—were murdered by the Nazis; I helped in the battle to create the state of Israel in the 1940s, and I have been involved in its concerns ever since. Nonetheless, I think differently from most of my contemporaries who make official Jewish policy and provide the accepted mass rhetoric. This book is a record of what I think, but why do I think these thoughts?

Two easy, and false, explanations of my views have been given by my critics: my opinions may be theoretically correct, but such judgments can be made only by someone who lives in a bookish ivory tower; the views in these essays are those of a woolly-headed liberal who—the refrain continues—does not know the "real" world. The first argument is simply not true to fact. Forty years as a congregational rabbi could not possibly leave one in ignorance of the pragmatic concerns of American Jews. In national and international Jewish life, I served six years as the national president of the American Jewish Congress, ten years on the executive boards of the Jewish Agency and the World Zionist Organization, and fifteen years as vice president of the World Jewish Congress. This is hardly the biography of someone who knows less about the political realities of world Jewry than any of the elected heads or appointed functionaries, past or present, of the Jewish establishment.

As for the currently dread word *liberalism*, the reader of these essays will soon discover that such an oversimplified label does not accurately describe what I think, and never has. To be sure, along with a large majority of American Jews, I remain concerned for the hungry and homeless. I continue to reject the entire notion that it is the duty for the government to bail out failing large capitalist enterprises, but a horrifying descent into socialism to help poor, failing individuals. My basic moral principle is biblical: Thou shalt not stand ignoring the blood of thy brother. Jews are commanded to treat others fairly, *especially* when it is inconvenient. Indeed, my assessment of the "Jewish interest," in matters both domestic and foreign, is that powerlessness is a curse, but power unrestrained by moral imperatives is an even greater curse. The Jews are a small people; they can survive in the world only when might—their own and others—is governed by the teaching that Hillel defined nearly two thousand years ago: "What is hateful to you, do not do to your fellow man."

It is clear to me that I think these thoughts because I was brought up in a rabbi's house. The Jewish experiences that shaped me were not ethnic memories and angers. I studied Talmud for many years under my father's guidance. I watched him and my mother feed the hungry, without any distinction, even when they themselves had little. I hope that these essays represent some echo of what they taught me.

With thanks

Writing a book is essentially a lonely occupation, but the task cannot be finished without the help of others. Most of the essays were written when I served as a member of the Department of Religion at Dartmouth College. I am deeply grateful to my colleagues for their many kindnesses. Ronald M. Green was chairman of the department when I was invited to Dartmouth in 1984. He has made a profound difference in my life.

Dean James Wright and his associate deans were most generous with help in covering the costs of preparing the manuscript for press. On the technical side my students, Meredith Katz and Joshua Wesoky, worked hard at all the tasks that are usually given to student assistants.

I am particularly grateful to friends and associates at Columbia University Press, a second home for many years. Kate Wittenberg and John D. Moore have been after me, jointly and separately, to do this book. Anne McCoy, Joan McQuary, and Roy Thomas were extraordinarily helpful in amending editorial slips and in the final organization of the text. I am delighted with the design provided by Teresa Bonner.

Obviously, all of the errors that remain are to be charged to my account.

Arthur Hertzberg

ACKNOWLEDGMENTS

I am grateful to the editors and publishers of the following publications for allowing me to use material appearing here in somewhat different form from my earlier writings.

Associated University Presses (London), "The Graying of American Jewry," in *Survey of Jewish Affairs*, 1983. *Christian-Jewish Relations, "Nostra Aetate:* Twenty Years On," September 1985. *Christian Science Monitor*, "An American Jewish Leader's Letter to Begin," June 29, 1979 (translation of Op-Ed article first published in *Ha'aretz*, June 17, 1979). *Commonweal*, "Another View of Church and State," November 30, 1984. Seymour Maxwell Finger, ed., "American Jewry During the Holocaust," 1984. Mimeo. Jewish Theological Seminary, "Why Did the East European Jews Come to America?" lecture presented at the Samuel Friedman Lectures. Johns Hopkins University Press (Baltimore), *Modern Judaism:* "The Emancipation: A Reassessment After Two Centuries," May 1981; "Gershom Scholem as Zionist and Believer," February 1985 (translation of article first published in *Ha'aretz*, May 6, 1982).

New York Review of Books: "The View from Cairo," July 26, 1980; "Begin and the Jews," February 18, 1982; "Reagan and the Jews," January 31, 1985; "The Triumph of the Jews," November 21,

1985; "The Return of Maimonides," September 25, 1986; "Israel: The Tragedy of Victory," May 28, 1987; "The Uprising," February 4, 1988; "The Illusion of Jewish Unity," June 16, 1988; "An Open Letter to Elie Wiesel," August 8, 1988; "The Impasse Over Israel," October 25, 1990. *New York Times*, "Begin Must Go," September 26, 1982. *New York Times Book Review:* "A Lifelong Quarrel with God," May 6, 1990; "Ahad Ha'am 100 Years Later," March 31, 1991.

Present Tense: "Merit, Affirmative Action, Blacks, and the Jews," Winter 1980; "Doing Unto Others," 17(1):14–15; "Zionism Revisited," March/April 1990. Westview Press (Boulder, Colo.), "Zionism as Racism: A Semantic Analysis," in Michael Curtis, ed., *Anti-Semitism in the Contemporary World*, 1986.

JEWISH POLEMICS

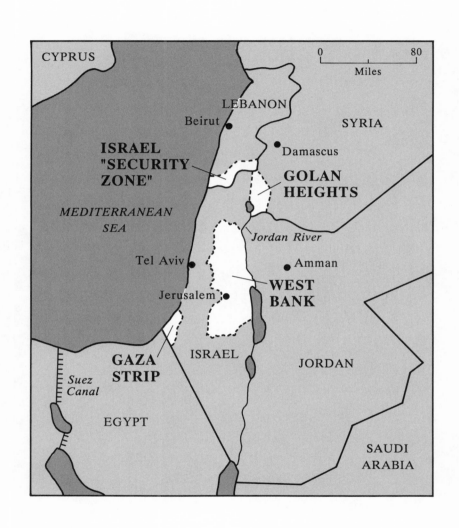

ONE

In Debate
with Menachem Begin

Israel's overwhelming victory in the war with all its Arab neighbors in June 1967 transformed the country, and the entire Jewish world. The Jewish state was now in control of all the land between the Mediterranean and the Jordan River, of the Golan Heights in the North, and of the entire Sinai Peninsula. The victorious Israeli government announced that it wanted to return all the captured territories, except for East Jerusalem, in return for an end to the Jewish-Arab conflict. The Arab League, meeting in Khartoum in November 1967, totally rejected any negotiation with the Israelis; it continued to regard the very existence of the Jewish state as illegitimate. Israel would, therefore, control the conquered territories indefinitely, but what would it do with them?

Opinions soon began to divide into two main camps. The "doves" believed that Israel should make as few changes as possible, holding the territories as bargaining chips in future peace negotiations. This school of thought knew that, whatever the shape of an eventual peace, Israel would require security arrangements. Some of the "doves" maintained that Israel would need up to 40 percent of the territory of the West Bank as buffer. Others thought that warning stations on the Jordan River and on the ridges would be enough. The "doves" have continued to disagree about the nature of security needs, but they all use the formula of "territories for peace." There is also no agreement as to what kind of Palestinian political structure the Israeli "peace camp" would prefer.

The other body of opinion, the "nationalists," saw the results of Israel's victory in the Six Day War of June 1967 as an unparalled historic opportunity: the Jewish state could now establish its rule over all the land of the ancestors. This view was inaccurate, however, because the actual biblical boundaries had extended into much of what is now Jordan and had ended at Beersheba—but the lack of historical precision did not matter. It was thrilling, after June 1967, to be able to drive to Hebron and visit the graves of the biblical patriarchs and matriarchs in the Cave of the Machpelah. This shrine had been closed to Jews for many centuries; it was now guarded by Israeli soldiers. Even "doves" could not imagine returning this holy place to its former status, of no access for Jews. The "nationalists" were soon insisting that Jews had a right not only to visit the shrine but to live in the city of Hebron, from which Jews had fled after a murderous pogrom in 1929.

The fundamental premise of the "nationalists" was that Israel had the duty and the right to retain the West Bank and Gaza as part of its historic heritage and that the Palestinians who lived in those territories would have to come to terms with Jewish sovereignty. Immediately after the victory, some secular nationalists formed an organization to retain the "Complete Land of Israel." Elements within the religious community proclaimed the victory to be a sure sign of messianic times, and after the war in October 1973 they formed "the Bloc of the Faithful" to help carry out the divine imperatives of the approaching millennium by establishing Jewish settlements in the West Bank, the biblical Judea and Samaria. To be sure, the Israeli government itself had established a string of paramilitary settlements in the Jordan Valley and on the crest of the hills in the middle of the West Bank, but these strongholds were defined as security measures, and they were placed as inconspicuously as possible. The "nationalists," and especially the religious among them, began to defy the government by moving into centers of Arab population. After some attempts in the mid-1970s to stop such actions, these "illegal" settlers were allowed to stay.

The battle over the future of the West Bank and Gaza was thus joined very early. In Israel and, even more, in the American Jewish community, the public debate revolved around the issue of security. It was morally comfortable to assert that a state is not required to commit suicide by giving back military positions from which its enemies could launch destructive attacks. The question whether any military or territorial advantages could really safeguard Israel, if it remained at war with the Arab world, could be finessed by being labeled woolly-headed. Moving the discussion of the West Bank and Gaza to the realm of security had another effect. It made it possible to avoid the ideological issue that was really at stake. Is the Jewish people commanded, by God and history, to pay any price to possess the entire land? Or, on the contrary, do Arabs have equal standing, with which Jews must seek compromise and accommodation?

In the United States these issues were raised around 1970 by a handful of younger people, who banded together in an organization called *Breira* (Choice), but their views were anathema to the mainstream of the organized Jewish community. The major exceptions within the establishment were Nahum Goldmann, who was then president of the World Jewish Congress, and Israel's first prime minister, David Ben-Gurion, in self-chosen semiexile in Sdeh Boker, in the southern desert. I shared their conviction that the Palestinians should not, and could not, be relegated to inferior status, or pushed out of the land. In 1971, when I was a member of the Zionist international executive board, I wrote an article for *Columbia Forum*, the quarterly of Columbia University, in which I argued the case for the creation of a Palestinian state in the West Bank and Gaza. Surveying the history of the conflict, I wrote:

> What we have been discussing is, in reality, a conflict between two nationalisms, Jewish Israeli and Palestinian Arab, each of which has a hinterland of supporters outside the immediate territory. . . . Despite all the changing circumstances, we are still back at first principles, which were already clear by the 1930s. The Jews and Arabs who feel

keenly about Palestine will ultimately, it is to be hoped, learn to live together with open borders, customs unions, and even political federation, but only after a long period of separation through partition.

When this essay was published, Golda Meir was already prime minister of Israel. Somehow my essay came to her notice. She let it be known that she ruled out a Palestinian state under any circumstances, and that she expected Jewish leaders abroad to agree in public with the position of the prime minister of Israel or, at least, to be quiet. Effectively, therefore, dissenting opinions in Israel were to be denied support in the world Jewish community.

This debate became more intense in the spring of 1977 when the Likud party, led by Menachem Begin, came to power. In July, not long after assuming office, the new prime minister was on his way to Washington. I saw him in Jerusalem before he left, and I conveyed a message to him from Jimmy Carter's White House: the American administration was deeply interested in helping to make peace between Israel and the Arabs. It was open to all suggestions from Israel about its security needs, but the White House was not hospitable to religious or ideological doctrines which entitled Jews—and never mind Arab sensibilities—to the "undivided land of Israel." Though we were old friends, Begin heard me out with increasing irritation. He replied that he was, of course, concerned about Israel's security, taking an expansive view of what that required, but Menachem Begin regarded it as his duty to educate all concerned (who had been badly taught for many years by his foes in the Labor party) in the true meaning of Zionism: it is a movement to create a Jewish state in all the ancestral land of the Jewish people.

In America, most of the Jewish establishment preferred to believe that Menachem Begin did not mean what he said, but I believed him—and I therefore went into public opposition. In a series of interviews and articles with the Israeli press during those weeks, I predicted that this maximalist nationalism would quickly lead to morally unacceptable actions, and that it would eventually bring political confrontation with Israel's main supporters in the West. I was soon counterattacked, on the well-known ground that Jews in the Diaspora had a duty to support the incumbent prime minister.

That argument really did not work very well for Menachem Begin. He had himself long been in opposition, and he even had begun to suggest in the mid-1970s, when he had little hope of winning office, that an advisory council be created of Jewish notables from the Diaspora to act as a brake on the unwise policies of Israel's socialist governments. Menachem Begin, who had thus suggested a "House of Lords" from abroad, could hardly demand complete obedience in the Diaspora now that he had become prime minister. This logic seemed incontrovertible to me, but it was ignored. The supporters of the Likud in Israel wanted to silence their opponents, at home and abroad, in any way that they could. The Jewish establishment in America wanted to avoid the issues. The Jewish press, which the establishment owned or controlled, was almost totally closed to any challenge to the official line that emanated from Jerusalem.

1. *An Open Letter to Menachem Begin*

During the first two years of the Begin regime, I was still sensitive to the argument that public criticism of Israeli policy would weaken it, especially in the United States. As the months passed, I realized that this silence was effectively depriving the internal Israeli opposition of support abroad. In an essay in 1978 I expressed outrage at a statement by Meir Rosenne, who was then Israel's ambassador in Paris, in which he had, according to press reports, termed a visiting delegation from Peace Now to be "traitors." I wrote:

> The raucous political processes of Israel's democracy and the debates within world Jewry should not be stilled in order to make the work of ambassadors easier. In the long run, the glory of an ambassador of Israel in Paris, London, or Washington is that he represents a state, supported by a Diaspora, within which the Jewish people argue and care in a democratic way. With such moral authority, ambassadors might find their tasks easier and not harder. . . . The ambassadors who are so worried about dissent might then discover that the cause of Israel will be more broadly based again among

people who do not necessarily equate their permanent and inalienable love for Israel with the immediate policies that the embassies, staffed by responsible civil servants, must defend each day.

Those lines were first published in Hebrew in the Israeli newspaper *Ha'aretz* and in an out-of-the-way journal in English, but I was nearing the public breaking point. It came the next year.

The Begin government had been encouraging settlements in the West Bank, but these were being placed on empty land to which the government asserted title. For the first time, in 1979, land was expropriated from its Arab owners for a new settlement, under the cover of "security." This was clearly a pretense, unless you accepted the Likud ideology that the West Bank needed to be possessed so that Israel might feel itself secure in all its ancestral homeland. I published an open letter to Menachem Begin in *Ha'aretz*; it soon appeared, with my consent, in several American publications.

▼

Dear Mr. Prime Minister,

The government which you lead has just expropriated privately owned land near Nablus to create a new Jewish settlement. Such an expropriation does not represent the overwhelming bulk of Zionist teaching. From its beginning more than a century ago, the Zionist movement has overpaid for land in order to acquire it with the assent of its owners.

The conscience of Israel and of the world Jewry, including your own in the early days of your service as Prime Minister, is not yet at peace with Biram and Ikrit, two Arab villages that were expropriated in 1948 for "temporary security reasons." You yourself have looked for ways of solving that problem by at least some partial return. You grieve over the pain of Arabs who were unfairly displaced in Northern Israel at a time of war; how can you now preside over such action near Nablus, while peace is being negotiated?

I know that you are aware of these feelings which I am voicing, and that you have already created the rhetoric to contain and silence them. What has been coming from you and your entourage in recent days can be summarized as follows: This new settlement is necessary for security and it is therefore not the business of people who do not know about such things, and especially of those who do not have to fight in the wars of Israel, to be critical. Second, there are many Jews who yearn to live in Judea and Samaria; it is unacceptable to surrender to Arab racism and agree that these territories shall be permanently free of Jews. Third, Judea and Samaria are an inalienable part of the biblical Israel, and Jews are therefore commanded to dwell there, trusting that God will protect and bless their efforts.

These arguments have been advanced publicly. What has been hovering over the discussion, privately, are two other motifs. One is a kind of circular argument about American Jews. We are told that criticism is dangerous because it weakens the pro-Israel forces; then we are told that, behold, the American Jewish leadership which has thus been silenced is united in total support of the Begin policy. There is also an allegation that criticism of the most provocative elements of Israeli government policy on the West Bank represents not true inner Jewish feeling but fear of or pandering to the administration in Washington.

These arguments are formidable, but I can neither accept them nor bow to them. To begin at the end of this list of fears, I cannot imagine that anyone in American Jewry is at this moment frightened of the Carter administration. You have reason to know, Mr. Prime Minister, that I am not alone among the critics of your policy on the West Bank who have fought against the Carter administration and all its predecessors on many occasions on behalf of Israel.

It is a delusion to imagine that American Jews are united behind your government's policies on the West Bank. They are at least as divided as are the Jews of Israel. Where indeed are the thousands who are clamoring supposedly to settle in Judea and Samaria? There is a comparative handful there, and many are known to have residences elsewhere in Israel. Are there no open spaces in the Galilee, where the Jewish majority is known to be fading, which require more settlers? If there are Jews who are indeed driven by the passion for Judea and Samaria, is there no vacant land anywhere except near Nablus? Does God really enjoin this enterprise? The rabbis of Agudat Israel's Council of Sages and the members of the Oz Ve-Shalom are

God-fearing Jews. They insist that God prefers peace and condemns provocative acts.

The really telling arguments are here, as always, the claim of security and the insistence that criticism by Jews lends comfort to our enemies.

I do not accept either argument. The security of Israel is of course—it has been said over and over again—something that is a matter of Israel to determine for itself. Yes, but which Israel? The Defense Minister (who would not endorse the creation of Elon Moreh), the defense experts of the previous government (who opposed it), or an incumbent Prime Minister who knows very well from personal experience that political and military considerations are interwoven and indivisible? I have not met anyone in recent days in the Jewish community, either Israeli or American, who believes that this new settlement exists out of primarily security considerations. Even those who are for it know that it is a political and ideological act.

Is dissent from the government position losing friends for Israel? I deny this. Indeed I insist that the contrary is true. The support for Israel in the United States, the deep love in which it is held in wide circles of American opinion, requires that the entrance fee to loving Israel be not necessarily assent to the policies of the settlers on the West Bank who belong to Gush Emunim ("the bloc of the faithful"). There is a liberal America that loves Israel precisely because it represents moral ideals and democratic living.

As a political leader, Mr. Prime Minister, you have complex problems in the management of a coalition which is divided internally and which leads an ideologically divided country. Perhaps Elon Moreh was an immediate tactical necessity for you on the way to the greater good of real peace by consent of all parties in Judea, Samaria, and Gaza. If so, my heart goes out to you for the difficulties of this moment.

Of course I continue to support you, like all Jews, as the leader of Israel. I shall continue to mount every barricade for the security of Zion. I will also continue to speak out against the excesses of right-wing ideology. It is today a necessary part even of that support that you be told that there are totally committed Jews, outside of Israel as well as within it, who disagree with the expropriation of Arab land. I hope and pray that Elon Moreh is an end and not a beginning. If it is a beginning, I have no choice but to say: this is not the way; "Zion shall be redeemed with justice."

1979

2. *The View from Cairo*

In 1980 I was invited by the then Egyptian ambassador in Washington, Ashraf Ghorbal, to give some lectures in Cairo at the government training school for foreign service officers. Peace had been made between Egypt and Israel in 1979, as a result of the Carter–Begin–Sadat negotiations at Camp David. Ghorbal wanted the younger professionals in Egypt's foreign service to understand both Israel and the world Jewish community better. The American embassy, over which two old friends, Roy and Betty Atherton, presided, was very hospitable. In a short visit I met many political leaders and opinion makers. The dominant view was that the peace between Egypt and Israel was the preamble to a warm, flourishing relationship between the two peoples and that, in the next stage, it would lead in a few years to a solution of the Palestinian question. I denied both propositions. The essay that I wrote was first submitted to a prominent journal of general circulation with strong links to the Begin government and to the American Jewish establishment. The essay was given a "pocket veto." It was never quite the right time to print it. I soon caught on that this journal had no intention of printing inconvenient truths, and so I took the text to an old acquaintance, Robert Silvers of the *New York Review of Books*. He accepted it immediately and printed it in the next issue. Thus there began a close and warm association with him and his coeditor, Barbara Epstein. The *New York Review of Books* became the home for many of my essays, some of which appear in this volume.

▼

After a visit of a few days in Cairo to talk with dozens of people about the possibilities of peace, I came away with answers that seemed surprisingly clear. Sadat wants peace; the intelligentsia does not want normal relations with Israel; and the ordinary people do not want war. So I was told. And whether they are accurate or not, these opinions appeared to be solidly rooted in the self-interest of those who are said to hold them.

Sadat is the most enigmatic of the three forces. It is possible and perhaps even probable that when he set events in motion by attacking Israel in 1973 and by inviting himself to Jerusalem in 1977, he had no clear conception of what the consequences for the Middle East would be. What is clear is that in both war and peace he was, and is, playing, above all, to what he thinks of as an American audience, the one that for him counts the most by far.

The large numbers of poor Egyptians have no spokesperson, no Gallup poll to record their views. What was striking was that every politician or journalist I talked to, including the young intellectuals who back the PLO, claimed that Egyptian young people would not want to fight again. One hundred thousand casualties in the various wars with Israel are enough. Moreover, the widening of the Suez Canal is now going forward and the cities on its banks are being rebuilt. A nation planning to make war would not be likely to block its route of attack in this way.

This does not mean that war is impossible. Some new pharaoh may arise who rejects Camp David. He may have missiles that can fly over the Canal and the entire Sinai Peninsula from deep within Egypt. Nevertheless, for the next decade, a long time in the Middle East, there seems very little possibility of an Israeli-Egyptian war.

This peace between Israel and Egypt does not, however, bring with it "normalization" either now or in the near future. The intellectual and professional classes seem overwhelmingly opposed to the exchange of ambassadors that has taken place and to carrying on regular trade and diplomatic relations, or collaborating on development projects. Aside from their sympathies for the Palestinian cause, they have other reasons for doing so. The wages of professors are low in Egypt; a teacher often makes ends meet by lecturing in Kuwait or elsewhere in the oil sheikdoms for very large fees. Technicians and researchers of all kinds need their jobs as consultants and temporary workers in the Arab world if they are to keep up their standard of living at home. Egypt's largest single source of foreign currency derives from the remittances of some two billion dollars a year sent back to the families of the quarter of a million Egyptians employed in other Arab countries. This "diaspora" is as large as, or larger than, that of the Palestinian technicians with which it competes for places throughout the Middle East. To interrupt these relations, even to cause a temporary tremor within them, would be disastrous not only to those who count on work abroad, but to the Egyptian state.

A few meetings between Israeli and Egyptian academics have taken place "under the table," but any Egyptian scholar who meets openly with Israelis has destroyed his bridges to the rest of the Arab world. In mid-April, a chair of Israeli-Egyptian studies was dedicated at Tel Aviv University, and an international colloquium was held there in honor of the occasion. Of fifteen Egyptians invited, two came. One was the cultural attaché of the Egyptian embassy in Israel, and the other was a famous retired scholar, aged eighty, who lives mostly in Paris.

Having been invited as vice president of the World Jewish Congress and as a historian, I was asked to give two lectures in Cairo, one to a group of middle-level diplomats, the other to university people interested in historical studies. No one made any secret of the fact that Israel and Egypt could not by themselves work out normal relations. That depended on the Palestinians, whose stamp of approval was required before full and open relations between Arabs and Israelis could begin to take place.

In the dealings of the Egyptian intelligentsia with the rest of the Arab world, matters of pride and self-confidence count for much. Cairo regards itself as the intellectual and academic center of the Arab world. Partly in order to maintain their claims to that leadership, the Cairo intellectuals, as some of them told me, feel they must show very openly their opposition to Sadat. They make the same arguments against him that can be heard in the rest of the Arab world—that the Camp David accord has not helped the Palestinians, and should be junked, and that pressure for an independent Palestinian state should now be the main task of Arabs everywhere. Whether they are university teachers or broadcasters or economists, the Cairo intellectuals and bureaucrats I talked to seemed to be waiting with some impatience for one of two things to happen—for Sadat either to succeed in the negotiations, by unexpectedly getting agreement to Palestinian self-determination, or to fail completely with the Israelis and thus free Egypt to pursue a new and tougher policy.

I had no trouble finding outspoken opponents of Sadat, even at official diplomatic parties. But my impression is that hardly a blade of grass falls among the bureaucrats and intellectuals in Cairo—even those who appear disaffected—that Sadat is not aware of and not able to fit in with his plans. Perhaps the leeway that Sadat is now giving to his various critics and opponents is more than "a safety valve for discontent," as it was described to me. He may also be orchestrating this very unhappiness as part of a campaign to bring pressure on Israel and especially on the Americans.

What lends support to these reflections is the argument currently being made by Egyptian diplomats in Washington, Cairo, and Tel Aviv: that if Israel does not concede more, then Sadat will be further weakened; that he will be in imminent danger of falling, thus removing from the Egyptian scene, and the Middle East, the one steady force for peace. The policies that would follow would be all the more hostile to Israel since the Egyptian intelligentsia and the technocrats who are so opposed to Camp David would have more of a voice.

If it is true that the Egyptian-Israeli peace depends wholly on Sadat's survival, then the Israelis would be right to regard the so-called Camp David process with sharp suspicion. But if you press the Egyptians, they will admit that peace—that is, a state of nonwar between Egypt and Israel—does not depend on Sadat's survival, that the basic contract between Egypt and Israel to end the fighting has been made. What is not secure, and indeed, has not even begun, is normal relations, which Sadat alone cannot deliver, and which the Israeli government, in view of its current policies, cannot possibly expect.

At Camp David, both Sadat and Begin must have known that whether normal relations between their countries could be worked out would partly depend on the Palestinian question. The differences in their respective interpretations of the Camp David agreement showed that it meant very different things to each of them. Were they simply fooling each other? Or, what seems to me more likely, did they badly misconceive each other's intentions?

Some of the officials I met in Cairo had their own explanation of Begin's behavior, one that seemed to me convincing. In their view Begin went to Camp David determined to be the magnanimous gentleman. The Sinai, including the settlements, the oil fields, and the road to Sharm-el-Sheikh—all this was hard for him to give up, but his ideological mentor Vladimir Jabotinsky had never laid claim to the Sinai as part of the land of Israel. What could be more gallant than to give up the Sinai in one grand gesture, thus accommodating to Sadat's demands, on the assumption that Sadat would then in his turn play the gentleman and allow Begin to retain territorial sovereignty over the West Bank? How could Sadat fail to recognize that the "undivided land of Israel" was indispensable both to the ideological purity and the domestic political needs of Begin?

It does not matter much whether Sadat thought, even briefly, that such a deal was possible. It should have been obvious that he could not settle the Palestinian question for Israel on terms favored by the Likud, however generous Begin's concessions on the Sinai. The most that Sadat could offer was exactly what the world knew he was offering at Camp David: concerted action among Israel, Egypt, and the United States to create, in a demilitarized West Bank, a Palestinian entity in some sort of association with Jordan. The Israelis may have believed that this was a rhetorical screen behind which Sadat hid his intention to conclude a separate peace. Sadat may have given them reason to believe this by emphasizing, then and since, how binding he considered the bilateral pledges never again to go to war. But it should have been clear that Sadat was able to offer peace in return for the Sinai, as he did, but nothing more.

The solution Sadat hopes for is that the Americans will put intense pressure on Israel; and there seems a fair chance that he is right, and that such pressure will become visible after the November elections, whoever wins. It is also possible that the rich Arab states, which have broken off political relations with Egypt but not economic ties, might create so many difficulties for Egypt over loans, trade, and other matters that Sadat would be in real danger of falling from power. At the moment this seems unlikely. For one thing, Sadat has been willing to act as the instrument of U.S. power in the region (it was from an Egyptian airfield that the C-130s flew in the abortive rescue attempt in Iran), and if he is deposed, the oil kingdoms that fear subversion or attack, and count on U.S. support, would feel much more vulnerable.

Time is therefore on Sadat's side. The United States is committed to supporting him, and already Egypt has very nearly overtaken Israel as the chief beneficiary of aid of all kinds. Many of Sadat's enemies in the Arab world now find the prospect of his successors much more frightening. And however short-lived it may turn out to be, there is something of an economic upswing in Egypt. During the next three years, while the rest of the Sinai is returned to him, Sadat is likely to grow stronger, not weaker—at least so long as he can keep the intellectuals and bureaucrats who might turn against him economically satisfied and politically quiet.

As for the Israelis, they can claim that their largely unpublicized contacts with the Egyptians are increasing, though not very rapidly, and it is therefore possible to imagine that, bit by bit, these will grow. They express the hope that their embassy in Cairo, now taboo for most Egyptians, will be less isolated as the days go by and that there will eventually be as much traffic from Egypt to Israel as there is from Israel to Egypt. But it is far more probable that rising anger over Israeli settlements on the West Bank will impede this progress, and that normal relations will, indeed, depend, as the Egyptians keep saying, on what is done for the Palestinians.

At Camp David, Sadat made Israel the only offer he could then have made good on: to undertake to lead much, and eventually most, of the Arab world to reconciliation with Israel, if Israel would join with him, the United States, and Jordan in creating some form of Arab sovereignty in the West Bank and Gaza. Had this happened quickly, Sadat would have emerged as "King of the Arabs." If what I heard in Cairo is true, he dreamed of this on the banks of the Nile, as he also imagined that, with peace, Israel would have a large part in helping to develop the Middle East. Not only did this not happen but Israel's relations with Egypt have been soured by the delay and by the growing hostilities on the West Bank.

What will happen now? The May 26 deadline on the autonomy talks will pass without progress. During his visit to Washington, Sadat suggested that, to save appearances, the governments involved make a new "declaration of principles." Some such rhetoric will probably be devised, while the basic problem will remain.

To put the matter bluntly, Begin and Sadat cannot give each other what he wants on the West Bank, and so the problem is inevitably getting worse. What seems likely from a visit to Cairo is that no successor to Sadat could be more forthcoming than he has been. The open question is whether, under the government to follow Begin, Israel will finally be able to negotiate with Egypt for a West Bank solution that Egyptians, Palestinians, Jordanians and Saudis would take seriously. Will the Camp David bargain for the West Bank, as everyone except Begin seems to have understood it—i.e., as a bargain granting the Palestinians real territorial autonomy—still be possible a year hence, whoever governs in Israel? There seems little reason to be confident about this, which makes it all the sadder that the opportunities that Sadat now claims were open were never pursued.

1980

3. *Begin and the Jews*

The essential line of the Begin government remained that the prime minister spoke not only for the political processes of Israel, but for all of world Jewry. The American Jewish establishment was sometimes uncomfortable, especially because it feared reactions in Washington to some of his statements or actions, but it spoke to him behind locked doors and in muted voices. The tales that came out of those meetings almost invariably reflected men and women who went into his office blustering as to how forcefully they would speak, and walking out not having dared to confront this charismatic figure.

The Likud party had just won an election, in the summer of 1981, by suggesting that it was "the national camp," thus implying that everyone who disagreed with it was an enemy of the Jewish nation. This slur had put the Labor party on the defensive. After this victory, the second Begin government felt much freer to behave according to its ideology. At the end of 1981, the Israeli government announced the annexation of the Golan Heights. Its purpose was to preempt any American pressure on Israel to return the territory to Syria as part of a process leading to peace. The prime minister had no doubt that the few Jews in the Diaspora who might doubt his wisdom could be labeled antinational. The formula had worked in Israeli politics; why would it not work in America?

▼

Menachem Begin's outburst denouncing the United States on December 20 is best understood as a scene from a bad marriage. "Are we a vassal state of yours? Are we a banana republic?" Begin asked when the United States suspended the strategic cooperation agreement with Israel following Begin's de facto annexation of the Golan Heights. The explosion was inevitable: each of the partners had entered into their strategic pact two weeks before with contradictory expectations.

Since Begin's speech, stories have appeared attributing its ferocity to his bad health—he was in great pain for several weeks before December 20; to jockeying with General Sharon for attention in Israel; to complicated domestic power plays in advance of the return of the northern Sinai to Egypt. Perhaps all the stories have some truth in them, for Begin is a master of political maneuver and uses public anger to serve a variety of purposes. But his harangue on December 20 was not primarily the outburst of an angry, tired man. It was a preemptive strike to neutralize his opponents, foreign and domestic, and it was effective.

When he drafted the statement Menachem Begin had not only heard protests from the American government about the Golan annexation. He also—as I was told in Jerusalem—had sharp messages of displeasure from some of his most ardent supporters among American Jews. That was something new for Begin. And what was new in his statement was his implication that he had taken over as spokesperson for the American Jewish community. He assured the American ambassador, Samuel Lewis, that American Jewry would fearlessly support him and would not be frightened by any implied threats of anti-Semitism from the Reagan administration. For Begin, this was an artful choice of ground on which to deal with Jewish opponents, especially in the Diaspora. Begin tried to suggest that while virtually all American Jews actually shared his moral and political concerns, some were, to quote an accusation he had made earlier at meetings in New York, "summer soldiers," fearful for their own position in the United States and lacking in Jewish courage and dignity. He implied that he could denounce the United States with complete support, even if some Jews were not forthright enough to make such statements themselves.

Begin's speech must thus be seen as a confrontation with world opinion, and within world Jewry, over the most basic issues. What kind of Israel is now being defined? Will it continue to be dominated by the kind of hawkish strategy that led to the annexation of the Golan? Are there even tougher Israeli leaders in the wings who, when challenged, will ultimately defeat Begin and Sharon in the game of King of the Hill? Does Begin's tough-mindedness define the true meaning of Zionism, and will American Jews follow him?

In the short run, Begin will prevail, both against the Reagan administration and within Israel and world Jewry. In view of the divisions within the Reagan administration, it is hard to imagine that the American government will successfully oppose an Israeli leader who knows exactly what he wants—i.e., a "greater Israel," including all the territory Israel now controls, with the exception, at most, of the northern Sinai after the Egyptians take it over on April 25.

After Begin's outburst, the senior officials in the State Department, led by Secretary of State Alexander Haig, moved to cool the tempers of the Israelis. Begin worried them but they feared even more General Sharon, who hinted a few days later that Israel might take military action on its northern border against the PLO and its Syrian patrons. The State Department wanted to find a way of passing over the incident of December 20 rather than widening the breach.

On the other hand, several of the senior advisers in the White House have anonymously been leaking word to the press that they are very angry with the Israelis and would like to punish them. Some of these White House staff members, and others in the Reagan administration, are sensitive to the views of those sectors of American business that have for years been engaged in large deals with the Arab states, and especially the Saudis, for construction, industrial development, and arms sales. Their views were made evident in the controversy over the AWACS sale and in the promotion, by Reagan himself, of the Saudi Eight-Point peace plan, with its "now you see it, now you don't" recognition of Israel. Begin's open confrontation with the Reagan administration, by increasing the threat of war on Israel's northern border, deterred those in the White House who would like to put an end to the "special relationship" with Israel. They dared not act right away, for Israel would then have had ample reason to throw off any remaining restraint.

So the State Department policy of patiently trying for an accommodation with Begin and Sharon has prevailed. If there is no preoccupying international crisis elsewhere, Secretary Haig can be expected to undertake shuttle diplomacy in February to infuse some life into the bogged-down discussions over Palestinian autonomy. These discussions are not likely to lead to an election on the West Bank before April 25. They will only serve for the time as a counterweight to Begin's action on the Golan. The Americans will at least appear to be reasserting to the Arab world that their commitment to autonomy for the West Bank is unaltered and unalterable.

The outlook for mid-1982 is darker. The Begin government has defined autonomy as "personal"; that is, the Arabs of the West Bank will be offered the right to deal with their local affairs, but they will have to retain Jordanian citizenship. Begin will not allow autonomy to apply to the territory of the West Bank, which will remain under Israeli rule. It does not matter to Begin that this interpretation of the Camp David agreement was repeatedly denied by Moshe Dayan and Ezer Weizman, who were the major negotiators for Israel; nor does he seem troubled that it has never been accepted by the Labor opposition in Israel or by Egypt or the United States. One cannot imagine the Begin government budging from its stand, for it is a fundamental principle of Begin's Zionism that the land west of the Jordan is indivisibly and inalienably part of Israel.

The kind of pressure from the United States that it would take to change this position would be opposed even by most of Begin's dovish opponents at home and abroad. An open threat to deprive Begin's government of U.S. support would, in their view, endanger the national morale and the very life of Israel. An Israel that could be delivered to a peace negotiation by such a U.S. threat would be a weak vassal state indeed. The situation on the West Bank is therefore likely to continue to drag on. Of all the players in the game, Begin is the one who is most likely to succeed in the immediate future, for he is increasingly making the cost of breaking his resolve too high for even his critics to bear.

What is more, Begin's attack on the American government was popular at home. Arriving in Israel just two hours after his statement was made public, I heard the same reaction again and again from the people I saw on my way to the hotel. *"Hu gever*: He is a man!"* Among intellectuals, opinion was much more divided. Everyone agreed that Begin's manners were deplorable, but most added that the Golan was vital to the defense of the Galilee. All were much concerned about the American reaction and about the possible loss of support for Israel in world public opinion.

By Tuesday, Begin was threatening to call a snap election, certain that he could win a clear majority. He would thus both end his dependence on his coalition partners and further weaken the opposition. This threat acted to keep everyone in line. The Labor party opposition is not only weak and divided but unable to arrive at a clear policy toward the occupied territories. My academic friends seemed deeply troubled, estranged. They were still partisans of the Zionist revolution, a revolution based on a moral passion for a better Jewish people; but they were more removed from mass opinion than ever.

At the Knesset, whether I talked to members of the opposition or of the government, there was not the slightest doubt that Begin had the votes he needed—not only to back his stand against the United States and for de facto annexation but to pursue his vision of a "greater Israel" in the future. The imponderable was the American Jewish community. Begin had done his best to neutralize any possible criticism from American Jews, but my friends in the Knesset were not persuaded that he had succeeded. They knew that Begin's Israel was near to passing the point of no return, to becoming a different country from the one its founders had intended. Would American Jewry support this different Israel?

The answer to this question is becoming clear: it is increasingly negative, but in a very complicated way. It seems evident that a majority of organized American Jews is opposed to Begin and the number is growing; but this opposition tends to be more silent than ever.

Fundamentally, Begin has been attempting to enforce within world Jewry the revisionist Zionism to which he is the heir. The great mission of a Jewish state for him—as for Revisionism's founder, Vladimir Jabotinsky—is to bring the Jews into the world of real power, thus denying the Gentiles the historic pleasures of mistreating them. It is this definition of the Zionist state that American Jewry is not buying, or buying only in part, even though dissent is muted.

The American Jewish community as a whole was persuaded to support Zionism after 1945 by the vision of a Jewish state that would redeem the victims of Hitler and build a benign society that could be "a light unto the nations." That this new state had to survive Arab attacks before it was created, and that the Arab world refused to accept it, made defensive military strength a necessity, and even a source of some pride, but the basic commitment to Israel remained, and remains, a commitment to the liberal dreams of Chaim Weizmann and David Ben-Gurion. In their last days, Weizmann in his Research Institute at Rehovoth and Ben-Gurion in a kibbutz in the Negev tried to suggest to the next generation that it hold fast to the earlier vision of Israel as a place of scientific and social pioneering. In their declining years, Weizmann and Ben-Gurion both thought that the looming danger to Israel was its increasing embourgeoisement, the rise of a new class that would soon become addicted to privilege. Neither of them expected that the countervision of an Israel respected, above all, for its military and strategic power would actually be installed in office and that such an Israel could reflect the mood of a new majority.

When the King David Hotel was blown up by the Irgun in 1946, the Zionist leaders presented it not as a great act in the cause of liberation but as the deed of a small faction led by Begin—which stood against the main principles of Zionism. The notion that it was the destiny of a "Jewish liberation movement" to regain the biblical borders of Israel and to assert its might in the world, thus recapturing Judaism's ancient dignity, was not the basis of the United Jewish Appeal, which asked American Jews to contribute to draining swamps and making the desert bloom, or of the Jewish lobby in Washington, which has traditionally argued that Israel is a moral cause, consonant with America's highest ideals—helping people to rebuild their lives, and making it possible for creative communities to flourish. The American Jewish community was led to Zionism primarily through the progressivism of Louis Brandeis and Henrietta Szold.

The countertradition, for which Begin now speaks, follows the confrontationist definition of Zionism. It claims that it will improve the position of Jews in the political world because it would base relationships on the facts of power rather than on vague humanitarian emotions. In its earliest versions, as far back as the writings of Theodor Herzl, this hardheaded school of Zionism has insisted, with far greater vehemence than most other Zionists, that it was confronting every individual Jew with a fateful choice: either come to the Jewish state and be part of the nation, or leave the Jewish community. In some later versions of this demand, the leaders in the Jewish state are charged not merely with creating conditions in Israel to receive many more Jews but also with managing Israel's policy so that the choice to settle in Israel would become more likely throughout the Diaspora. So, for example, after years of debate, Israeli leaders have finally persuaded the international Jewish relief organizations to limit severely the help extended to those Russian Jewish émigrés who do not choose to go to Israel.

Confrontation in the name of Zion—with the non-Jewish world and within Jewry—is, thus, a "historic necessity"; it is part of the process of restructuring the Jewish people. Enough, says this school of thought, of this strange anomaly, a scattered people which has reconstituted part of itself in the land of its ancestors, and still harbors everywhere a peculiar combination of particularist feelings and universalist ideals. Enough of an Israeli people always inhibited by tensions and anxieties.

Last summer in Israel, this clash of ideals was being discussed night after night by audiences that went to see a play staged dramatically in a subterranean stone chamber near the Jaffa Gate to the Old City. Words taken largely from Josephus, with a bit of Talmud added, were used to reconstruct a debate over the destruction of the Second Temple in the year 70, at the end of the Roman War. Who was to blame? The antagonists were the Zealots, who kept insisting that Jewish dignity demanded Jewish armed revolt against the Romans, for Jewish power would somehow prevail, and Jochanan ben Zakkai, the leading rabbi, who counseled political prudence and insisted that the cost of war with the Romans would be strife among the Jews and the destruction of Jerusalem. The American Jewish visitors in the audience were clearly against the Zealots; the ushers and some of the Israelis seemed to be rooting for them.

Traveling in the two countries, I have been struck by a converging sense of fear on the part of the more cosmopolitan minority of Jews in Israel and what clearly seems the majority of American Jewry. Such people fear for Begin's Israel. The lesser part of their concern is that Israel's great friend, America, may tire of its alliance. The far greater dangers, for them, are that Begin and Sharon may really get what they seem to want, that Israel will become America's only ally in the Middle East, that its current borders will be the place where the boundary is firmly drawn against Soviet power and influence, that Israel will become a coguarantor of America's interest in the Persian Gulf.*

Anyone who loves Israel should fear for its very life if this were to come about. Contrary to the grand strategists in Jerusalem, an

---

*Author's note: Here, and in the next essay, "The Uprising," the argument presumed the continued existence of the Soviet Union as a superpower opposed to American interests in the Middle East. The disintegration of the Soviet Union has inevitably changed the strategic situation in the Middle East. The United States, the remaining superpower, is less concerned with the threat of the Soviets to its interests in the region. Washington is ever more mindful of internal currents within the Arab world which might lead to instability and increased hatred of the West. The Bush administration therefore went to war against Saddam Hussein, and it is pushing for a settlement of the Israel-Arab conflict. The arguments of Israel's hardliners, that a "strategic ally" is entitled to its own definition of the territory that it needs, are now ignored. The "special relationship" between Israel and the United States rests again on intangibles, such as shared humane values. Therefore, Israel's continuing rule over two million unwilling Palestinians continues only at the cost of fraying the last tie that binds Israel to many of its friends, both in America as a whole, and within the Jewish Diaspora.

untidy region, increasingly neutralized—in which some progress was made toward separating the West Bank from Israel—would be a far safer place for Israel itself. The seemingly valorous image of Israel and America marching hand in hand to hold the line in the Middle East against tens of millions of enemies, both Arab and Soviet, risks becoming a modern version of Zealotry and promises similarly disastrous results.

During the last five years, there has been a perceptible weakening of support within the world Jewish community for Begin's Israel. In the United States, of the funds raised by major Jewish appeals, the proportion going to Israel has fallen from about 60 percent to less than 50. Polls have consistently shown that most American Jews do not support the policy of continuing occupation of the West Bank. The facts are there for all to see: American Jews try to support the present government as best they can, fearing that Israel as a whole might be damaged; but they keep demonstrating privately and sometimes publicly that they wish this Israeli government were not in power.

My own fear is not that Begin will fail but that he will succeed. His foreign minister, Yitzhak Shamir, has made it clear again that Israel's sovereignty over the West Bank is not negotiable, and that only personal autonomy for its Arabs can be considered. No matter what else happens in the autonomy negotiations, Begin's government will insist on having control over land and water on the West Bank— and land and water are the central issues.

In a few years, therefore, Israel will consist, internally, of three main groups. First, a strong electoral majority for the Likud made up largely of Jews of North African origin; second, a minority, consisting of most of the Jews of European origin, increasingly fragmented across a wide spectrum of political and social beliefs; and third, a growing minority of Arabs who will be increasingly sullen and perhaps mutinous, and who will have the support, however hedged, of every Arab state.

If the Begin government succeeds, and Israel becomes America's principal strategic ally in a turbulent region, it will have to be accommodated in any changes of American strategy, or in some possible global deal with the Russians, while ruling nearly two million Palestinians. Begin's brilliance as a politician is that he has made it difficult for the United States, or for the opposition in Israel, to stop his progress toward such a prospect, which cheers him while it frightens the majority of American Jews.

Whatever may happen in the immediate future, the Jews of the world can no longer choose to be silent. The Israelis who see themselves as the architects of Israel's grand strategic power are risking its existence. The Israelis who are bringing about confrontation between Jews and Gentiles, and between Jews and Jews, are risking its soul.

1982

4. *Begin Must Go*

In March 1982 Israel invaded Lebanon. The name of the operation was Peace in the Galilee; the announced purpose was to clear out the Palestinian enclave in southern Lebanon, to a supposed depth of 45 kilometers. In actuality, the war soon developed into a political exercise through military means, with its centerpiece the creation under Israeli auspices of a government in Lebanon dominated by the Christian Phalange party headed by Bashir Gemayel. In the last days of August, Gemayel was installed as president of Lebanon, but he was assassinated within a few days. In revenge, several hundred armed men of the Christian Phalange entered two Palestinian camps at the outskirts of Beirut—Sabra and Shattila. They slaughtered at least one hundred or perhaps a few hundred (the number remains in dispute) of its inhabitants. This outrage took place under the eyes of the Israeli army, which had permitted the Phalange forces to enter the camps.

Menachem Begin's first reaction was to disclaim responsibility: "Gentiles kill gentiles and the Jews are blamed." In Israel pressure built to a mammoth demonstration, the largest in Israel's history. Some 400,000 people were in the streets of Tel Aviv on Saturday night, September 25. American Jewish reaction, especially within the establishment, was muted and loyalist.

But there was a moral issue involved. Jews had no right to look away and disclaim responsibility for a pogrom. During the early hours of Friday morning, September 24, I wrote what I felt and gave it to the editors of the Op-Ed page of the *New York Times*. They printed it on Sunday. Yom Kippur, the solemn fast of the Day of Atonement, in which Jews beg forgiveness for their sins, began that night.

▼

Menachem Begin may not resign tomorrow or next week, but he has lost the power to govern effectively. A Prime Minister of Israel can survive blunders at home, deep strains with the United States, and disagreements within world Jewry. He cannot remain in office if he has squandered Israel's fundamental asset: its respect for itself and the respect of the world.

Menachem Begin and Defense Minister Ariel Sharon can no longer govern because they have sullied and divided the armed forces. Israel is not a militaristic country, but the army has a very special place in its life. Everyone, with few exceptions, serves in it and remains in the active reserve, with regular recalls to temporary duty, until well into middle age. From its beginning, the Israel Defense Force has taught the principle of "the purity of arms"—that military operations must be conducted with honor. In July, the most decorated and youngest colonel, Eli Geva, asked for a transfer from the front to avoid having to order actions in Beirut that might harm civilians. The response by Begin and Sharon was to drum him out of the army in semidisgrace. A high officer who wrote an anonymous article in support of Colonel Geva was tracked down by army intelligence on Sharon's orders and cashiered. Nor would Begin and Sharon listen in August to 2,000 reserve officers who asked for withdrawal from Lebanon and an end to the siege in Beirut.

It is clear now, beyond any doubt, that Sharon soon knew what was going on in the Shattila and Sabra camps and so did some of the highest officers of the army. The head of the staff college, Brigadier General Amram Mitzna, has resigned in protest and others will surely follow. Most men and women in the army are like the protesting officers. They are not like the handful who obeyed Sharon's orders to close their eyes last week in Beirut. The Israel Defense Force will not remake itself in Sharon's image.

Begin and Sharon can no longer govern because they have lost the trust and regard of the moral and political elder statesmen of Israel and of world Jewry. The President, Yitzhak Navon, called on Monday for an independent investigation of the Beirut massacre—two days before the Knesset debate in which Begin categorically rejected the idea as a political assault on his government. On Thursday, after the Knesset vote, Mr. Navon's request was echoed by his predecessor, Ephraim Katzir; by Ephraim Urbach, president of the Israeli Academy of Arts and Sciences; and by the Israel Bar Association. In the Western world, Jewish protests and pressures for a judicial investigation were led by Edgar Bronfman, president of the World Jewish Congress; by the ecclesiastical and lay leaders of British Jewry, Chief Rabbi Immanuel Jacobovits and Greville Janner; and by a growing list of Jewish organizations in America and elsewhere. As a vice president of the World Jewish Congress, I know, from information flowing into our offices, that the Jewish world is more upset by the Begin government than ever before. On Friday, in a special cabinet meeting, Begin reversed himself and announced the appointment of a limited investigating committee, but the situation is already beyond repair. Like Richard M. Nixon in the midst of Watergate, Begin is no longer governing. He has been engaged in "damage control" and his room for maneuver is dwindling by the hour. So long as he remains in office, Israel's leaders, including some of his own adherents, no longer trust his judgment or really believe in his legitimacy.

Begin and Sharon can no longer govern because they have lost the power to speak for Israel among its friends. The most precious asset of Israel, its credibility, is now severely damaged. Even before the massacres, I heard on all sides, from army and government people, in Israel last summer, that the government was not telling the full truth about the operation in Lebanon. It announced in June that it was moving northward to insure the "peace of the Galilee" by an advance of 25 miles, but everyone in Israel, and Washington, knew almost immediately that the military plans had long been made for a much more extensive action. During the operations, the army spokesperson, who had always been believed in the past, was not taken seriously even by Israel's own soldiers, who were listening to Radio Lebanon for truer accounts of what was happening in their own sectors. On the highest levels in Washington, the personal word of Begin and Sharon is not trusted. This has not happened before to any Israeli leaders.

Jews, in a few hours, will be observing the total fast of the Day of Atonement. They will ask God and man for pardon, but this is granted only if they clear themselves first of sin. This cannot happen so long as Israel, the center of the Jewish world, is led by those who refuse to acknowledge guilt. Israel is a great and moral country; it deserves better leaders.

Begin and Sharon must go.

1982

TWO

In Debate with Israel

Only now that these essays have been organized together as a book am I aware that I have been engaged in a two-front battle with the "hawks." In the essays in the first chapter I insisted on the moral responsibility of Jews to treat Arabs with decency. But there is the second and more pragmatic matter: war and peace. Can Israel best survive at war with hostile neighbors, or should it seek compromise, in hope of defusing the hostility? Can the enmities ever be ended? Menachem Begin and his successor as prime minister, Yitzhak Shamir, succeeded in creating a large constituency in Israel and the Jewish world for the tough-minded option. But throughout the 1980s, polls kept showing that, two to one, the American Jewish community preferred dovish options, and so did the majority in Israel. Even the leaders of the American Jewish establishment, when polled privately, were "doves." The essays in this chapter were written about the issues of war and peace. They represent the largely surpressed views of the majority of world Jewry.

5. *The Tragedy of Victory*

The hinge on which the history of Israel turned was the victory during the Six Day War in June 1967. This event had radical repercussions in the United States and in the Soviet Union, the homes of the two largest Jewish communities outside Israel, as well as in the rest of the Diaspora. Twenty years later, in 1987, I assessed the impact of that victory on all world Jewry.

▼

Less than a month after the Six Day War, at the beginning of July 1967, I heard David Ben-Gurion speak at Beit Berl, the "think tank" of the Israeli Labor party. Ben-Gurion was, by then, no longer a member of the party he himself had founded, and he had even given up his seat in the Knesset, where he ended his political career, a faction of one. In June 1963 he had finally retired to Sdeh Boker, a rather primitive kibbutz on the edge of the desert in the Negev.

The Ben-Gurion who walked into the meeting had about him the air of a prophet who had walked out of his tent to die, but had paused on this last journey to tell us truths that the less farsighted could not see and that only a man possessed by the spirit would dare tell. He warned his listeners against the euphoria that had swept the Jewish world in the aftermath of the Six Day War. Ben-Gurion insisted that all of the territories that had been captured had to be given back, very quickly, for holding on to them would distort, and might ulti- mately destroy, the Jewish state. He made only one exception of consequence: the Israelis should not relinquish control of the whole of Jerusalem. Ben-Gurion's most striking assertion that night was that he did not expect immediate peace with the Arabs; for its own inner health, he said, Israel needed only to give back the territories very soon in return for a workable set of armistice arrangements.

A reporter from Israel's news service, ITIM, was present. A few short lines of the speech appeared the next day in the Israeli papers. What Ben-Gurion had to say about returning the territories, and his solemn warnings against being emotionally overwhelmed by victory, were read in Israel as only another one of the angry outbursts of the founding father, who had now become a public scold.

Israel went on to rejoice in its new power and its new sense of space; no longer could one drive the length of the country in four hours. Levi Eshkol, the prime minister of Israel, offered the Arabs, shortly after the war was over, the return of nearly all the territories, if they would recognize Israel and negotiate peace. The response of the Arab League at a meeting in Khartoum in November 1967 was three resounding noes: no recognition of Israel, no negotiation, and no peace. And yet most Israelis, and almost all their friends, did not believe the Arabs. It seemed beyond doubt that the vanquished would soon realize how badly off they were, and would sue for peace. In such a negotiation, almost all Israelis thought that they would undoubtedly have the power to make themselves more secure by returning less than all the territories captured in the war.

Now, twenty years after the heroics of June 1967, Ben-Gurion's speech at Beit Berl, his wrathful cry that the most glorious of Israel's victories could turn out to be even more poisonous than defeat, has become my most vivid memory of Israel in 1967, when, along with hundreds of thousands of others, I visited the West Bank for first time, drove freely through the Sinai, and even brought home as a u-venir from the Golan Heights a plate of instructions in Russian from the wreck of a Syrian tank. I am more and more persuaded that the old man I heard that night twenty years ago was more prophet than angry octogenarian. It would, I now believe, have been better had the Six Day War ended in a draw and not in a series of stunning victories. And yet the full effect of the war on Israel cannot be understood unless we begin with the important, even positive, changes that were the results of this victory. The euphoria of victory lasted for years, and not without cause. The Six Day War gave Israel, and the world Jewish community which rallied around it then as never before, something more important than victory, or captured territory, in which to take satisfaction. It gave the Jews, for the first time, a sense of power.

Throughout the centuries since the destruction of the Second Temple in the year 70, the physical existence of the Jews has depended on the goodwill of others. In 1948, the Zionists proclaimed the State of Israel and defended it in a costly war (6,000 dead and many more thousands wounded, out of a population then of 600,000), but its power was modest. In 1956 Israel went to war against Egypt, to end raids by fedayeen guerrillas into its territory from Gaza. This military campaign was coordinated with the British and the French, who had their own reasons for attacking Egypt; they wanted to regain control of the Suez Canal, which had been nationalized by then Colonel

Gamal Abdel Nasser. Despite military success, which took the Haganah all the way to the Suez Canal, the war went badly for Israel, at least emotionally. The British and the French withdrew under American pressure, and they hastened to disavow any connection with the Israelis. By February 1957 the Israelis were forced, by American and Soviet pressure, to go back to their original borders. Israel benefited from the protection of a United Nations force that was interposed on the border in Gaza, and the fedayeen raids ended. But the deeper lesson of this venture was that Israel's valor was a minor factor in a world in which even middle-sized powers, such as Britain and France, seemed negligible.

During the next decade, between the withdrawal in 1957 and the war of June 1967, nothing happened to change Israel's perception of itself as still a "Jewish" state, that is, a community that could do little according to its own will: the Americans and the Russians held the ultimate veto power. In 1967 Israel chose to go to war when Lyndon Johnson was suggesting yet another formula for "buying time," when Charles de Gaulle was denouncing the Israelis as aggressors, when the British were on the borderline between neutral and unfriendly, and when it was feared that the Russians might intervene to support their two major clients, then, in the Middle East, Egypt and Syria. Israel's decision to go to war was an act of daring, and of faith in its power to complete the action before those who might veto it could intervene.

On June 12, 1967, when the fighting stopped on all fronts, Israel was, for the first time, the modern heir to David. It had slain visible Goliaths, and it had defied the even larger giants lurking behind them. Even nonbelievers spoke of miracles. In a very deep sense, the exile of the Jews, which had begun with the destruction of the Temple in the year 70, ended in the Six Day War. This victory "cured" Jews of the shame of powerlessness. They were now admired among other nations, and they could admire themselves, as a people of valor, and of independence.

Israel and the Jews of the world were transformed after 1967 by the "normalcy" of power, but not entirely for the better. On the positive side: in the Diaspora, the most striking immediate expression of the new Jewish spirit was in the Soviet Union. A handful of dissidents had begun to agitate in the early 1960s for the right to emigrate to Israel, and they had been supported by a few small groups in the United States and in England. At least overtly, the State of Israel had not been at all involved in these efforts; it had diplomatic relations with the Soviet Union which it did not want to endanger. The success of Israel in the June 1967 war was incendiary; it made Jews believe they could prevail against mighty powers. Everywhere, both inside and outside, Jews began to fight more boldly, and without apology, for the right to leave the Soviet Union.

The Soviet Union has had reasons of its own for allowing some 275,000 Jews to leave so far, such as its announced desire to get rid of some "troublemakers" and its continuing wish to get something from the West in return. Nonetheless, it is clear that the Soviets did not wake up one morning to decide suddenly to let some Jews out. This battle was undertaken and essentially won by Jews who had been moved by Israel's victory in 1967.

The effects on the self-image and actions of American Jews have been striking—and ambiguous. In the first decade of Israel's existence, support of the state had largely been a private matter, an internal concern of the American Jewish community. The relatively modest contributions to Jewish fund-raising were enough to help pay Israel's deficit (especially because very large amounts of money were then coming from German reparations). The United States government had made almost no contribution either to the budget or to the armed strength of Israel, and American Jews had not even thought of making a political fight for aid. When President Eisenhower insisted in the winter of 1956 that Israel had to back down during the Suez crisis, the leaders of American Jewish organizations preferred to counsel Israel to heed him rather than oppose the wishes of the leader of the United States.

Since 1967, despite the immediate and enormous outpouring of Jewish money, the need for economic and military support of Israel by the American government has become a prime political issue in the United States. It was made so by the organized Jewish community, which had no inhibitions about going public even during the turmoil and disarray of the Vietnam War years. It was not simply that the Arabs were less popular than they had been before, for, on the evidence of all the polls, their reputation, though not high, remained fairly stable throughout the 1960s and beyond. The change in American Jewish policy had something to do with the increasing power and self-confidence of Jews in American life; but it is undeniable that the worldwide acclaim for Israel in 1967 and thereafter added cubits to the stature of American Jews. The "Jewish lobby" was no longer spoken of in whispers, and its official leaders no longer pretended that they advanced their cause only by gentle persuasion.

This new forthrightness on behalf of Israel has brought Jews, as a community, more prominently into the American political process than they had ever been before. The Jewish lobby, particularly the American Israel Public Affairs Committee (AIPAC), has fought both Republican and Democratic administrations, not only on behalf of Israel but also against almost every attempt to do something for any of the Arab states.[1] Paradoxically, these very ethnic, parochial efforts by Jewish organizations have served to move their leaders into the main current of American politics. The Jewish lobby, especially when it has been most intransigent, has acquired power enough to place it among the forces with which even the most powerful American politicians must reckon; senators have good reason to believe that they risk their seats if they antagonize AIPAC and its allies, and similar fears have been felt in the White House itself. The style of pro-Israel political advocacy in the United States has been determined by an exaggerated sense of power; suggestions of compromise are denounced by the lobby as weakness; only total support of the Israeli government of the moment—or sometimes of policies even more intransigent—is deemed to be "good for Jews."

This expression of the post-1967 spirit has been clearest in the relations between Israel and the Diaspora. The American Jewish community cast itself very early for the role of chief priest of the temple of unqualified admiration of Israel. If Jews were now to be proud and unafraid everywhere, then Israel, which was the source of this pride, could not ever be seen as wrong. It was irrelevant that within Israel itself criticism had begun to rise as early as the speech by Ben-Gurion I had heard three weeks after the end of the Six Day War. Respected Labor party leaders such as Lova Eliav and Yitzhak Ben-Aharon, each of whom had served as secretary general of Histadrut, strongly argued that Israel could and should take the risks of withdrawal from the West

Bank in order to achieve peace. American Jews did not read the Hebrew press, and those who quoted it to them were dismissed as the bearers of treasonable tidings from writers on the fringe of Israeli society.

The result has been that successive governments of Israel knew that they had a "blank check" from organized American Jewish opinion, at the very least because unquestioning support of the Israeli government was seen in the United States as the necessary emotional base for the work of Jewish political activists and the fund-raisers. That American Jewish opinion should be open to the pluralism one finds among Israelis; that realistic, independent, and critical views of Israel would provide a better and more honest basis for relations between American Jews and the Israelis; and that such a relationship would be a much more solid, lasting, and self-respecting expression of Jewish pride—these ideas are only now becoming conceivable among organized American Jews. Perhaps twenty years, or more, is not too long a time to wait for emotions of pride to move from chest-beating to debate. But it has, in my view, been a costly period both for Israel and American Jews.

To turn now to the developments in Israel itself: in the first nineteen years of the existence of Israel, Menachem Begin was a figure on the fringe. In the 1950s he had threatened the negotiators of the reparations agreement with West Germany (and especially Nahum Goldmann) with death. Before, in 1947, after the United Nations resolution establishing a Jewish state in international law, Begin had declared permanent "war" against the partition of Palestine. Until 1967 most Jews in Israel, and elsewhere, regarded such ultranationalist notions as absurd. After 1967 the rhetoric and the practice of aggressiveness, in the name of Jewish nationalist purpose, seemed ever less absurd to more and more Jews.

I found out that this transformation had begun in the most heartbreaking moments of my weeks in Israel right after the Six Day War. I visited a close friend, Dr. Hayim Yahil, an urbane and politically liberal diplomat, a former director general of Israel's foreign office who had been a lifelong member of the Labor party, and who had lost a son in the battle of Jerusalem. He knew where the young man had fallen, but he had not been able to bring himself to go to that spot outside the wall of the Old City. I took him there in the early evening of my second day in Jerusalem. We stood at the side of the road, with buses going by, so that there was not even an instant of quiet, and together we said the kaddish. Much later that night, at home, after I had told him about Ben-Gurion's speech, he answered: "Can we give back the land for which young men like my son died?"

Dr. Yahil had already taken the first steps to found the League for the Undivided Israel, of which he was chairman until his death a few years later. A major demand of this group was that Jewish settlements had to be extended into the West Bank. These efforts began in 1968. The Israeli army created farming units at strategic points in the valley of the Jordan. These were manned by soldiers doing national service; but soon there were unauthorized settlements as well. A handful of Messianic believers sneaked into Hebron in 1968, supposedly to celebrate Passover at the tomb of Abraham, Isaac, and Jacob. They refused to budge, and the army protected them.

The government of Israel was then still in the hands of the Labor party, and it was to remain so until the election of 1977. The Labor politicians were unwilling to confront such unauthorized settlers. No settlement was ever removed by force until Menachem Begin and Ariel Sharon were in office and reluctantly withdrew from Yamit in the northern Sinai in 1981, in order to comply with the Israeli-Egyptian peace treaty.

The Labor politicians permitted a few illegal Jewish settlements on the West Bank because, so they asserted, the relatively small number of settlers would be a negligible obstacle to peace negotiations—but this reason was only part of the truth. The other, perhaps deeper, cause for the passivity of Labor was that many of its leaders had themselves been transformed by the Six Day War. When they were young, before they had acquired desks in Jerusalem and chauffeur-driven cars, most of the leaders of the Labor party had been among the founders of the kibbutzim in the 1920s and 1930s. As Ben-Gurion had shown by his move to the kibbutz of Sdeh Boker in 1963, the tradition of pioneering gave these Labor Zionists a strong and confident sense of identity and a claim on the right to govern. By the 1970s, Israel had become a consumer society, and the children of the founding families were leaving the collective settlements. After the 1967 war, the only element in Israel that insisted on settling in places where Arabs might shoot at them was the right-wing, religious members of Gush Emunim. By now, of course, most of the settlements on the West Bank are bedroom communities for Tel Aviv and Jerusalem, but the earliest settlers there were full of ideological fervor, and they proclaimed they were carrying out a religious mission to reclaim the entire "land of Israel" for the Jews.

These settlers, who were so alien to the Labor Zionists in ideology and motivation, nonetheless reminded them of their youth when they stole by night into Arab areas to create new Jewish positions. As the years have gone by, the relationship of the Labor party to Hayim Yahil's claim to "the undivided land of Israel" has thus become ever more ambiguous. The official position is that the Labor party is willing to trade "territories for peace," but there is no map on which its many factions agree. The Labor party today contains representatives of the entire spectrum of Israeli opinion, from ultrahawks who are de facto annexationists to doves who agree with Ben-Gurion's advice on withdrawal. Labor, which was in control of the government for the first decade after the Six Day War, did not resist the temptation of Israel's newly won power. Levi Eshkol had intended to keep the captured territories much as they were before, with minimal interference by the occupying army, so that they could be bargaining chips for peace; but he died in 1969. His successors, Golda Meir and Yitzhak Rabin, had a much more grandiose vision of Israel's new power. They allowed and sometimes encouraged more and more restrictive control of life in the occupied territories because they did not believe that the Arabs could ever rally enough counterpower to call Israel to account. The idea that the territories could be central to a bargain with the Arabs receded.

During the 1970s, the rhetoric about the Arabs was becoming ever more negative in Israel, and it was not limited to ultranationalists. Most Israelis were sure after 1967 that the Arabs were feckless blusterers and that Israel would always maintain intellectual and technological superiority. One can find evidence of this view in the Israeli press of the early 1970s, but it was, for me, most pointedly expressed in a meeting with Golda Meir in 1972, when, as prime minister of Israel, she was at the height of her reputation. That year a number of efforts were made to reopen the Suez Canal so that the oil tankers from Saudi

Arabia, Iran, and the other states in the region would not have to go around Africa on their way to Europe. The benefit of this proposal to Egypt was that it would again have been receiving some hundreds of millions of dollars in income a year from the tolls of the canal. The benefit to Israel was that a reopened canal, even after an Israeli withdrawal of a few kilometers (while retaining the whole of the Sinai), would represent a de facto agreement by Egypt not to make war on Israel again. This offer was transmitted to the Israeli government through numerous channels. Historians still argue whether the proposal came to nothing because the Egyptians withdrew their support of the idea or because the Israelis were intransigent. When I, as one of the backdoor messengers, came to Golda Meir to tell her of the offer, she suggested that she need make no concessions to the Egyptians because they were schlemiels; the next year, on Yom Kippur Day, these schlemiels crossed the canal in force.

The bitter losses suffered in the Yom Kippur War remade attitudes in Israel toward the Arabs. Now even the Palestinians could no longer be dismissed. Acts of terrorism, such as the massacre of Israeli athletes at the Olympic Games in Munich and the bloody attack on a school in Maalot, both in 1972, horrified Israelis, but they also changed the image of the Palestinians from hapless adversaries to people to be feared.

And yet the basic legacy of the Six Day War remained. Since 1956, as I have said, it had been widely believed in Israel that what the country wins in war it usually losses at the diplomatic table. In 1956, General Dayan had marched through the Sinai in one hundred hours only to be pushed back by the diplomats. The Yom Kippur War of 1973 was further "proof" of this proposition. No one had tried to stop that war while the Israelis were losing. The Americans and the Russians enforced an armistice and saved the Egyptians from total defeat only after General Sharon had succeeded in crossing the canal into Africa. The only time that Israel had not been done out of the fruits of victory— so many, if not most, Israelis thought—was in 1967, when the military success had been swift and complete.

The ultimate military result of the victory in June 1967 was the war in Lebanon, which began fifteen years later almost to the day, in June 1982. Begin called the invasion a "war of choice," and not one that was waged for immediate defensive needs. General Ariel Sharon, who was the minister of defense, went to war over the objection of most of his general staff, and without fully briefing the cabinet, in pursuit of a "grand design": to establish a Christian-dominated government in Lebanon that would depend on the Jewish state for its survival; to weaken Syria; and to sweep the Palestinians in Lebanon into Jordan, where they would create such disorder that the Hashemite dynasty would fall and Jordan would become "Palestine," finally absorbing the inhabitants of the West Bank. Sharon seems to have sold all this to Begin piecemeal, on the promise that it would be a short and cheap war which would produce grandiose results. It was to be a replay of the glorious days of June 1967.

The enchantment of the memory of 1967 was such that Sharon, a brilliant combat commander, completely missed the difference between tank maneuvers in open territory, in which great battles could be won in a few hours, and the grinding, interminable demands of street fighting in a sprawling city like Beirut. He understood even less that the attempt to reenact the Six Day War in Lebanon in 1982 was predestined to fail, for both political and moral reasons. In Israel and in the Western world, the events of 1967 had been perceived as a defensive action. The war of 1982 was seen, with nearly the same unanimity, as an attempt to end the Palestinian problem through force—and never mind what might happen to the Palestinians as they fled before their enemies, the Christian Lebanese and the Israelis. Sharon and Begin had learned the wrong lesson from the Six Day War. There was something parvenu about the attempt to shoot down Palestinian nationalism by an incursion into Lebanon. The power that had been acquired in 1967 was now being flaunted, and misused, in a cause that the nations on which Israel depended would not accept.

For the Jewish world generally, the most striking effect of the Six Day War was a religious one. Before the war the official rabbinate in Israel had declared that the creation of the state was "the first root of the Messianic redemption." This formula is the climactic assertion of the prayer for the State of Israel that is recited at Sabbath and holiday services in most of Israel's synagogues—but until 1967 it remained a prayer and not a call to action. In June 1967, a small band of religious Messianists were transformed from impractical dreamers to armed prophets. They were going to bring the "end of days" now, and others began to join them.

Almost immediately, these Messianists succeeded in transforming the religious Zionist parties, and not only in Israel. Until 1967, the religious Zionists had been on the defensive; they had fought to pre-serve an enclave for religion in the State of Israel. They needed money for their educational institutions, and they wanted to establish Orthodox Jewish practice as the law of the land, at the very least in such matters as marriage, divorce, and conversion. The religious Zionists had achieved these limited goals through a long-standing political alliance with the Labor Zionists. The State of Israel was run, during its first thirty years, by secular, pragmatic social democrats, almost all of whom, from Ben-Gurion to Golda Meir, never entered a synagogue; but these nonbelievers guaranteed the religious minority their limited but con-siderable enclave in the Jewish state in order to be sure of their support in coalition governments.

The armed prophets who appeared in 1967 very quickly chased out the older, quietist leadership of religious Zionism. The political leader of this young guard was Zevulun Hammer, who was then a firebrand—though he is now, as minister of religion in Israel's coalition cabinet, considered too moderate by his former associates and followers. The official leader of the religious Zionists, Dr. Yosef Burg, ceased being a moderate, at least in public: he moved very far toward accepting the proposition that these were Messianic times and that the commandment of this hour was to reunite the holy soil of Judea and Samaria with the rest of the Promised Land.

The religious parties have split and resplit in the last twenty years. It is true that their proportion of the vote in Israeli elections has not risen but has remained static at something under 15 percent. None-theless, in their new form as radical Messianists, the religious parties have become a far greater force in Israeli politics than they used to be. The near-equal division of forces between Labor and Likud has made all these smaller parties more important. Each of the two main blocs has continued to court them as possible partners in a "narrow" coalition. The radical Messianists have succeeded in moving Israeli politics to the right. So long as Labor had hope of enticing the religious groups back into an alliance, it effectively postponed and avoided the question of exchanging territories for peace. Meanwhile, more and more "facts on the ground" have been created on the West Bank by settlements, control of land and water, and integration with the Israeli state apparatus. Meron Benvenisti, a former vice-mayor of Jerusalem, may well be right that such developments seem irreversible. If so, a settlement with the Palestinians has been made immensely more difficult.

There is no way of knowing whether more modest policies following the Six Day War would have produced a better result for Israel, for the Jews of the world, and for peace in the region. As it is, the results have been ambiguous when they are not discouraging. True, some Palestinians on the West Bank and a few Palestinian leaders have said they accept the principle of the partition of Palestine, which they utterly rejected before and immediately after 1967. Some say that they are now ready to settle with Israel for a state in the West Bank and to accept that such a state be circumscribed by near total disarmament, so that it should not threaten Israel. These moderates, however, are not now likely to produce such an offer from the Arab side. But even if they could, the power of the right wing in Israel has grown sufficiently so that a deal of this kind, which would not have been conceivable without the victory of 1967 and would have been accepted gladly in May of that year, is no longer acceptable to Israel's internal factions. Boldness and intransigence are depicted by the right-wingers as the sole legitimate heirs of those glorious days. Did not Menachem Begin win the election of 1981 by proclaiming himself to be the leader of the "national camp," thus relegating all those who were more moderate to the semitreasonable fringes?

There is an even more painful truth: an attempt by Israel to settle with the Palestinians in a compromise requiring the return of most, not even of all, of the West Bank would undoubtedly lead to civil disobedience, and worse. This would happen not only in the name of ultranationalism and religious Messianism; a deep undercurrent in Israeli life would cling to Hayim Yahil's conviction that holding on to the territories is the debt that the present owes to the heroes of 1967.

Every suggestion that has been made in the last decade for imaginative diplomacy for peace has been vetoed in Israel, although Israeli military leaders such as General Yehoshafat Harkabi and General

Aharon Yariv have argued for years that Israeli withdrawal from the main occupied territories could be negotiated in ways compatible with Israeli security. (This was the view I heard expressed several times in the mid-1970s when I lectured at Israel's army war college.) A de facto coalition of right-wing ideologues and of Labor hard-liners continues to feel, as Golda Meir did, that peace is something that Israel will confer on the Arabs, on its terms, as an act of largesse. It is this immodesty, this exaggeration of power, that is the underside of the shining glory of 1967.

Still, it is worth emphasizing that during the twenty years since the Six Day War the Arabs have sinned against peace more than Israel. Had they taken up Levi Eshkol's offer in 1967, they could have had a settlement far more favorable than any they are likely to get now. The signals from Arab moderates in recent years have again and again been rejected by Arab hard-liners, who have used terrorism as a way of announcing that they are not ready for any version of peaceful settlement.

To a sad and unsettling degree, Arabs and Israelis have become mirror images of each other. In each of the camps, it is seen as advantageous in internal politics to block movements toward peace. In early April, Vice Premier Shimon Peres went to Spain on yet another of many trips in search of backing for a peace conference; en route, he was denounced by Prime Minister Shamir as a fool for whose failure Shamir prayed. In late April, Yasir Arafat paid for a show of unity by the PLO at its meeting in Algiers by breaking the PLO's link with Jordan and announcing the continuation of "armed struggle" against Israel and its installations abroad.

And yet, sinful though the Arabs have been, blaming them does not diminish Israel's burdens, for it needs peace more than the Arabs do. Israel has now become an American dependency, because it cannot maintain both its standard of living and the state of war without at least $3 billion of American aid annually. Israel's society has been altered, and distorted, by its being an occupying power; as the Palestinians on the West Bank become ever more numerous and more restless, Israel is in danger of becoming the Belfast of the Middle East. A more frenetic exercise of power cannot solve these mounting problems. Israel has no intelligent choice but to pursue peace.

It is easy to forgive a people that has had only twenty years to change its sense of itself from victim to victor. Unfortunately, the twentieth century has given Jews, and everybody else, very little time to absorb change. The tragedy of the last twenty years is that the new Jewish power has not been more open to the counsels of moderation.

1987

6. *The Uprising*

The *intifada*, the uprising by Palestinians against the Israeli occupation, began in December 1987. Most Palestinians believed that this bold expression of their national cause would force Israel to negotiate. Moderates in the Jewish community hoped that the time had finally come for peacemaking. My own reactions were pessimistic. I believed that, as before, a dramatic occasion would slip away into the continuing morass of the intractable politics of the Israeli-Palestinian conflict. Regrettably, this pessimistic assessment was not disproved by events.

▼

During the spring of 1948, as the war between Jews and Arabs in Palestine was becoming even bloodier, the American ambassador to the United Nations, Warren Austin, is reported to have asked: "Why can't the Jews and the Moslems learn to practice Christian charity?" Like Warren Austin, the columnists and commentators who have been writing and speaking about the recent unrest that has spread from Gaza to all of Israel have been preaching at Jews and Arabs, asking them to behave reasonably. Many are calling for the establishment of a Palestinian state in the West Bank and Gaza; others are backing the "Jordanian option," that is, the redividing of the West Bank between Israel and Jordan. All have talked about the need for flexibility and a change of heart on both sides.

Moderate, reasonable people, including many Israeli writers and intellectuals, have been advising a peace of mutual recognition for more than twenty years, since June 1967 when Israel conquered the

West Bank and Gaza. Why is that old advice being repeated now? Many commentators seem to think that the recent outbreaks, and the harsh methods that the Israelis have used to contain them, have caused such a strong reaction in Israel that, after two decades of stasis, it will begin to detach itself from Gaza and the West Bank. The Palestinians, it is claimed, are ready to compromise their ideology, which requires the return to them of all of Palestine, on the day that Israel offers to negotiate with them.

That the recent riots and protests are likely to have such an effect is a foolish illusion. There was, however, something new about them. The Arabs of pre-1967 Israel never joined in mass demonstrations against the government, and until this December there had not been an Arab general strike, not even for a day, since Israel was founded in 1948. But Israelis have long memories. Before the state was created, during the 1920s and 1930s and into the 1940s, there were long periods of guerrilla warfare in Palestine, and the Arabs called many general strikes. The price that the Arabs demanded for ending the war between the communities was agreement by the Jews to stop Jewish immigration. The Jews found war preferable, especially since they had the military force to contain the other side. The Arabs in Israel were able to mount a brief general strike in December but they are far less threatening than their predecessors, who assailed a far weaker Jewish community before 1948—and the Jews now control the apparatus of the state.

There is another new element in the present outbreaks. Until the mid-1980s the most dramatic terrorist attacks were made by PLO teams from outside Israel's borders, while the Arabs under Israel's control have been relatively quiescent. In recent years there have been few PLO incursions, but the number of violent incidents within the borders of the undivided Israel has grown dramatically. The protests of mid-December, started by angry young people within the territories, were the strongest expression so far of homegrown Arab violence against the Israelis. According to the most reliable reports, the outbreaks were spontaneous; help from the PLO came only after young Arabs in Gaza set the demonstrations in motion. The thousand or so political prisoners who are being tried by Israeli political authorities are almost all young men between their mid-teens and mid-

twenties. These demonstrators have grown up under the Israeli occupation, as have their sisters and younger brothers who were with
them when the rocks and Molotov cocktails were thrown.

During the first outbreak, when television cameras were turned
on, it looked disgraceful for armed soldiers to be firing at teenagers
and women. A day or two later, the government made it clear that
it was rounding up young people who were easy to find, and who
could be jailed or deported into Lebanon. Israeli military authorities
were, in fact, visibly pleased by the lack of expertise among the rioters
they have in custody. The Israeli press and recent polls suggested
that the Israeli public was not only much relieved that the riots were
contained but confident that future outbreaks are likely to be contained more professionally, that is, with less deadly force, and therefore
with less embarrassment to themselves. A poll in the conservative
daily *Yedioth Aharonoth* on December 25, 1987, however, showed
that 69 percent of the Israelis surveyed favored harsher security measures in the territories and 47 percent said that since the riots they
took a harder line toward the Arabs.

This is not the mood of a country about to change its fundamental
policies. The current disorder tends to push the moderates, or many
of them, closer to the hard-line nationalist camp, if not into it. The
familiar cry is heard that one cannot make concessions or negotiate
while terrorists are attacking the forces of law and order. This is
precisely what the leaders of the Labor party in Israel, Vice Premier
Shimon Peres and Defense Minister Yitzhak Rabin, have been saying.
They are clearly afraid that, if they were to be perceived as "giving
in to terrorism," the Likud party could defeat them in an election.
Menachem Begin won in 1981 by appropriating the slogan "national
camp" for his party and thus forcing the Labor party to "prove" that
its more moderate policies were not antinational. "Giving in to terrorism" is a slur that would instantly be applied to Labor if its leaders
sounded in the least bit daunted by the task of quelling the distur-
bances.

Once Israel returns to "normal" (i.e., to a situation in which scattered acts of violence are the accepted norm), it is highly unlikely
that the more moderate Israeli political leaders will move any more
boldly than they have before. Why risk domestic political turmoil—

which any serious concessions would create—when the situation is quiet? This is the Catch-22 of the moderate Israeli politicians: they are trapped into "national unity" by Arab violence, but they also prefer not to fight both the Likud and each other (for there are both hawks and doves in the Labor leadership) when the pressure is off.

Shlomo Hillel, the speaker of the Knesset, is the leader of the Labor hawks, who, in his calculations, make up about half (twenty-two) of all the Labor members of the Knesset. Hillel was quoted in the Israeli papers on January 1 as demanding that Peres not go beyond the official platform of the party, which rules out the return of much more than half of the West Bank and insists on Israeli military control of all the territory west of the Jordan. Hillel left no doubt that in the view of the Labor hard-liners, Peres had been speaking much too broadly in his various calls for negotiations.

In view of these political pressures Shimon Peres' recent calls for an "international conference" to consider a peace settlement were heard in Israel as a message to the superpowers, and especially to the Americans, to bring pressure on the Arab nations to consider moderate solutions, and thus help him prove that "moderation pays." He hoped that the Americans would thus dislodge enough marginal votes to make him prime minister in his own right. The Americans refused, and Peres never had the votes in the Knesset, or in the country, to support a serious shift in the Israeli position. It was and remains the accepted wisdom among practically all Israeli political observers that a new election would produce the same political stalemate that exists today, with the possible exception that Labor might lose a few seats if some of its own more hawkish members decided to join the right. It would take someone with the appeal and authority of De Gaulle or Ben-Gurion (i.e., someone who does not now exist) to bring Israel to détente with the Arabs, or at least with some of them.

The Palestinians are no more united than the Israelis. The Jordanians do not want a Palestinian state on the West Bank and Gaza since it would be a threat to the monarchy. Over 60 percent of Jordanians are Palestinians, whose loyalty to the king is likely to be diminished by a Palestinian government in Ramallah, on the West Bank. The more militant factions of the PLO will continue to be at war with both Israelis and other Palestinians, in pursuit of an undivided Palestine under their control. The groups of angry young people who have been making themselves visible on the West Bank have carried the Palestinian flag in their demonstrations; but according to recent reports they have not for the most part been close to the PLO, even as many have continued to say, in a kind of incantation, that it is "the sole legitimate representative of the Palestinian people."

In addition to the young Palestinians who have been rioting, a more sophisticated leadership has appeared. Hanna Siniora, the editor of *Al Fajir* in East Jerusalem, and Mubarak Awad, an Arab-American who heads an institute in the West Bank to study nonviolent politics, have called on Palestinians to engage in nonviolent civil disobedience by refusing, for example, to pay taxes or to buy Israeli products. The leader of the moderate Israeli Peace Now group, Tzaly Reshef, has said, "We need to hear moderate voices on the other side that will give us, the doves, the feeling that our minimum demands for security and survival will be met." This plea may perhaps be answered by Siniora and Awad and their supporters. But Arab moderates remain a minority, an endangered one, and Peace Now has yet to show it can become more than a marginal force in Israeli politics.

The PLO leadership has also explored new positions. There are rumors of a meeting somewhere in Europe during the last days of December between representatives of the PLO and leaders of the riots in Gaza and the West Bank. The PLO apparently offered help so that it might claim a share in the "victory." On the international scene, moreover, Arafat has suddenly become more visible and more forthcoming. According to *Ma'ariv* of January 1, 1988, Arafat told a Kuwait newspaper that the Palestinians must remember that "there are Jews in the land." In a separate interview in the *Washington Post* of January 4, 1988, he talked optimistically of setting up a Palestinian government in exile to negotiate a Palestinian state with "the presence of UN forces for any period" that Israel required on the Palestinian side of the border. Such actions and statements by Arafat serve to remind the maximalists among the Palestinians, who want the undivided land of Israel, that there is no hope of achieving Palestinian aims except through compromises with the Israelis; but no political program that he can announce will have even the grudging assent

of all the various Palestinian factions. Palestinian unity exists so long
as they are at war with Israel; it falls apart the closer they get even
to talk of a political solution. The more formidable obstacle to a
Palestinian state is that it is opposed by the Israelis and the Jordanians,
both of which feel threatened by it, and by the Americans, who remain
unconvinced that such a state would be peaceful and that it would
stay out of the Soviet orbit.

The tragic truth is that both Israel and the Palestinians have fewer
problems with violence than they have with peace. The inner politics
of both camps have been conditioned by at least two generations of
resisting and fighting. The cycle of violent protest followed by repression may become more frequent. A continuous, unrelenting civil war
is not yet in view; even if it were, there is the example of Belfast to
suggest that communities can live with horror, even for centuries,
without undergoing the revulsion that would lead both sides to sanity
and peace.

Why, then, don't the superpowers try to stop this growing tragedy,
for only they have the power to do so? The reason is that they prefer
not to pay the price that it would cost them to apply convincing
pressure for peacemaking in the Middle East. The last serious initiative to come from Washington was announced in September 1982,
when President Reagan endorsed the goal of Arab autonomy on the
West Bank. That proposal soon died and American policy since then
has been dominated by one recurrent concern: to keep the Russians
out of the Middle East. When Peres first called for an international
conference, his friend George Shultz refused to support him; such
a conference could not possibly take place, even if the superpowers
were present formally only at the ceremonial opening, without the
kind of parity and connection between Russians and the Americans
that Shultz did not want.

There has recently been some change in American foreign policy
thinking. The Middle East was discussed in the many talks that led
up to the summit meeting between Gorbachev and Reagan, and the
Americans now say they are ready to accept the Russians as a party
to negotiation if, as a State Department official said to me some weeks
ago, "they promise to be helpful and constructive." This formula
seems to mean that the United States would be delighted to have the

Russians' blessing for what they are likely to perceive as continuing American dominance in most of the region.

Recent statements by the American government about the riots in Israel contain no signs whatever that the United States has a new policy. The White House and the State Department have urged the Israelis to be more circumspect and sophisticated in containing the demonstrations; the United States voted in the UN Security Council to condemn Israel's decision to deport Palestinians. But these seem no more than gestures to save face with America's friends in the Arab world. America's formal position remains, as it has for years, that there must be a political solution giving separate status to the West Bank and Gaza, which the United States continues to call "occupied territories." Beyond this the Americans have taken no diplomatic initiatives, and there are no signs that they are willing to do more than invoke the long-rejected Reagan plan of 1982, which called for autonomy on the West Bank without being specific about its political character or future.

The Americans, however, could return to the only existing peace treaty between Israel and an Arab state, the Camp David agreement of 1979, which Menachem Begin signed with Anwar Sadat. Israel then agreed to hold talks on "sovereignty" after a five-year interval of autonomy for the West Bank and Gaza. There never was a period of autonomy, the five years are long past, and even the first talks were never held. The Egyptians have not insisted on them but have contented themselves with getting the Sinai Peninsula back. The Palestinians denounced the Camp David scheme as being too narrow, because it did not mention the possibility of an independent state. The Jordanians refused to cooperate because they had been left out of the Camp David negotiations. The United States, following the Reagan initiative of 1982, made several unsuccessful attempts to construct a joint Jordanian-Palestinian delegation to negotiate with Israel. The Americans should try again, and much more vigorously, emphasizing that autonomy talks are still called for by the agreement at Camp David. This would be the only diplomatic initiative that the Israeli right-wingers cannot veto. Begin himself agreed to autonomy talks, and Prime Minister Shamir has said repeatedly that this is the only path to a settlement he is willing to take.

Do Israel's right-wingers mean what they say? Begin essentially undermined his own agreement to autonomy talks by acting against the spirit, and probably even the letter (that is still subject to dispute), of the Camp David accords when he planted Jewish settlements throughout the West Bank. In the minds of Israel's right wing, autonomy means hardly more than the right of Arab municipalities to control their firemen and garbage collectors. Israel meanwhile decides on land and water policy and continues to change the character of the administered territories. But if autonomy talks ever begin, with the Americans acting in their capacity of guarantors of the Camp David agreement, could such negotiations be confined to the Likud's version of their limits?

Yitzhak Shamir and his advisers are well aware of this question. As a member of the Knesset in 1979, Shamir voted against ratifying the Camp David agreement. He saw it as the beginning of the end for Israeli rule over the West Bank and Gaza. We can imagine that Shamir, notwithstanding his public statements, is today far from enthusiastic about the kind of negotiations with the Arabs that the Camp David agreement calls for.

We can also imagine that recent events have not made King Hussein more eager to get the West Bank back. If it were returned to his rule, Gaza would come with it. He would thus be faced in both regions with a new generation of Arab activists, the very people who took part in the riots, who do not much like him, and who certainly do not regard him as the leader of Palestinian nationalism. Gaza is even more intractable than the West Bank. Under Egyptian rule, it was kept in quarantine; the Egyptians did not permit residents of Gaza to cross into Egypt except with rare special permission, and they made it clear that Gaza was not part of Egypt. The Israelis have been more open; they have made use of tens of thousands of workers from Gaza, and they do considerable business across the border. Gaza remains more and more densely populated with angry Palestinians who are without hope. It is widely, and reliably, rumored that the Israelis several times sounded out the Egyptians about taking Gaza back, and were refused. This festering territory, which neither Egypt nor Israel can digest or keep quiet, is hardly likely to appeal to Jordan.[2] Even in the face of the recent riots in Israel, all the parties concerned are calculating that their short-run interest is to do nothing. Reviving the Camp David talks is certainly worth trying, but no one should have high hopes that the opposing sides will bring to them the qualities necessary for a compromise. Meanwhile, people are being killed, and untold other lives, both Israeli and Arab, have been distorted by the occupation. It is painful to think of Arab young people growing up with little hope and of the young Israeli conscripts patrolling the sullen cities of the West Bank and Gaza. One hundred and sixty reserve officers and men recently announced, according to the *Jerusalem Post* international edition of January 9, 1988, that they would "refuse to take part in suppressing the uprising and insurrection in the occupied territories."

Meanwhile, as the short-run calculations of all the invoked parties persuade them, one by one, to do nothing, there are more awful terrors that are imaginable, just over the horizon. As the situation hardens, rocks and stones will not necessarily be replaced only by revolvers. During the last few weeks I have several times heard officials in the United States and Israel talk about sophisticated devices of terror, including atom bombs miniaturized into suitcases, being introduced before long. I hope they are exaggerating; but it is hard to see what would prevent such developments if current trends continue.

The conflict between Israel and the PLO was once a quarrel between two Western-style nationalisms, both of which considered themselves expressions of secular ideologies. Both Jews and Arabs are increasingly being pushed into the embrace of religious extremists who see themselves as prophets armed. What could be more dangerous—as we can see from the behavior of Iran in its war with Iraq—than the willingness of young people to be slaughtered in battle for the sake of the Jewish or the Muslim God? It is not for nothing that some rabbis of the Talmud, as they contemplated the prediction that the Messianic Era would be preceded by murderous war, cried out: "Let the Messiah come but I will not welcome Him."

Everyone with whom I have talked in the past few years about the Middle East—and, at various times, I have met with leaders of all the different camps—agrees that stalemate leads to disaster, but no one seems to have summoned up the political will to say that a settlement can no longer be postponed. After each visit to the Middle East, I return more pessimistic. Prophets of gloom rarely like the words they utter: they feel compelled to describe a despairing vision in the hope that someone will act to prove them wrong.

1988

7. An Open Letter to Elie Wiesel

In the early months of the *intifada*, Arab demonstrators were being killed at the rate of thirty a month. To be sure, the rock-throwers endangered lives, and a few Israelis were killed, but the use of force was disproportionate. The apologists for Israel's policies kept finding ways of blaming the deaths of even the most innocent Palestinians on the demonstrators: if they had not been demonstrating, none of this would have happened—but how else were the Palestinians to call attention to their cause? Had not the Jews in the Soviet Union been demonstrating against the regime, to call attention to their demand for equality and for the right to emigrate? The issue was again that of a double standard of justice; we could countenance repression of Palestinians, but if Jews were the victims of such actions, we would cry out before the world.

▼

Dear Elie,

You and I met almost half a lifetime ago, in the late 1950s, when you had just written your first book, *Night*, and I had just finished my own first book, *The Zionist Idea*. In those days, very few in America were much interested in either the Holocaust or in Zionist ideology, and so we established a comradeship of the ignored. Much more important, we were among the few who still spoke Yiddish, as we continue to do when we meet, for neither of us can let go of the world of our childhood.

You will remember what I told you about my own family. On my mother's side, she and her children were the only survivors. Her father, all of her brothers and sisters, and all of their children were murdered in Poland. On the eve of Yom Kippur, in 1946, when it was certain that all were dead, my mother lit thirty-seven candles in their memory. You, as the only survivor of your family, became part of my life. I entered your life, so you told me, because I carried with me, then and to this day, the guilt of my own good fortune, that my parents emigrated from Poland in the mid-1920s and brought me to the United States as a child. We are, both of us, part of what little is left of the Chassidic communities of your birthplace in Sighet and of mine in Lubaczów. I can never really enter into the heart of the child—you—who spent his bar-mitzvah year staring out from a bunk in Auschwitz, but our obligations are the same. What have we both learned from the murder of our families? How must we live in their memory? You and I read and reread Bible and Talmud: what do the sacred texts command us to think, to feel, and to do?

Jews are deeply troubled these days by Israel's behavior and policies in answer to the *intifada,* the uprising of the Palestinians against occupation by Israel. Both in Israel and in the Diaspora, many—you and I among them—have been agonizing in public (and, of course, even more in private) about the rocks and firebombs hurled by Palestinians, which have been answered by beatings and shootings by Israelis. You have deplored these excesses by both sides, but you have then thrown up your hands and said: "I don't know what Israel should do. Give up? They cannot give up" (*International Herald Tribune,* January 11, 1988). Therefore, so you imply, the Israelis must, at first, beat and shoot the uprising into subjection. And yet, you have expressed deep understanding of "the anger of young Palestinians." You have added that the Palestinians who are "treated as nonpersons" have a right to "have chosen violence as a means of attracting attention to their existence and their means of obtaining national identity" (*New York Times,* June 23, 1988). You have deplored "the extremists in both camps."

I have looked in your statements for definition of who are these extremists, and I have found many paragraphs about Arabs who practice terrorism. You have even quoted from a Palestinian poet, Mahmoud Darwish, who has "recently stirred up angry passions in Israel" with a poem which is read as demanding that all the Jews get out and leave Palestine, including Haifa and Tel Aviv, to the Arabs. These passages of yours seem to require some balancing comments. You know of the incantations by Meir Kahane and his followers that the Jews are commanded to expel Muslims and Christians from the Holy Land. That a former chief of staff, Raful Eytan, called the Palestinians "crazy bugs" has, surely, not escaped your attention. I wonder whether you, and I, would have been silent if a Russian general had uttered a comparable slur about Jews demonstrating in Red Square. More seriously, you know that the prime minister of Israel, Yitzhak Shamir, has been saying that he will not return a single inch of the West Bank to Arab sovereignty; he has, thus, stalled even the beginnings of negotiation.

You are so eloquent in talking about the faults of the Arabs, and so mute in talking about the faults of the Jews. You yourself have told us that this silence, this imbalance in your utterances, is not an accident. You have argued that Israel has many enemies; it is an endangered state and therefore one should defend and even excuse its conduct lest criticism give weapons to its enemies. That estimate of Israel's strength is not as self-evident as you make it appear. It is rhetoric that Israel's hard-liners, the Likud and the parties to the right of it, like to use, for it helps to excuse intransigence—but this is not the view of Israel's moderates. Abba Eban knows as much about Israel's real position in the region as any one alive, not least because he serves, now, as chairman of the Foreign Affairs and Defense Committee of Israel's Knesset. Speaking last March in Jerusalem to a meeting of the New Israel Fund, Eban said: "We have reached a point in which we can say that Israel has never been stronger in power and in quantitative measure. Never has Israel been less existentially threatened. Never has Israel been more secure against external assault and never more vulnerable to domestic folly. The major perils that now face us come from within ourselves. And they would emerge from the stupendous folly of attempting to enforce a permanent Israeli jurisdiction over the one and a half million Arabs in the West Bank and Gaza." Eban went on to argue—and he has said this repeatedly, since, in speeches both in Israel and in the United States—that all who care about Israel will help her best by uttering the very criticisms that you, Elie, exclude. Eban, of course, speaks from the point of view of Israel's Labor party. You seem to have accepted the position of the Likud.

You have suggested that some of the Jewish critics of Israel's conduct, and especially those who live outside the state, are "intellectuals who had never done anything for Israel, but now shamelessly use their Jewishness to justify their attacks against Israel." This may be true of a few individuals, but is that all that you, who are so morally sensitive, have heard in the outcries of the critics? Why have you not been able to find space, so far, in any of your writings or statements to suggest that there are Jews in the world, from the very center of doing and caring for Israel, who have expressed outrage at such actions as dynamiting houses in the Arab village of Beta? These villagers had tried to protect Jewish teenagers on a hike against stone-throwers. In the melee a girl was shot by accident by one of the Jewish guards. The army then blew up fourteen houses, not to punish the guilty but to appease the angry hard-line settlers in the West Bank. You were not among those who said anything in public after this, and after all too many other such incidents. Are such figures in the Diaspora as Sir Isaiah Berlin and Philip Klutznick, and hundreds of others like them, who have suffered for and with Israel all their lives, and who have spoken up in criticism of actions which they could not countenance, so negligible that they can simply be ignored? Is the moral agony of such men and women an irrelevance, with which you need not deal?

Any public criticism, so you say, lends aid and comfort to Israel's enemies; Israel wants to decide without any interference from abroad. But is this the only view in Israel? Are the reserve generals and colonels of Israel, more than 130 of them, who have launched a public campaign for territorial compromise, and who are pointedly critical of the occupation of the West Bank, enemies of the Jewish people? They keep saying that only compromise can end the conflict, and that repression is unworkable. Four of these generals have recently been on tour in the United States, to enlist support of such views among all those who care about Israel. Is it a betrayal of Israel to heed these men?

As you know better than anyone, silence is a form of interference.

In all your writings you have insisted no one has the right to be silent in the face of injustice, any injustice. Those who throw up their hands and, in your own recent defensive words about Israel, "would like to believe in miracles," have abdicated responsibility. This is all the more an abdication now, because there is no demand from Israel that the Jews of the Diaspora be silent. On the contrary, that half of Israel which is led by Shimon Peres has been saying over and over again that it is the responsibility of Jews who care to speak their minds.

On May 18, Shimon Peres made the point unmistakably when he spoke to the leaders of the Jewish establishment organizations in New York: "Whoever wants can be involved. We are a free people." He made it clear beyond any doubt that dissent and criticism did not in any way weaken commitment to Israel. The other half of Israel, which is led by Prime Minister Yitzhak Shamir, has not really asked the Jews of the Diaspora to leave the decisions to Israel. The most effective device of these hard-liners has been to suggest that any criticism of their position is a self-hating assault on the state when such criticism is uttered by Jews, and that it is a form of anti-Semitism when spoken by non-Jews. This strategy is used even in Israel. The Likud likes to call itself the "national camp," and to insist that the moderates are not sufficiently patriotic and are enemies of the Jewish people. You, Elie, do not believe such canards, but I must ask: Aren't you lending aid and comfort to this view? Aren't you, in fact, helping the Likud?

On this question of keeping silent, I cannot agree with you even on the matter of non-Jewish opinion. Yes, as you say, there are critics of Israel who wish it ill, but are those the only ones? You know as well as I that the majority of Israel's supporters in the world love it because it represents humane and prophetic values, and that they are deeply troubled by the stalemate and by the exercise of repression as the only policy. Is Jean Daniel, who addressed an open letter to you in Paris after your first declaration of noninterference, an enemy of the state of Israel—or is he a friend trying to recall Israel to its moral nature? Do you, Elie, really want to suggest, even by implication, that all of us are obligated to speak out on every moral issue in the world, but that not even the best intentioned, whether Jews or non-Jews, have a right to say a critical word about Israel?

There is an answer to your repeated question: "What are we to

do?" We must act justly, especially when such action seems impru-
dent and embarrassing—because there is a Jewish moral tradition. This
Jewish morality has taken one form, recurrently, throughout the ages.
Even in bad times, when Jews were under fierce attack, the moral
teachers gave us no exceptions. The prophets knew that Assyria and
Babylonia were far more wicked than Judea, but they held Judea to
account, even as the Assyrians and the Babylonians were advancing.
"Only you have I known among all the nations of the world; therefore
I will hold you to account for all your sins."

There were other voices in the days of the prophets. Amos and
all the rest were opposed, generation after generation, by prophets
who belonged to the royal courts, who assured the king that his
conduct, in the light of his circumstances, was beyond reproach. The
biblical prophets were hounded and harrassed as traitors who weakened the resolve of a small people—but their "treason," and not the
prudence of the court prophets, is our unique Jewish tradition. While
the official soothsayers denounced the enemies of the king, the prophets whom we revere followed after Nathan, who dared to confront
King David with his murder of Uriah and the stealing of his wife.
Nathan defended this Hittite stranger against a divinely appointed
Jewish king: "You are the man," he said to David; you are morally
responsible.

In the memory of the Holocaust, we have been reminded by you,
Elie, that silence is a sin. You have spoken out against indifference
and injustice. Why are you making a special case of Israel? Do you
think that our silence will help it? If you do, your love has blinded
you. The texts that we study and restudy teach the contrary. "Israel
will be redeemed by righteousness, and those who return to it, by
acts of loving-kindness." To be silent is an act of misplaced love.
Such silence gives free reign to the armed zealots of ages past, and
of this day. Several times in our history, the armed zealots have led
the Jewish people to glorious disasters. Encouragement by silence, as
some of the rabbis did when the Zealots declared war on Rome in
the first century, has a long history of being tragically wrong. We
dare not repeat this mistake. The excesses of the zealots may succeed
today, briefly, as they succeeded for a moment several times before,
but such excesses lead again, God forbid, to disaster. Teachers of

morality must not indulge the zealots today, and not only because zealotry does not work. To suppress the weak because of our own supposed weakness is against the very essence of our tradition. Moses taught us in the desert, when we were a bunch of ex-slaves, that we should not oppress strangers, for we had been oppressed as strangers in the land of Egypt. This injunction is unconditional.

Because I have been reading you for many years, I have learned from you to think, at least sometimes, in haunting images. I am haunted by one incident. Several days after the incident in Beta, an Israel patrol tried to stop some Arab youths to question them. They had not even been throwing rocks, so they were guilty of nothing except not wanting to stop. These young men were fired on, and one was killed. Now I know, as you do, about the dangers for Israeli soldiers in the West Bank and Gaza; I have nieces in Israel's army, to whom I have said that their moral obligation does not include allowing themselves to be slaughtered—but firing on those who are unwilling to be questioned is another matter entirely. How can we be silent?

I agree with you that *ahavat Yisrael*, the love of the Jewish people, is a great virtue, but I can find little trace in all the Jewish texts through the centuries that this love must be uncritical. Even Levi Yitzhak of Berdichev, the chassid who constructed defenses of the conduct of the Jews, was not silent about their misdeeds. He accepted the moral responsibility to lead. "Love can bend a straight line"—it can mislead the lover, so that, with the highest motives, he does grave injury to his beloved. You, Elie, care far too much about the Jewish people, and about Israel, to indulge falls from grace and, de facto, to lend comfort to zealots. At the very least, if you are persuaded of the views of the Likud, you must, in fairness, cease being so dismissive of the political and moral views of the moderate, larger half of the Jewish people, which rejects the politics and morality of the hard-liners.

Elie, you belong on the other side. Let me remind you of the saying that both of us have quoted many times, and sometimes at each other, especially in those early years when we were closest. Menachem Mendel of Kotsk, that tortured chassid of the last century, once said that when the Evil One wants to destroy us, he tempts us

not through our wicked desires but through our most virtuous incli-
nations; we then do good deeds at the wrong time, in the wrong
intensity, and in a context in which they do devastating harm. I think
that your love of Israel, these days, is falling into the moral trap that
Menachem Mendel described. Elie, you do not belong where you
are these days. You belong on the other side. You belong among
those who speak truth, even to Jewish power, and who do not look
away because of real or invented Jewish weakness. The truest love
of Israel and the Jewish people is to remind ourselves that, in strength
or in weakness, we survive not by prudence and not by power, but
only through justice.

1988

THREE

In Defense of Political Zionism

In its modern form, the Zionist movement began a century ago. Its political purpose was to create a Jewish state in the land of the ancestors, and for that state to settle down in peace among the Arabs. The state has existed since 1948, but it is still far from having achieved peace with the Arabs. Most Jewish discussion blames the Arabs for their intransigence and avoids the subject of Jewish intransigence. In the essays in the first two chapters of this book, I chose not to take this easy, and safe, option. It is the responsibility of Jews to remove the motes from their own eyes; they should not take refuge from self-criticism by pointing to the beams in the eyes of their adversaries.

Even in their own favorite realm, the politics of power, the hardliners are wrong. They offer no conceivable vision of peace with the Arab world. Their favorite formula, that "Jordan is Palestine," supposes that such a Palestinian state would accept Israel's annexation of the West Bank, and that the Palestinian government in Amman would be willing to receive hundreds of thousands of new refugees fleeing across the Jordan River. Laying aside all the moral and political objections, would Israel, at the end of such a process, have peace? A Palestinian state in Transjordan is likely to be a much greater threat to Israel than a demilitarized state on the West Bank, which would be wedged between Israel and the existing Hashemite kingdom of

Jordan and carefully monitored by both powers. A three-state solution, with some form of economic consolidation, is better for Israel than an angry Palestine created on the ruins of the state of Jordan.

But I have reason to believe that the hard-liners do not really care about creating a Palestinian state in Jordan. The formula "Palestine is Jordan" conveniently masks their basic view, that no significant political concessions need to be made to the Arabs; Israel is, and can remain, sufficiently powerful to withstand the Arab world. This proposition seems foolhardy to the point of madness. In the aftermath of Saddam Hussein's firing Scud missiles at Israel's population centers, it is clear that only a few members of an enemy force need to be technologically advanced. A semiliterate soldier or terrorist can be trained to push a button that will launch a missile from hundreds of miles away, and that weapon need not have been built by its users. The only hope for the future is comprehensive peace. Making peace in the Middle East is a risky endeavor with many pitfalls, but it is less dangerous than the delusions of the hard-liners that Jewish power will always prevail.

The Arab delusions are at least as disastrous. Almost all Arabs continue to insist that Zionism is not a valid form of nationalism, and that it has no conceivable claim on any part of the Holy Land; the Jews have no deep roots in the land of their ancestors from which they have been largely absent for many centuries. If the Palestinians refuse to accept the existence of the Jewish state, it will somehow disappear. This notion is even more unlikely than the hope of the Jewish maximalists that the Palestinians would eventually disappear from the political map: that they would tire of the struggle, and, even if not, they would become one of the many lost causes which the world forgets.

As a Zionist moderate, I have defined myself by disagreeing with the extremists on both sides. In the first two chapters of this book, I broke lances with the Jewish ultranationalists. In the following essays, I debate the Arab hard-liners. I suggest not some grandiose, ideological vision, but rather a pragmatic path to untidy accommodation. For over two decades, I have been saying to Zionists and to Palestinians alike that they continue to talk past each other. Their ideologies do not clash; they simply never meet on any common ground. The way out of this dilemma is to define the conflict in such fashion that Jews and Arabs are forced to talk about the same issue. I have proposed a model that comes from American domestic politics: the Zionist state was conceived by the world community as an act of "affirmative action," of one-time redress for ancient wrongs. Jews have hailed this act as just, and Arabs feel injured by the cost to them—but these are questions that Jews and Arabs can debate with each other, and among themselves, in the same universe of discourse. The elaboration of this idea is to be found in the essays below.

The extremists on both sides, to whom I have suggested this moral and political model, know very well what it means—that they have to give up their maximalist demands and their ideological purity—and few on both sides have seemed eager to move toward such pragmatism. But if the world community is ever to nudge Jews and Arabs to peace in the Middle East, it will have to be in the name of untidy decency. Once, on an occasion when I shared the platform with a very distinguished Palestinian scholar, he said the following: "The Jewish God may have told the Jews that they are entitled to the land of Israel, but Allah did not tell me so." I responded: "Allah may have told you that all of the land to which the teachings of Islam has been extended rightfully and permanently belongs to Muslims, but I did not hear him speaking Hebrew." But the divine language is, perhaps, neither Arabic nor Hebrew, as spoken by maximalists on both sides. I believe that it is the Esperanto of moderates who work for accommodation.

8. In Debate with the Arabs and Their Friends: "Zionism Is Racism"— A Counterattack

In 1975 the General Assembly of the United Nations passed a resolution asserting that "Zionism is racism." This action was an expression of Arab frustration that Israel continued to exist. The large majority for this slur came from the then third world allies of the Arab states. A political quarrel was, thus, moved to a far more dangerous level. If the state of Israel could be described as inherently racist, then the Arabs did not need to negotiate with it. They were justified in using every possible means, including terrorism, to help it fall. Many Jews have responded to such rhetoric by asking: If the Arabs can see Jews only as racists, then how can Jews ever think of making peace with such enemies?

▼

Modern Zionism existed by the 1830s, very near the dawn of nationalism in Europe, as a revolutionary force, but it lay dormant for a half century. During the middle decades of the nineteenth century, it was still widely believed in Europe, and especially by Jews, that Western liberalism was on the rise and that it would eventually reach even tsarist Russia. The Jews were on the way to achieving, everywhere, equal rights in law and equal treatment in society. The question of Jewish nationalism, which posited the return of many, or even most, Jews to the land of Israel, was deemed to be a theoretical dream.

Zionist nationalism became a serious political option as a result of a rising anti-Semitism in Europe in the last decades of the nineteenth century. The most virulent Jew-hatred, including large-scale pogroms, was native to tsarist Russia, but it existed everywhere in one form or another. In France, groups that hated the results of the French Revolution expressed themselves in the anti-Semitic incitements of the Dreyfus Affair. In Germany, Richard Wagner gave currency to Aryan racialist doctrines, which were soon expressed in politics by the pan-German movement. In Austria, Karl Lueger led an anti-Semitic party to repeated victories in Vienna before and after the turn of the century. In Hungary and Bohemia, the "blood libel" was revived; it is the ancient canard that Jews slaughter Christian children before Passover in order to use their blood in the baking of matzoth.

Many Jews wanted to believe that even these attacks were a last gasp of dying Jew-hatred, but some, such as Leon Pinsker in Russia in 1882 and Theodor Herzl in Paris and Vienna in 1895, decided that the renewed anti-Semitism was not a passing phenomenon. This hatred had declared Jews to be aliens in Europe; it had asserted that Jews were members of an alien people which was not assimilable.

In the 1880s and 1890s the justification of Zionist nationalism changed. It had begun, in mid-century, as a plea to Jews to labor for their national liberation and equality, just as the other nations in the world (e.g., Greeks, Italians, and Hungarians) were doing. By the end of the century, under the impact of anti-Semitism, Zionism faced the uniquely troubled relationship between Jews and Gentiles. Theodor Herzl, who founded the Zionist movement in 1897, did not merely appeal to the Jews to cease being a minority and become a "normal" nation. He addressed himself to the powers of the world, to persuade them that it was in their interest to help found a Jewish state. Thus the nations would solve a problem of their own; they would end the turmoil caused within their own borders by negative encounters between Jews and non-Jews. Turning to the Jews, Herzl argued that a state of their own would be an act of redress for the many centuries during which Jews had lived as a minority. As for the Arabs, Herzl asserted that whatever discomfort such a creation might cause the local Arabs of Palestine would be more than counterbalanced by the good that an advanced Western society, the Jews, would bring to the entire region. He emphasized, of course, that the Jewish state would conform to the highest standards of morality in its treatment of non-Jews within its borders.

In the language of our own day, Herzl's Zionism was a plea for "affirmative action." He was himself, culturally and religiously, a highly assimilated Jew. There is nothing in his writings of the pathos and passion of a deep relationship to the Jewish past. The "Jewish problem" for him was exclusion of Jews by the Gentile majority, and he wanted to correct it once and for all through Zionism. He knew that it would take unusual effort, which would be attended by temporary injury and dislocation of Jews and of Arabs. Once this act of state building was completed, normalcy would prevail and the relationship among all the peoples involved would proceed along common norms. It would require no special consideration for anyone, and any lingering persistent tension would vanish.

This view of Zionism was held in the next generation by Vladimir Jabotinsky. He knew that the creation of a Jewish state in Palestine would cause some discomfort to the Arab inhabitants of the land. Jabotinsky had much less hope than Herzl that Arabs would easily accommodate themselves to the new reality, and he even proposed population transfer, with Jewish help, for those Arabs who did not want to remain in a Jewish state; but Jabotinsky insisted, as Herzl had, that those who did remain would be treated as equal citizens. Zionism was a moral imperative for Jabotinsky because, as he asserted, without at least one Jewish state—and only one was possible or desirable—the existence of the Jewish people in the modern era was severely endangered; on the other hand, the loss by the Arab people of some thousands of square miles of territory, and even of some places that it had held dear, would not in any serious sense endanger the continuity or vitality of Arab nationalism and religion. Jabotinsky argued before the Peel Commission in the British House of Lords in 1936 that the failure to achieve a Jewish state might be the end of the Jews; therefore, whatever had to be done to safeguard the continuity of Jews and their culture was morally justifiable, provided the maximum care was taken to limit the injury that this might cause to other interests.

The case for Zionism as defined by Herzl and his followers made it possible for the movement to enter the arena of international politics. To be sure, Herzl's formulation was not universally accepted, even by Zionists—at least not in its pure, theoretical form. In logic, Herzlian Zionism could have accepted any territory that might be made available to Jews. The Jewish National Movement need not necessarily have centered all its attention on regaining the ancestral land of Palestine. In his essay *The Jewish State*, Herzl himself suggested an unpopulated stretch of Argentina, and he was willing, in 1903, to accept the British offer of possible Jewish settlement in Uganda, at least as a temporary solution to the vast needs of the Jews who were being persecuted in the Russian empire. The majority of Herzl's followers did not, however, allow him to take so purely rational and formal an approach. To them Zionism meant Zion, and no place else. Unlike Herzl, even the most secular Jews among the majority of the Zionists had cultural and emotional roots in the Jewish tradition and historic experience; only the emotions about "the return to Zion" could arouse their deepest and most fervent energies.

In a very interesting way, these nonrational facts themselves became part of the demand that Zionism posed to the world as part of its plea for "affirmative action." The cultural Zionists, those for whom the national endeavor was more than merely a solution to the problem of anti-Semitism or a regularization of the political status of Jews in the world, analyzed the internal situation of Jewish culture and tradition and came to quite pessimistic conclusions. These required radical action to save Judaism—however that might be defined—for the future, not only for Jews but also for the world. This argument was made primarily by a Jewish intellectual, Asher Ginsberg, who wrote under the pen name of Ahad Ha'am. The essence of his argument was that Jews, like all Western people, were now living in a postreligious age. The function that religion had once performed, to encase and preserve the Jewish people in a scattered Diaspora, it could no longer discharge in an age of growing disbelief. Hence a new center of Jewish energy was required, one in which the majority culture was Hebraic. In such a center, the Jewish spirit would survive, in contemporary redefinition. Ahad Ha'am believed that this center would provide a new energy for the Diaspora. It is not necessary to analyze Ahad Ha'am's theories or to measure them against the evolving reality of Zionism and Israel. It is enough for our present purposes to note that the conception of the renewed Jewish settlement in Israel as critical to the revitalization of Judaism and to the preservation of the Jews as a people (even as Zionists differed about their definitions of Judaism) became central, early on, to Zionist argument.

The basic contention of cultural Zionism is thus, in its own way, a plea for "affirmative action": if the world wants the Jewish experience not to vanish or, at the very least, not to be distorted, there must somewhere be a place where that experience does not always exist under the pressure of some other culture, in an endless majority/minority situation. The interest of the world as a whole in the preservation of one of its major traditions, the spiritual heritage of the Jews, requires an unprecedented act of one-time favoritism. All the other major traditions were entering the twentieth century in places where each had a normal home—that is, where the majority lived within the culture and had only to face the task of adaptation to modernity. Only the Jews had no such center; only the Jews lived always under the pressure of another, the majority, culture. Therefore, it could justly be maintained that it was not only in the Jewish interest but also in that of the world at large that such a Jewish national home should exist.

In November 1917, the British government issued the Balfour Declaration, which ranged the greatest power of the day, the leader of the soon-to-be-victorious Allies, on the side of Zionism. In its very language, the Balfour Declaration was an act of redress, of affirmative action. The British cabinet which had decided on this pro-Zionist action accepted the idea that a nonresident people, the Jews (they were then perhaps 10 percent of the population of Palestine), had larger rights in the land than the resident Arabs, because the Jews, scattered around the world, had a national need to return to the land of Israel. The declaration also tried to limit the hurt such an action might cause to those who were affected by it; it specified that the rights of the Arab inhabitants of the land were to be respected.

In fact, a balance between these two clauses of the Balfour Declaration has not yet been found, either in law or in politics or in military fact. Those who have fought against this action have used every means from armed struggle, including terrorism, to intellectual defamation in an effort to destroy the Jewish state. The assertion that "Zionism is racism" is the newest, and most flagrant, attack. This defamatory slogan is being used by Arabs, who have been joined by anti-Western forces in the Soviet Bloc and in large parts of the third world. Jews have been so angered by this incitement that any form of criticism of Israeli policy, even when uttered by proven friends and sometimes even when stated by Jews, has become, among some Jews, the subject of another equation: all criticism of Israel is defined as anti-Semitism and it is therefore equated with the canard "Zionism is racism."

Much of the criticism of Israel does, indeed, mask a wish that the State of Israel should not exist at all—but it is a self-defeating exaggeration to equate all criticism of Israel's policies with anti-Semitism. There is a legitimate argument within Israel, in the Jewish world as a whole, and among the friends of Israel as to whether annexationist policies on the West Bank are in the best interests of Israel, of peace in the Middle East, and of sound future relationships between Jews and Arabs. Ronald Reagan and François Mitterrand are not enemies of Israel; they are both opposed to the annexationist policies in which the right wing in Israel fervently believes. It is not an assault on Israel to question some of its policies, echoing moderate or even left-wing opinions in Israel itself, and it is vile and harmful to brand all such questioners as traducers of Zion. The Jewish people have enough enemies without adding to their number those who are critical friends.

But the slogan hurled by Israel's enemies that "Zionism is racism" is unforgivable. It is ironic, and even tragic, that most of the hostile forces which lament this charge are themselves making claims on the world in accents comparable to those of Zionism. The moral demand for special consideration, for major acts of redress for past wrongs for which present generations are expected to pay, are being ever more insistently made by various forces of the third world. No one seriously believes that the bulk of the third world countries will ever repay the vast loans, which amount by now to many tens of billions of dollars, that they have taken from governments and banks in the West. This transfer of capital is justified by the argument that these countries were colonized and exploited by their Western masters in previous centuries and that the money is a form of recompense for past wrongs.

To the degree to which such a claim can be sustained, a claim based on the memory of injustice inflicted on a helpless people by a foreign oppressor, the Jews are actually the prime example. The "colonialist" attack on the Jews was different only in geography from those experienced—and remembered—by the third world. The Roman conquerors of Judea in the year 70 enslaved and exiled most of its Jewish population. After that, the Jewish Diaspora has existed until recent generations under exploitative laws. Jews were excluded from most economic pursuits; they were taxed much more heavily than anyone else, and were often victimized by pogroms, or worse. The only strikingly comparable situation is that of American blacks, who were victims of slavery in a country to which they were dragged by force. American blacks insist, quite correctly, that their experience is at one with the pain inflicted by colonialism on peoples all over Africa, Latin America, and much of Asia.

The passion of Jews for self-determination and for dignity as a people—the Zionist ideal—is a prime example of recoil from colonialism. Anti-Semitism, medieval and modern, was colonialist oppression of the Jewish minority by the Gentile majority. Those who make the case for special consideration for the third world, in the name of anticolonialism, cannot defend the principles that justify their demands without accepting Zionism, for it is a parallel demand for "affirmative action." "Zionism is racism" is thus a fraudulent assertion. It can be understood only as a political tactic, and a very nasty one at that, in the Jewish-Arab confrontation. This attack must be resisted, and exposed.

1986

9. *In Debate with Jewish and Palestinian Extremists*

Of the making of many books on the conflict in the Middle East, there is no end. In October 1990, I wrote in the *New York Review of Books* about some of the recent writing. The subjects, and the authors, ranged across the entire political spectrum. Most of that essay was devoted to two works, one by John Quigley, explaining and defending the Palestinian position at its most extreme; the other book was an unfriendly biography by Robert I. Friedman of Rabbi Meir Kahane, the founder of the Jewish Defense League and the leader of the extremist Kach party in Israel. (Friedman's book and my comments about it appeared before Kahane's assassination in New York on November 5, 1990, and before the war in the Gulf.) In this essay, which is given here in shortened form, I continue to argue for dealing with the Zionist enterprise as a form of "affirmative action."

▼

Is the Zionist state legitimate? Is the Palestinian state legitimate? Most Arabs deny the legitimacy of Israel. The Arab argument grew more passionate earlier this year as it became clear that the PLO's expressed willingness to negotiate with Israel was not leading to a Palestinian state, and many Palestinians concluded that Israel remained implacably opposed to Palestinian nationalism. When I spent some time this summer on the West Bank, even before Saddam Hussein became the hero of the Palestinians there, the young people with whom I talked were no longer listening to their parents, or even to the supposed leaders of the *intifada*.

The mood in Israel, too, was changing radically, in the direction of more intense nationalism. Even the left was adopting the language of fervent patriotism. The main reason for this change was the vast new immigration of Jews from the Soviet Union. The Zionists in the Labor party and the parties further left refused to join the Palestinians in proposing limits to the new immigration, which Palestinians feared was tipping the balance against the possibility of a Palestinian state. Most of the Russian Jews would have preferred to come to the United States, and few were moving into the West Bank. But they were rapidly occupying scarce housing in Israel, and the cheaper, government-subsidized housing on the West Bank was becoming more attractive to other Israelis.

In the encounter between Israelis and Palestinians the divisive issue was still—as it has been throughout the history of the conflict since the 1870s—the question of Jewish immigration. One of Israel's best-known left-wing polemicists, the journalist and politician Uri Avnery, who has been advocating a Palestinian state since 1948 when he was a soldier in Israel's war of independence, wrote this summer that his mother had come to Israel from Russia; he could not now say to his cousins from Pinsk that they should not be allowed to come to Israel, too. If he were to agree to such a policy, Avnery wrote, he would be declaring his mother's arrival to have been illegitimate and his own presence in Israel to be the result of usurpation. Throughout Israel the "right of return," which guarantees that unrestricted numbers of Jews can settle in Israel, was again being asserted as a fundamental principle that all Zionists share.

This Zionist principle was not extended to the Palestinians. Even the most outspoken members of the Zionist left, such as Shulamit Aloni, the leader of the Civil Rights party, could not accept the possibility that a large number of Palestinians would return to Israel; and many were not at all sure that they would welcome a totally unrestricted return to the West Bank, though Aloni recently has been bold enough to ask: "Why should the Palestinians not hail Saddam Hussein? What have we, even in the 'peace camp,' done for them?"

Aloni was responding, in an interview with *Ha'aretz* (August 27, 1990), to the news that Yossi Sarid, one of her most respected colleagues in the peace movement, had written in *Ha'aretz* ten days before that while he still favored Palestinian self-determination and the end of the occupation, he was angry and disappointed with the PLO for its support of a leader who "murdered tens of thousands of 'regime opponents' without blinking an eye." "Let them call me," Sarid had said, implying that they should do so after they get over their infatuation with Saddam Hussein. In her answer, Aloni said that a settlement with the Palestinians was not a reward for good conduct and that, moreover, the continuing war with the Palestinians was debasing Israel.

The deep issues in the conflict between Arabs and Jews are now being stripped of the customary obfuscation of liberal rhetoric on both sides. The Palestinians are asserting their right to an Arab state, and they continue to blame the Western powers, and particularly the United States, for helping to inflict Zionism upon them. The Israelis insist that only anti-Semites would dare question the legitimacy of Israel's existence. The most liberal members of both camps agree that the Israelis and the Palestinians are facts of life, and that some kind of solution for their coexistence must be worked out. But most people in both camps think it is not morally necessary to accept this view.

The most extreme case for the Palestinians that I have seen recently is *Palestine and Israel: A Challenge to Justice* by John Quigley, a professor of law at Ohio State University. The closest he comes to finding some validity for Zionism is when he acknowledges that the mandate to govern Palestine, which the League of Nations gave to Great Britain in 1922, contained an endorsement of a "Jewish national home in Palestine." But that endorsement must be qualified, he argues, because the Zionist leader, Chaim Weizmann, failed at the Versailles conference in 1919 to get the Allies to use the phrase "historical right" to describe the Jewish claim to settle in Palestine; the Allies had settled for a reference to the "historical connection" between Jews and Palestine.

It is not at all clear how much difference the distinction between these two phrases makes to Quigley, because he finds the Balfour Declaration as a whole, in the words he quotes from Quincy Wright, an international lawyer who visited Palestine in 1925, "a gross violation of the principle of self-determination, proclaimed by the Allies." It was a gross violation, for Quigley, for Wright, and for most Arab Palestinians, because the people living in the territory designated as a Jewish homeland in the Balfour Declaration were never effectively consulted; if they had been, most of them could not have wanted a Jewish homeland to be established in Palestine. For Quigley, virtually everything that the Zionists did to establish their presence in Palestine was illegal.

Quigley attacks the validity of the UN resolution 181, of 1947, which called for the partition of Palestine, and which the Zionists accepted and the Palestinians rejected, on the ground that a resolution by the General Assembly is only a recommendation; it has no enforceable authority. In his discussion of the 1948 Israel-Arab war Quigley seems uneasy. He thinks that the Palestinians, as the existing majority in 1948, had the right to defend themselves against a rebellious minority, the Jews, who were trying to create a state of their own. He suggests that Israel's claim to any territory at all is open to question, and that the claim certainly does not refer to the territory gained in the war:

> The duty to restore the preexisting situation requires Israel to repatriate the Arabs it dispossessed. This means allowing them to return to their original areas. Not only the Arabs who left Palestine but the substantial numbers who took refuge in 1948 in the Gaza Strip and the West Bank have a right to return.

Israel's fight with the Arabs in 1948 was "a war of aggression," for which not only the state, but even individual Israelis are responsible.

The main problem with Quigley's book is his selective use of international law. It is true that the Jews were a minority in Palestine in 1948, but were they, then and earlier, by law and by right, as he suggests, entirely subject to the will of the majority? Had they no ethnic or religious character, no history and no active community life of their own in Palestine, and no ties to other Jews, of which international law could and should take into account? The concept of "minority rights" is hardly mentioned in Quigley's book, even though the League of Nations and its successor, the United Nations, have labored long to find ways of protecting minorities against unfriendly majorities.

In criticizing Israel, Quigley invokes the "new law" made at the Nuremburg trials that individuals are responsible for committing illegal acts that were ordered by national authority: individual Israelis, in his view, are personally guilty if they followed orders to expel Arabs. This "new law" made by the victors at Nuremburg is valid, but "new law" made by the League of Nations in the 1920s and the United Nations in the 1940s to grant Jews national rights, and ultimately a state, is invalid. (Nor does it matter that the Jewish settlers agreed in 1947 to live peacefully in a limited part of Palestine in areas where they were the majority, and that they were attacked by the surrounding nations and the Palestinians. I wonder whether Quigley would argue today that the national character of French Canadians can be defined, or even obliterated, by a simple plebiscite based on majority vote of the English Canadians.)

Quigley's references to the Arab states in the region are also ahistorical. All the Arab states, without exception, were creations of the arrangements after the First World War when the victors carved up the Ottoman empire. Their boundaries are artificial. Their very existence as separate states and not as parts of the pan-Arab realm was imposed by the victorious Western powers. This accident of diplomacy created the modern Middle East, as David Fromkin points out in his important book, *A Peace To End All Peace: Creating the Modern Middle East*, 1914–1922. Quigley seems to believe that the West had no business deciding who was to rule in the Middle East after the fall of the Ottoman empire. That was a matter for Arabs alone, he writes, and never mind the concerns, claims, and rights of all the other peoples—Jews, Kurds, and a variety of Christians—who were in the region. Quigley seems to think that states should be born by immaculate conception, and that outside powers have no right to protect or promote their interests—at least not when it comes to helping the Jews to a stake in Palestine. One problem with this approach to the conflict in Israel and Palestine is that it is far removed from reality, both past and present, and that it offers no basis for making peace.

At the other extreme, Meir Kahane is the subject of a biography by the journalist Robert I. Friedman, *The False Prophet: From FBI Informant to Knesset Member*. Friedman's account of Kahane's personal life and his political record is devastating. In Palestine, Kahane's father had been a member of the right-wing nationalist group, the Revisionist party. Kahane himself was trained in a Talmudic academy in Brooklyn and was ordained an Orthodox rabbi there, but soon left his congregation for a strange career as a demagogue and an underground man.

We learn from Friedman's impressive research that Kahane led a double or triple life. He wrote polemics for the Jewish press, often attacking blacks as enemies of the Jews, as well as sports articles for a Brooklyn daily paper, and he appeared to be the pious father of four children. He was also a secret FBI informant on leftist groups, and a philanderer who posed as the Presbyterian "Michael King"; one of his lovers committed suicide when he rejected her. Friedman also shows that after Kahane organized the Jewish Defense League in 1968, both the Mossad Israel's intelligence agency, and Shamir, who had recently left the Mossad, knew about the JDL's campaign of harassment against Soviet consulates and other Soviet targets.

Kahane left for Israel in 1971 after being indicted for manufacturing weapons, perhaps for use against Soviet consulates. When some years later, on October 11, 1985, Alex Odeh, an official of the American-Arab Anti-Discrimination Committee, was murdered by a bomb, and a string of other bombings occurred, it was suspected that they had been carried out by the JDL, of which Kahane was still the leader. Friedman reports that "the FBI is said to have one informant whose testimony can link Kahane to planning sessions that took place before two of the 1985 bombings, including the murder of Alex Odeh. The informant, however, refuses to testify publicly."

The accuracy of Friedman's account, which describes Kahane's lack of personal honor and his sponsorship of thuggery, has not been challenged. The larger question, however, is how to assess Kahane's political significance as a leader of a highly visible faction of the Jews both in the United States and in Israel. In America to this day, as Friedman shows, Kahane supporters have included some respectable figures in the Jewish community. An uncle of Kahane's, Isaac Trainin, who was a high official of the New York Federation of Jewish Philanthropies in the 1970s, told Friedman that "at least twelve of the twenty or thirty people sitting on the dais [at a dinner of the Federation] . . . had given Kahane $10,000 or more. They would curse him in public, but give him money under the table."

Is Kahane a major figure in Israel? Is he, as Friedman says at the end of his book, the direct heir "of the broad stream of the Orthodox Zionist Right"? Friedman himself supplies the evidence and the arguments to balance this conclusion. Kahane moved to Israel in 1971, in part to escape being tried for several offenses in the United States. On arrival, he refused to join the leadership of any of the right-wing parties, preferring to stay "in business for himself." He organized an Israeli JDL, which began its public career by threatening Arabs with death if they did not leave Israel. This has been his obsessive theme. In an interview with Friedman in 1979 he said that he would be willing to deport Arabs in cattle cars in the middle of the night.

In 1977 Kahane ran for the Knesset and was badly beaten. He lost again, but in July 1984 he finally won a seat in the Knesset. His support, Friedman tells us, came not from Gush Emunim, the principal representative of the West Bank settlers (he got only 5 percent of their votes), but, as Friedman puts it, from "Israel's poor, undereducated and underemployed Sephardim."

There is truth in both of Friedman's seemingly contradictory assessments of Kahane's importance. The Jewish right wing, religious and secular, both in the United States and in Israel, is more divided than Friedman suggests.[3] A current best-selling book in Israel, *Rabbi Shach*, is an account by the journalist Moshe Horowitz of the ninety-three-year-old leader of a major wing of the ultra-Orthodox movement in Israel. Shach believes that the occupied territories are not worth the lives of the Jews who are endangered in the West Bank and Gaza; for the sake of peace with the Palestinians, Shach would accept return of the territories to Palestinian control. He is vehemently opposed to the notion of Kahane and other ultra-Orthodox, both in Israel and abroad—including the followers of the Brooklyn rebbe of Lubavitch—that the apocalypse is near, and that the settlements must be protected and the Arabs expelled in order to prepare for the arrival of the Messiah. Even among those who expect the Messiah to come soon, no one imagines that Kahane will be found in his immediate entourage. Friedman acknowledges that Kach, Kahane's political party, "is a one-man show and it will die with Kahane."

Kahane is just as unlikely to take over the secular parties of the right to any significant degree. Vladimir Jabotinsky, the founding father of the Likud, was a thoroughly secular figure who would have nothing whatever to do with religion. For that matter, there was not a single religious believer among the most ultranationalist group of all, the "Stern Gang" of the late 1930s and the 1940s, which was founded by Abraham Stern, and to which the young Yitzhak Shamir belonged. Joseph Heller, professor of political science at the Hebrew University, in the first detailed analytical history of this group, *Lehi: Ideology and Politics*, 1940–1949 (it is in Hebrew), describes how the Stern gang took as its model Jozef Pilsudski of Poland, a populist Catholic authoritarian with a socialist past, who was willing to ally himself with Japan and Germany in order to advance the Polish cause. The Stern gang thought of itself, as Kahane does now, as the cutting edge of ultranationalism, but nobody in the group respected the political authority of rabbis.

Even today, the alliance between the ultra-Orthodox and the Likud is a matter of political convenience: neither Shamir nor Sharon is ever in a synagogue unless he has to make a speech. They have succeeded in persuading at least half of Israeli voters, and perhaps more, that Jews must have all the land up to the Jordan River, and they use the very arguments that Begin used in his speech defending the new settlement in Elon Moreh. Like Begin, they say that Zionism requires the Israelis to create an impregnable, fortified position for themselves in the sea of Arabs, and that it is no less virtuous to create a Jewish majority on the West Bank during the coming decades than it was to do exactly that in Haifa and Jaffa–Tel Aviv during the 1920s and 1930s.

Among such Israelis, the "transfer" of the Arabs is now supported in polls by some 40 percent. And yet I do not believe that these people subscribe to Kahane's idea of midnight expulsions of Palestinians. The number favoring "transfer" have risen dramatically during the *intifada*, but few believe that such action is possible. The changing opinion is largely an expression of frustration. In any event, were Israel to embark on a policy of "transfer," the leader in charge would be someone who is regarded by its society as indigenous—former generals such as Ariel Sharon, Rechavam Ze'evi, or Raful Eytan—and not someone like Kahane. The right-wing parties took the lead in excluding Kahane as a "racist" from the last Knesset election. In their mind, he is from the gutter, or at best an obnoxious import from America, and a competitor from the fringe whom they want to silence.

Nonetheless, Friedman is right to emphasize that Kahane poses a threat to Israel's democracy. His appeal to circles beyond his immediate supporters in Israel, and in America, is a warning of what might happen if the conflict between Jews and Arabs in the Holy Land continues and becomes even more embittered. This is Friedman's important theme. It is not that much of Israel is already following Kahane, but that to describe Kahane as Friedman has is to ring "the alarm bell in the night." If turmoil increases in the Holy Land, it is not entirely absurd to suggest that Kahane could become the Goebbels, or at least the man who prepares the way for the Goebbels, of an angrier and more frustrated Israel. Friedman's book is an impassioned warning that Jews, who like to think of themselves as heirs of the prophets, must take heed not to be debased by zealots.

One of the saddest elements of the conflict is that only the maximalists, on both sides, have clear-cut positions. The Palestinians believe that the Jews should not be in Palestine at all and they are willing, at best, to acknowledge the unfortunate fact of their being there. The Likud believes that it has already conceded the land east of the Jordan to the Arabs and that western Palestine is the least amount of territory to which the Jewish nation is entitled.

The Zionist moderates in the Labor party have not been able to define how much less than all of the undivided land in Israel is enough—and on what basis. The critics of the moderate Zionists, both within and outside the Jewish camp, remember very well that while Chaim Weizmann and David Ben-Gurion accepted the principle of partition, each, when he was at the height of his powers, believed that the Jews should obtain land by stages until, or so they undoubtedly if privately hoped, Israel would possess all of Palestine. In *The Arab Question and the Jewish Problem*, published in Hebrew in 1985, Joseph Gorni reached the somber conclusion that the Labor party, which was the main actor in creating the Jewish settlement in Palestine, became "more than any of the other parties, the primary incarnation of the Zionist danger," in the mind and experience of the Arabs.

What principles define the policy toward Arabs of "moderate Israelis"—and the policy toward Jews of "moderate Arabs"? Almost all the writers whose work I have discussed here agree that neither side has worked out a satisfactory theory to reconcile the two nationalisms with the imperatives of peaceful coexistence. The only theoretical approach that I keep suggesting to help resolve the conflict is that of affirmative action on behalf of minorities. Zionism began by asking for, and getting, what amounts to affirmative action to help a landless and long-persecuted people return to its ancient homeland. The Palestinians are now demanding special consideration for, and redress of, their own grievances; they are saying that they refuse to accept the fate that a cruel world usually accords to losers in territorial wars. In any case of affirmative action, there is no clear limit that defines how much is enough. The degree and kind of reparations that the oppressed receive is determined by a combination of power they can bring to bear and the moral discomfort they cause.

Affirmative action was a policy born in American domestic politics, and I do not want to appear to suggest that it can be applied mechanically to the conflict between Jews and Arabs in Israel/Palestine. Palestinians maintain that they owe the Jews of the world no reparation for the injuries done to them by the Western anti-Semites, or even for those Jews suffered in Muslim countries. In reply it can, of course, be argued that those who pay the price for affirmative action are usually not those who inflicted the injuries. In the second place, affirmative action usually implies that an existing majority provides redress for a minority. In the conflict between Palestinians and Israelis, each group is, in its own mind, an aggrieved minority. But the essence of affirmative action is that hard cases require complicated answers, which can be devised more easily in untidy practice than in neat theories.

Most of the writers whose books I have discussed advocate a charitable pragmatism that reflects, I believe, the dominant faith of Western intellectuals—but the two camps are prevented from such accommodation by the strength and passion of their ideologues. Nevertheless, hope will not die, even these days when nationalism and intransigence are in the ascendant in both camps. The moderate pragmatists have not all run for cover. A few months ago, at the very height of the *intifada*, Bishop Michel Sabbah, the first Arab to be appointed Latin Patriarch of Jerusalem, published a pastoral letter in which he asked for a two-state solution: he took a stand against Palestinians who would deny the Jews a homeland. In mid-August 1990, soon after the crisis in the Gulf began, a group of Israeli and Palestinian moderates met together in Jerusalem and restated their view that Israelis and Palestinians should accept each other's national existence and national equality.

It would perhaps help if everybody would stop thinking about a definitive settlement. The partition of Palestine, when it was first proposed as a solution in 1937 by Great Britain's Peel Commission, was not conceived as permanent. The commission imagined that Jews and Arabs needed a period of separation leading, or so it was hoped, toward a subsequent stage when they had learned to accept each other and might then actually live together. This hope was very much in the minds of those who took part in the United Nations decision of November 1947 to create two states. It is largely forgotten that the two states were expected, from their very beginning, to function as one economic entity. The principle of partition would be easier to carry out now if the arrangements were made subject to regular review by Israel and Palestine after periods of five or ten years.

This suggestion is not identical with the "confidence building" delay of three to five years, which was built into the Camp David accords in 1979. That proviso was designated as the period between preliminary agreement on West Bank autonomy and negotiations for a permanent solution. What is being suggested here is a two-state solution, subject to periodic rethinking and renegotiation. Such an untidy and even unprecedented arrangement might encourage a situation in which the ideologies on both sides would gradually become obsolete. More than ever before, one must remember the hope of the radical Zionist movement, Hashomer Hatzair, in its beginnings, and of Martin Buber and Judah Leon Magnes, that some form of binationalism will emerge in the region.

I have little hope that progress will be made through any of the existing processes. Jews and Arabs are not likely to be soon negotiating across the same table. The Americans, under pressure from the Israeli lobby in the United States, were always reluctant to force them to do so, and especially now, because the PLO has sided with Saddam Hussein. I do not believe that counterpressure from America's allies will be sufficiently intense to move Washington to do more than to try to cajole Israel's Likud government. Bush and Gorbachev, in agreeing in Helsinki on November 9, 1990, that they would cooperate to push their clients toward a solution of the Israel-Arab conflict, seemed to be reviving the idea of an international conference of all interested parties. But both Yitzhak Shamir and any of his likely successors will probably resist attending such a meeting. They would have to be very much more frightened than they are at present.

Nonetheless, the tide of another, much more serious fear is rising in Israel. Saddam Hussein will not prevail, and the Arab world will remain divided between the powers who want to maintain the status quo and insurgents with very different goals, including Iraq, Libya, and the PLO. Israeli society, however, is increasingly troubled by the knowledge that the deepest tide running in the region is the anger of the have-nots. Even after Saddam Hussein is gone, America, Israel, and Arab national leaders will have to reckon with tens of millions of Arabs who will be increasingly hungry, and increasingly angry. The Palestinians are a special case, as are the Jews, but both are part of a larger problem. Resources will have to be redistributed in the Middle East, or more and more of the hungry and resentful will try to arm themselves with the terrible weapons that Saddam Hussein is now brandishing. No matter how the crisis ends, Israel will be in ever greater danger in a region of growing hate. It can afford to be made the scapegoat of the discontent of the Arab poor even less than it can survive forever with the anger of the Palestinians. The real threat to Israel is no longer the PLO; it is the pan-Arabism of the poor. Israel's very life depends on making peace with the Palestinians, and thus opening the door to the Arab world as a whole. For its own sake, and for the sake of the world, Israel must soon join in helping the people in the entire region to achieve more decent lives.

1990

10. *Zionism Revisited*

The essence of Zionism is the revolt of Jews against eighteen centuries of powerlessness. To flee their persecuters, Jews needed permission to save themselves from those who controlled the ports of refuge. A state in the hands of Jews means that this people has again acquired ports of its own and doors it can open for Jews in need. From the very beginning of the Zionist enterprise, to this very day, even as the factions keep clashing on every other issue, bringing Jews home to their land is the affirmation all Zionists share.

▼

The Russian Jews are coming, but some Israelis would rather they stayed away. Benny Suissa, a leader of the poor in the slums, insists that money should be spent on improving their housing and on getting them jobs (Israel's rate of unemployment has risen beyond one in ten), and not on newcomers.

The complainers are wrong, and they will not prevail. Suissa and his constituents are in Israel because earlier settlers risked their lives in the 1930s and 1940s to bring in "illegal immigrants" that the British Army and Navy fought to keep out. After 1948, secret emissaries from Jerusalem made paths to Israel for Jews in flight from hostile Arab states. I was in Israel in 1949, when there was little to eat and tens of thousands of newcomers had to live in tents. In those heroic days the immigrants were brothers in need, with whom one shared, and not competitors for welfare checks.

The complainers, Israel's version of "nativists," are not a new phenomenon. In the early 1970s, as the first hundred thousand Russian Jews were arriving in Israel, young soldiers and their brides were complaining to the government and to the executive board of the World Zionist Organization (on which I sat in those years) that some of the money being used to settle the Russians should be spent on providing housing for newly formed families. At the very beginning of modern Zionist settlement in Palestine, in the last decades of the nineteenth century, the earliest settlers of the "old *Yishuv*" wanted the Zionists to stay away, for they were upsetting the Turks and bringing trouble with the Arabs. In the 1920s, when Palestine was in a severe economic crisis, few new immigrants came, and those who did were not universally welcomed.

But the basic institutions of the Zionist movement, and the Jewish people as a whole, remained unshakably committed to the notion that Zionism means providing a home for Jews. This idea is enshrined in the very terminology of Zionism: to come to Israel is not simply to change addresses; it is *aliyah*, "ascent" to a higher plane.

Concerning unrestricted immigration to Israel, there is no difference between hawks and doves. The hawks hope that the Russians will go to the West Bank and increase the hold of Jews in the disputed territories, while the doves want new immigrants for the Galilee, part of pre-1967 Israel, where Jews are losing their majority. But Yitzhak Shamir, the leader of the right, would remain a passionate proponent of immigration even if not a single new immigrant went to the West Bank, and Shimon Peres, the leader of the moderate left, would not call for an embargo on newcomers even if many of them insisted on living in the occupied territories. The battle about the future shape of Israel's society continues, with unabated passion, but the right of all Jews to come to the land is the unshakable and uniting principle. It has to be, for Israel was created as an answer to Jewish powerlessness. It was conceived as the one place to which Jews could come as a right, one that was guaranteed by the power of a sovereign Jewish state.

Some Zionists have known from the very beginning that the existence of the right of Jews to return to the land of their ancestors would create problems with the Arabs and that the "return" would inevitably wreak injustice. States are not born immaculately, as the Native Americans and Tories of the Revolutionary era could have attested. America has not always looked like the land of the Founding Fathers. It has also been the land of nativists, of the Ku Klux Klan, and of Joe McCarthy. But the indwelling, self-correcting impulse of the American tradition is democracy.

Zionism has not always been, and it is not now, the movement of Theodor Herzl, who imagined a purely secular, democratic state, or of Ahad Ha'am (Asher Ginsberg), who was troubled about the pain of the Arabs, late in the nineteenth century, near the beginning of modern Zionism. The Israeli state and the Zionist ideal, which is its reason for being, contain many other impulses, and some are as unlovely as Benny Suissa's expression of self-interest. But, even on a bad day, Zionism remains a movement about saving Jews from oppression and assimilation, and from the indignity of having to beg for some place of refuge in the world. Zionism is a movement for the creation of a decent, just society for everybody, and not only for Jews, in the Jewish homeland. And Zionists remember, even when some of them try to forget, that they can achieve their vision of a Jewish state not by repression but only through peace with the Arabs.

Zionism is as disfigured, and as much alive, as the ideal of democracy.

1990

FOUR

In Defense of Cultural Zionism

The modern Zionist movement was not only about politics; it was also about culture. As late as the last years of the eighteenth century, Jews still thought of themselves as an extended religious and national community, and that religion was Orthodox. A century later, when modern Zionism began, Jews had become factionalized into several versions of the Jewish religion, and into secular nationalism and a variety of other ideologies. In the new age, apart from shared grief, what held Jews together? The dominant response among the Zionists was that Jews shared a national culture, and that the various factions would ultimately accommodate themselves to this new self-definition. Among Jews, modern Zionism, when it began, was resisted both among the Orthodox and the Reformed; they maintained, in separate ways, that the Jews were, above all, a community of believers and that they could not be transformed into a secular nation.

Among the Zionists themselves, the meaning of a national Jewish culture became, and remains, a subject of profound and impassioned debate. Some insist that the religious tradition is, and must be, superseded by a completely secular national culture. At the opposite extreme, some Orthodox believers have perceived Zionism as a temporary, secular instrument in the hands of God on the way to achieving the messianic redemption of the Jewish people. The mainstream of Zionist thought continues to define contemporary Jewish culture as a blending of, or perhaps a compromise between, the inherited religious tradition, and contemporary secular life. As is clear from the essays in this chapter, I belong to this third opinion. Chaim Weizmann, the first president of the State of Israel, invented the term "synthetic Zionism" to describe moderate political and cultural views, such as mine, advanced in this chapter and the one before.

11. *Ahad Ha'am,* 100 *Years Later*

The founder of spiritual Zionism, Ahad Ha'am, is both a profound influence on all modern Jewish thought, and half-forgotten. I have been deeply influenced by his thinking and his persona. Writing a century after he appeared on the literary and intellectual scene, I tried to come to terms with his legacy.

▼

Hundreds of books and articles about Israel keep appearing each year, analyzing and reanalyzing its foreign policy and internal politics from every conceivable point of view. But very little has been written about Israel's culture, and it remains a mystery, except perhaps to Israel itself.

Yet a national culture is developing there, one that is in constant tension with the literature and values of the classic past. So, for example, the poet Yehuda Amichai keeps struggling, line by line, to write about everyday life in spare, modern Hebrew, but he knows that almost every one of the words has a history that goes back to the Bible. The contemporary life that he lives amid the stones of ancient Jerusalem, and the very words that he uses to describe that life, cannot be bound by the past, or escape from it.

This tension is not new. It did not first arise after the state of Israel was declared in 1948. How to create a contemporary culture out of the earlier religious heritage has been a central problem of Zionism for at least a century.

This "question of Judaism" was sharply defined in the late 1880s by a young writer, Asher Ginzberg (who always wrote under the pseudonym Ahad Ha'am, which means "one of the people"), ten years before Theodor Herzl convoked the First Zionist Congress (1897) in Basel, Switzerland, to deal with the "question of the Jews"— that is, with their need to escape persecution. The very distinction between the "question of Judaism" and the "question of the Jews" was made by Ahad Ha'am. He became the central figure of "spiritual Zionism," in contrast to Herzl's political Zionism. Martin Buber, Judah Leon Magnes, and Gershom Scholem were, in their various ways, among Ahad Ha'am's disciples. Contemporary Israeli writers and intellectuals such as Amnon Rubenstein, A. B. Yehoshua, Amos Elon, and Amos Oz are under his influence or, like the Israeli historian David Vital, they write in conscious opposition to his politics.

This spring marks one hundred years since Ahad Ha'am's first visit to Palestine, from February to May 1891. He looked then with deep concern, but with few illusions, at the beginnings of Zionist settlement. A century later, it seems appropriate to think about the paradox of why he is so central to Israel to this day, and so unknown elsewhere. Is it because questions that he raised a hundred years ago continue to be painful?

Ahad Ha'am (1856–1927) began writing in 1887 in the Jewish intellectual center of Odessa, where he immediately became famous among those who read modern Hebrew, the language in which he wrote. His very first essay, "This Is Not the Way," created a stir and a scandal. Ahad Ha'am chided the Hovevei Zion (Lovers of Zion), the first Russian Zionists, who were busy raising a few rubles to help the handful of Jewish farming settlements they had founded in Palestine. Ahad Ha'am maintained that the Lovers of Zion offered the persecuted six million or seven million Jews of Russia no vision that could sustain them. He did not believe that even a Jewish state would bring a permanent end to anti-Semitism; he offered, instead, the vision of a revived Jewish national culture in which all Jews, everywhere, would find pride and meaning.

Ahad Ha'am was deeply ambivalent about political power, even as he knew that Jews had to acquire some in order to survive. He was a modern intellectual, a Rabbinic scholar who had turned agnostic, and yet he insisted that Jewish ethical values were absolute, that they could not be changed or flouted. His ultimate faith was his sense of belonging to the Jewish people, but the most strident expressions of Jewish nationalism evoked his anger.

From the beginning of his career until his death in Tel Aviv in 1927, Ahad Ha'am was unavoidable. He was different from all his contemporaries in Hebrew letters. Everyone, both admirers and enemies, knew it. His very style and use of language compelled attention. The attempt to make the Hebrew language into a modern instrument had begun a century earlier in Berlin, in the circle of Moses Mendelssohn, the founding father, among the Jews, of Haskalah, or Hebrew Enlightenment. This effort produced its greatest resonance in the next century in Eastern Europe, where novelists, poets, and essayists demonstrated that Hebrew could be used to express the concerns of modern men. But almost all these authors employed a language that was largely archaic and arcane. Their Orthodox fathers and grandfathers had written, or were still writing, medieval Hebrew, in which a writer was judged by how many allusions to the Bible and the Talmud he could weave into his text. The new Hebraists wrote not about the Talmud but about love and war, and about the conflict between science and religion, but their language and style were still half-medieval.

Ahad Ha'am was himself deeply learned in all the traditional sources, but he wrote in an unadorned Hebrew. He used no pyrotechnics of style to hide his thought. A self-taught polyglot who read voraciously and wrote easily in Yiddish, Russian, German, and English, he refused to publish in any of these languages. His aim was to raise modern Hebrew literature to the level of the best writing in Europe. And in his hands, the language of Hebrew prose finally, and irrevocably, left the Middle Ages.

Ahad Ha'am became a writer while believing he was only a temporary sojourner in the "temple of literature." He expected to make his living as a businessman. But by 1895 he had lost his money and turned to editing, pouring his energies a few years later into a new monthly published in Warsaw, which he called *Hashiloah*, after the biblical river that "flows quietly." The name was chosen to suggest that the journal would not be strident in tone but firm in direction. In the six years that he edited *Hashiloah*, Ahad Ha'am rewrote every article, insisting, often in vehement exchanges with authors, that their style had to be uncluttered and their intellectual content precise. To appear in Ahad Ha'am's monthly meant a writer had arrived; he had satisfied the severest taskmaster, its editor. At *Hashiloah*, Ahad Ha'am made his clear Hebrew the norm for modern Hebrew prose.

Ahad Ha'am was the most modern of Hebrew writers, not only in language but also in thought. He accepted Darwin's account of the evolution of humankind and was deeply influenced by the ideas of Auguste Comte and Herbert Spencer. He no longer believed the Book of Genesis, nor that God had created the Jews and then set them apart; on the contrary, the Jewish people, in his view, had given authority to their unique moral values by inventing the God who commanded them. For Ahad Ha'am, Moses may never have existed, and even if he had, the quest for the historical Moses was irrelevant. He said that the Jews, in the biblical writings, had constructed a hero who represented their image of themselves at their best. Moses was no builder of empires. He did not even lead his people across the Jordan to begin the conquest of the promised land. He was a human being and not a demigod. He knew anger and rage. To the very end of his days, at the age of 120, he was still sexually potent. Moses was the supreme representation of Jewish virtue, because he was undaunted by failure and defeat and because he never compromised a principle. There is, of course, more than a hint of autobiography in Ahad Ha'am's version of Moses.

These heresies were instantly challenged by the Orthodox rabbis in Eastern Europe. But even followers of Ahad Ha'am found themselves in disagreement with him. Judah Leon Magnes, who was the rabbi of the Reform Temple Emanu-El in New York City during the early years of the century, left that pulpit in order to establish a "reconstructed" synagogue. Magnes wrote to explain his ideas to Ahad Ha'am. The master replied by agreeing that such a synagogue should be "a haven of Jewish knowledge" and not the purveyor of "phrases of unctuous piety," but he insisted that religion was of secondary value for Jews. "It is possible to be a Jew in the national sense," he wrote, "without accepting many things in which religion requires belief."

At the very core of Ahad Ha'am's thought was a metaphor borrowed from Darwin and Spencer: peoples are to be compared to individual biological entities; nations, like individuals, are organisms that have wills to live and that adapt to new circumstances, or die if they do not. The Jewish people had survived in the Diaspora, Ahad Ha'am contended, by using religious law as the binding tie of community. Because that force was weakening in the modern era of disbelief, he said, religion no longer was preserving the Jewish people. Jews needed to find some other source of communal energy.

Ahad Ha'am's solution was a "spiritual center" in Palestine—an elite community to be established not as a haven for refugees, but as the laboratory within which the Jewish spirit would make itself contemporary. He did not envisage this elite community as an academy divorced from life. On the contrary, the high-minded members would be farmers and businessmen. Their lives would demonstrate the spiritual and moral values of the reviving Jewish national culture. Ahad Ha'am's center would be the place where Jewish life would be lived at its most intense. Incandescence would radiate out from it to all the Jews of the world, and the Jewish people would use national culture as they once used religion, to insure their life everywhere.

This analysis of the "question of Judaism" justified far more radical ideas than Ahad Ha'am was willing to countenance. Arguably, if the Jewish soul was weakening, Ahad Ha'am's secular, national culture was not necessarily the only medicine. Some younger writers, disciples of Nietzsche, proposed the superman to replace the prophet or scholar as the form in which to cast the new Jews. The Jewish people might rejuvenate themselves, they claimed, by turning to physical prowess and to reawakened joy in all that the senses could experience. Ahad Ha'am printed the most talented of the Jewish Nietzscheans, Micah Josheph Berdyczewski, in *Hashiloah,* but he answered in the tone of an offended rabbi. The Jewish people did need new forms, Ahad Ha'am conceded, but these could not be antithetical to the nature of the Jews. Ahad Ha'am knew, without feeling any need to defend this knowledge, that the Jews were inherently and irretrievably the bearers of the prophetic moral teaching and they had no right to betray their nature. "The secret of our peoples' persistence is that, at a very early period, the Prophets taught us to respect only the power of the spirit and not to worship material power."

Judaism, Ahad Ha'am kept insisting, was unique. The central theme of its history, he said, was "that Judaism was born in a corner and has always lived in a corner. . . . History has not yet satisfactorily explained how it came about that a tiny nation in a corner of Asia produced a unique religious and ethical outlook, which, though it has had so profound an influence on the rest of the world, has yet remained so foreign to the rest of the world, and to this day has been unable either to master it or to be mastered by it."

Ahad Ha'am was thus rooting the doctrine of the chosen people in the mystery of Jewish history. This agnostic's passion reminds the reader of George Santayana's respect for the authority of the Roman Catholic Church and his love for the beauty of its forms, even after he had lost the faith. Similarly, I once gave some essays of Ahad Ha'am to Paul Tillich, the Protestant theologian, after I heard him identify God with man's "ultimate concern," and then insist that though he, Tillich, did not believe in the doctrine of the Incarnation, Jesus was the prime symbol of the highest human values. Tillich recognized the parallelism between himself and Ahad Ha'am; they were both former believers who wanted to preserve the values of their youth, even if they no longer believed with their heads. "Cultural Christians" like Tillich have become ever more prevalent in the Western world. Ahad Ha'am is the founding figure of cultural Judaism.

Ahad Ha'am's passion for Hebrew culture and tradition made it impossible for him to welcome the father of political Zionism, Theodor Herzl. A case for Herzl's Zionism could be made on Ahad Ha'am's own premises: if the Jewish people required new verve and forms, Herzl's demand to turn all Jewish energies into reestablishing a state could evoke a renaissance of the tired Jewish spirit of the kind Ahad Ha'am was calling for. Ahad Ha'am did, reluctantly, attend the First Zionist Congress that Herzl convened in 1897, but he pronounced himself to be "a mourner at a wedding." In the essay he wrote about that event, Ahad Ha'am argued, as a realist, that the millions of Eastern European Jews could simply not be moved as a whole to Palestine. In that undeveloped land, there could be space for no more than a minority of those who wanted to flee poverty and persecution. Most of those who were running from Russia would, and should, go west, and especially to the United States, to better their personal circumstances. Only a selected elite, he said, should move to Palestine to establish the spiritual center.

Every one of Ahad Ha'am's major disciples disagreed with him. Chaim Weizmann, the future first president of Israel, at 17, adopted Ahad Ha'am as a spiritual master. Nonetheless, Weizmann understood that the weakening of religious faith was not the only crisis confronting the Jews. Most Jews, learned or illiterate, resented their powerlessness in the face of persecution and pogroms, of living in a world where they depended on the goodwill of others for their survival. Herzl had offered the dream of a nation-state in Jewish hands. It was a transforming vision.

But Ahad Ha'am did succeed in grafting his views about power and about the nature of Jewish culture onto the Zionist movement and the state it created. Herzl insisted that Zionism should have only one purpose, the establishment of a state for the victims of anti-Semitism. He refused to link the political effort for a Jewish state with the question of culture, even a renascent culture in Hebrew. Herzl lost that battle to a group of Russian Zionists who were, almost without exception, friends and disciples of Ahad Ha'am. They kept pressing, ultimately successfully, to make the revival of the Hebrew language a central aim of Zionism; they prevailed in 1901 at the Fourth Zionist Congress, three years before Herzl's death, in adopting the founding of a university in Jerusalem as a major project.

When the Hebrew University was opened in a solemn ceremony in 1925, Hayyim Nahman Bialik, the most important Hebrew poet of the time and an ardent disciple of Ahad Ha'am, spoke in the spirit of his master: "We have come to the conclusion that a people that aspires to a dignified existence must create a culture; it is not enough merely to make use of a culture—a people must create its own, with its own hand and its own implements and materials, and impress it with its own seal. . . . We must therefore hasten to light the first lamp of learning and science and of every sort of intellectual activity in Israel, ere the last lamp has grown dark for us in foreign lands. And this we propose to do in the house whose doors have been opened this day upon Mount Scopus."

Classrooms for teaching all branches of culture and laboratories for all the sciences were valid successors, Bialik asserted, to the academies for the study of Talmud. But, Bialik said, the new national culture had to contain, and to remember, the Jewish past, and especially its classic religious literature.

Bialik and Ahad Ha'am have prevailed in Israel. The final examination that all Israeli high school students must pass in order to be given their diplomas requires knowledge of the entire Bible and an acquaintance with ancient and medieval religious literature. Ahad Ha'am's formulation of Israel's culture continues to be challenged and even defied, but his outlook is bred into the bones of the large majority of Israelis.

Yet despite his impact on Israel's culture, Ahad Ha'am is almost totally unknown in the West. Perhaps fifteen essays have been translated into English from the four volumes in Hebrew into which his work was collected some seventy-five years ago. Many of his letters (a six-volume collection was published in Hebrew in the 1920s) are first-rate essays, but only a few pages have ever appeared in English. The last biography in English, by Leon Simon, was published in 1960. The only scholarly conference about him that resulted in published papers in English took place in 1980 at the University of Toronto. Meanwhile, Herzl continues to be the subject of new major biographies, most recently by Amos Elon in 1975 and Ernst Pawel in 1989.

The situation is all the more remarkable because many American Jews, when they are challenged to explain their relationship to Israel, often invoke the spirit of Ahad Ha'am, not that of Herzl. They maintain that Israel is their spiritual center and that it gives meaning to their lives in the Diaspora. The few who have actually read Ahad Ha'am know that he intended the spiritual center in Zion to provide the rest of the Jews not with the reason for political activity but with the knowledge of a renascent Hebrew culture. The memory of Herzl shuttling among the Kaiser in Berlin, the Sultan in Constantiople, and the cabinet in London in search of a political patron for the Zionist movement is comforting to political activists. Ahad Ha'am is a more difficult role model, for he presupposes the need for a contemporary Jew to be learned in both Jewish and European culture.

Above all, Ahad Ha'am was a moralist. He argued that the Jews had devised a morality that was different from everyone else's. In his one essay on Judaism and Christianity he maintained that Judaism was concerned less with the individual than with the moral stature of the people, whereas Christianity was centered on the individual. He was even willing to admit that "individual salvation certainly makes a stronger appeal to most men, and is more likely to kindle their imagination and to inspire them to strive after religious and moral perfection" than Judaism, which strives to make the Jewish people into a spiritual elite on the way to perfecting all of humanity.

This distinction is, of course, debatable. Judaism does not ever forget the individual, while much of Christianity continues to seek the evangelization of the whole world so that, in the age of the Second Coming, all the ills of society would disappear. Ahad Ha'am seemed to know that he could not easily sustain his thesis about the uniqueness of Jewish ethics. In 1906, when his fiftieth birthday was being celebrated, he was asked to come to the United States to teach at Dropsie College in Philadelphia, a newly established institution of Jewish learning, and to write the book on Jewish ethics that he had long wanted to do; but he refused. His métier was not theory of ethics, but its application.

Thus, in the spring of 1891, writing from Jerusalem, Ahad Ha'am was the first Zionist intellectual to raise the question of the Arabs. There were 3,000 Jews then in the farming settlements of Palestine and perhaps 10,000 more in the cities, among 300,000 Arabs, most of whom were farmers. And yet, Ahad Ha'am predicted that conflict between Jews and Arabs was probable and perhaps inevitable. The Arabs, he insisted, were not "wild men of the desert" who would remain inert and uncomprehending while the Zionists built their community. "If in the course of time," he wrote, "the Jewish holding in the country should develop significantly and encroach in some degree on the Arabs, they will not easily give up their position." The clear meaning of this warning was that Palestine was not, as some early slogans proclaimed, "a land without a people" waiting for a "people without a land." All his life he kept insisting that both prudence and justice commanded the Zionists to make peace with the Arabs.

A century later, such views are dominant among the Israeli intelligentsia. One representative figure, the novelist Shulamith Hareven, wrote in this spirit on March 15 in *Yedioth Aharonoth*, the mass-circulation Tel Aviv daily: "The boundaries that will determine our future are not geographic. . . . The true boundary is, rather, the knowledge that there is a limit to power. The respect that we need will not come through conquest by the sword: it can be obtained only through respect for others. Our ultimate hope is not for the undivided land of Israel, but for an Israel that is undivided in spirit and at peace with itself." Ms. Hareven shares such rhetoric with even younger writers, like the novelist David Grossman, and with many other voices. They speak the language of Ahad Ha'am.

Such views are disconcerting to the Jewish establishment both in Israel and in the United States. Practical people know that intellectuals, everywhere, are usually to the left of the government in power. In Israel, however, the intellectuals matter to the politicians, for even the pragmatists there must keep asking themselves questions about fundamental values: Is Israel a state like all other states, or must it make unique demands on itself? What is the place of the Jewish religion in a largely secular, modern society? What shared values, aside from the defense of the state, bind all the Jews of the world, wherever they might be? Issues like these erupt into public debate in the United States only occasionally, when an immediate interest is involved, as with the repeated downgrading of the liberal forms of Judaism by the Orthodox in Israel. The continuing struggle to define a modern Jewish culture is largely avoided here, perhaps for the very reason that upset the Lovers of Zion in Russia when Ahad Ha'am began the debate a hundred years ago. To talk of problems, and to export differences of opinion to the Diaspora, is supposed to be bad for the unity of the Jews.

Ahad Ha'am did not think it was. He was not remote, in an ivory tower, uninvolved in the real world. On the contrary, he knew the spiritual center that he affirmed would need political power and a productive economy. He said many times that the spiritual center would exist only when the Jews became a majority in Palestine. In fact, during the negotiations with the British from 1915 to 1917 to support Zionist aims, Ahad Ha'am advised Weizmann to fight for maximalist guarantees for the Jews. The formula he preferred for the Balfour Declaration was "Palestine as a Jewish national home," and not the more ambiguous statement that was finally issued favoring "the establishment in Palestine of a national home for the Jewish people." But he always contended that Zionist needs had to be realized while maintaining respect for the feelings and rights of the region's Arabs. He kept insisting that power could be squandered unless a people understood and abided by their values.

On this point, the question of faith, Ahad Ha'am was at both his strongest and weakest. The author and scholar Gershom Scholem was among those who understood him best, and disagreed with him. Scholem shared with Ahad Ha'am an ultimate mysticism about the meaning of the Zionist endeavor. In Scholem's words in the 1960s, "there are those who see in the secularism of our lives and in the building of the Zionist state the expression of the mystical meaning of the secret of the Universe." But Scholem could not accept Ahad Ha'am's' agnosticism: "So long as the belief in God is a faith which cannot be destroyed by any ideology, it appears to me that the absolute secularization of Israel is inconceivable. The continued wrestling with this process of secularization, with both its positives and its limitations, seems to me to be creative and determining."

Every significant Jewish thinker of the last century has argued with Ahad Ha'am. He defined, for them, the fundamental human questions: the source of community, the meaning of faith in a disbelieving world, and the relationship of morality to power. The translation of all his work into English is long overdue.

1991

12. *In Debate About the Diaspora: Gershom Scholem as Zionist and Believer*

Is a completely secular Jewish culture possible, even in Israel? In formal terms Ahad Ha'am said yes, but he contradicted himself. On the doctrine of the "chosen people," he had denied the existence of the Jewish God Who did the choosing, and yet Ahad Ha'am had insisted that, for some mysterious and unfathomable reason, the Jews were indeed unique; they remained the "chosen people." Gershom Scholem, the founder of modern Jewish study in the Kabbalah, chose to break a lance with the secular side of Ahad Ha'am's teaching. Scholem asserted that a true Jewish culture is not possible without the faith in God. Scholem moved much closer to Ahad Ha'am than he perceived, or perhaps than he was willing to admit, in insisting that the very secular life of Israel had mystical meaning. (On both these points, see, just above, the concluding paragraphs of the essay on Ahad Ha'am.)

Zionist secularism was expressed at its most extreme soon after the creation of the state of Israel by the "Canaanites." A few writers and intellectuals wanted to break with all the Jewish past, and especially with the moral teachings of the prophets of the Bible. They proclaimed themselves to be aborigines on the soil of the homeland, "natural men." On the other extreme, the ultra-Orthodox, who have been growing in numbers in Israel and in the Jewish world, have been insisting that true Jews must totally exclude modern culture. Jews must live within the realm of the Halacha, at its strictest, waiting for the Messiah. The mainstream of Zionist thought has rejected both extremes. But a modern national culture in balance with the religious past is still in the process of becoming—and it is increasingly endangered by the factionalism on both the secular left and the religious right.

▼

Then came the fundamental shift in perspective. It came with the rise of the national movement. We found a firm place on which to stand, a new center from which there appeared utterly different, new horizons. . . . The new slogan was: to view our history from within . . . to rebuild the entire edifice of Jewish learning by the light of a Jew who lives within his people and has no longer purpose but to view problems, events and ideas, in their true light, within the framework of their significance for the Jewish nation.
—Gershom Scholem,
"Mi-Toch Hirhurim al Hochmat Yisrael,"
in Devarim be-Go

Gershom Scholem was barely thirteen when he began his revolt against the assimilation of Jews in Germany. He soon found his way to rabbis who taught him classic texts. These men not only knew the Jewish law; they believed it and obeyed it, and under their influence the young Scholem thought seriously that in order to enter Judaism he ought to follow after them. "Nonetheless, after I got to know the orthodox life up close, and after years of ambivalence, I decided not to adopt it," so Scholem told in his autobiography, *From Berlin to Jerusalem*.[4] However, the tension remained unresolved for some years more. In the Hebrew edition of the autobiography there is even a picture of Scholem in Jerusalem in 1925 sitting on Sukkoth inside a Sukkah with his head covered, studying the Zohar. Scholem had been attracted to the Kabbalah very early, but here too he never agreed to study it from within—that is, even briefly to suspend scholarly distance and become a Kabbalist. In Jerusalem the young Scholem encountered a scholar of the Kabbalah, of the older kind, who offered to teach him if Scholem would agree to listen and to ask no questions, to enter the world of the Kabbalah on its own terms. Scholem refused, even though he continued to hold frequent long conversations with this Kabbalist. His earliest path toward Jewish scholarship led him to the work of the nineteenth-century founders of modern Jewish studies, the *Wissenschaft des Judentums*. In fact, he had begun to return to Judaism as a thirteen-year-old under the influence of his reading of a short popular version of Heinrich Graetz's *History of the Jews*, which persuaded him that this was indeed his people and that he ought to identify with it. Nonetheless, despite his continuing admiration for Graetz, Scholem's work on the Kabbalah began as a counterattack on his first teacher. In 1945 Scholem completed his avowed break with most of the leading figures of the *Wissenschaft* school, for he accused them, in a stinging essay, of lacking any passion for continuing Judaism. Their historical studies, so Scholem insisted, had been done to classify and entomb the Jewish past, to write its epitaph.[5]

At one point or another in Scholem's career he thus rejected, in whole or in part, German culture as not his own; the Halacha, the law of the rabbis, as a set of prescriptions under which he would not live; the Kabbalah, a world that fascinated him and to which he devoted his life, but also one he would affirm as having living value only in the most oblique ways; and modern Jewish historical scholarship, the scientific study of the Jewish past, to which he clearly belonged in his method even as he rejected his predecessors. In Scholem's own lexicon the word *dialectic* is to be found with great frequency. Sometimes this word in Scholem's usage really means ambivalence—that he himself was the field of battle within which opposing forces were at war.

All of these various elements within Scholem were to find their resolution in Zion. Zionism, and not his scholarly studies of the Kabbalah, or even the redefinition of the whole of Jewish history in the light of those studies, is the center of Scholem's intellectual and moral endeavor. The nascent Jewish community in Palestine was the place within which this latterday Archimedes chose to stand in order to forge his lever with which to move the world. He was thus able to live out the paradoxes of breaking both with Germany and with Western liberalism, while never severing contact with the very culture that he has rejected; to be a supreme incarnation of *Wissenschaft des Judentums* while entombing his predecessors, for some of whom he had more than a passing admiration; and to believe in God, with enormous respect for both the Halacha and the Kabbalah, while identifying and affirming the secular life of Israel.

Scholem's ship arrived in Palestine in 1923 in the port of Jaffa a day late, and so he landed on Yom Kippur morning. He hinted on occasion in conversation that perhaps there was some significance to this accident. He never hid his certainty that his journey was a paradigm for other people like himself in the Jewish world. In his autobiography Scholem quoted a letter he wrote to a friend at the end of 1924, not much more than a year after he arrived in Palestine, in which he said that "here something more important is happening than anywhere else in the world."[6]

This conviction did not lead him to distancing himself from his many friends in the Jewish intelligentsia whom he had left behind in Europe. On the contrary, he maintained and increased these connections in the six decades of his life in Zion. On his side these relationships were colored and even dominated by the desire to draw his friends after him to Zionism—that is, not merely to an ideology but to *aliyah*, to casting one's lot with the renewed national community in Palestine. In his close friendship with Walter Benjamin, Scholem worked hard, and unsuccessfully, to convince Benjamin to come. He even arranged a Hebrew University grant to pay for his preliminary Hebrew studies in Germany, but Benjamin soon went off into Marxism. Scholem, ever the Zionist, warned Benjamin that he would find no home there or anywhere else except in the Judaism he was rejecting.[7] Of one of the friends of his youth in Germany he wrote a kind of epitaph, in his autobiography: that she would have been a particularly valuable addition to the new Jewish life being born in Palestine, and it was especially regrettable that she did not come.[8] In his later years when most of his visitors among the Jewish intelligentsia were from English-speaking lands, he himself never overtly raised the question of *aliyah*, but his wife Fania almost invariably did.[9] I can bear personal witness to his increasingly sad, but demanding silence, and of her underscoring in words the meaning of what he was not saying.

In his youth in the 1920s, Palestine was indeed the home for a striking number of creative Jewish intellectuals, far more than could be expected in a population of perhaps 80,000 Jews. The young Scholem had no doubt, then, that it was the home of the bravest and the best of Jewry. As the years went by, and especially after the creation of the State of Israel, comparable intellectual forces did not come from the United States, the last available reservoir of free Jewish population. The intelligentsia in the expanding America after World War II were less troubled by immediate threats of anti-Semitism, or by feelings of otherness, than any previous generation of Jewish intellectuals in the Diaspora. Nonetheless, Scholem believed that his journey would eventually be taken by many. There were more than hints in his conversations, and in occasional comments in his essays on current themes, of the notion that contemporary America might be Weimar Germany. Scholem never seemed to be sufficiently certain of that analysis to insist that anti-Semitism was inevitable even in America, that even there Jews would ultimately be excluded from the majority culture. In a roundtable discussion of the *Galut* (the Diaspora defined as "exile") in *Ma'ariv* in 1963, he was willing to imagine the possibility of a people that does not regard the Jews living among it as alien. If the Jews cooperate by forgetting that they are in any sense in exile, then assimilation follows.[10] He had American Jewry particularly in mind, among which, in the floodtide of its post-war success in American society as a whole, the word *Galut* had become unfashionable even among the Zionists.

Even though he was willing to imagine successful large-scale assimilation of Jews in the United States, Scholem insisted that America was not really different. The central question was not the possibility of anti-Semitism, which would inhibit assimilation, but rather personal authenticity. The post–World War II intelligentsia in American Jewry reminded him of the kind of people that he had known in Germany. At their most Jewishly and visibly involved, American Jewish writers made their careers out of describing the discomforts in the counter-pulls of Jewish and American identity; but this had already been done in Germany in the 1920s by such figures as Jakob Wasserman, who had written a very pained and famous book, *My Way as German and Jew*. The description of this tension in Philip Roth's *Portnoy's Complaint* made Scholem very angry. He denounced the book in 1969 in two letters to *Ha'aretz*: Roth's portrayal of Jewish marginality was simply pornography; it furnished material for anti-Semites and "the Jews would yet pay dearly for this book." Scholem was a bit uncomfortable about the last remark, for it was out of character with his unapologetic stance, as a Zionist, before the Gentiles; but he nonetheless "had to describe a fact."[11] What seems to have prevailed here is the dominant and lasting motif in Scholem's Zionism: the quest for wholeness and authenticity, which was the healthy antithesis to Jewish marginality in the Diaspora, however well or badly that marginality might express itself.

The contributions of American Jews to movements of social protest and the prominence of many individuals in all fields of the larger culture was simply a repeat of earlier experiences in Europe. Scholem had rejected Jewish assimilation in Germany because, even if it worked, it represented the erosion of the true Jewish self. Of course he knew that many of his friends and contemporaries had once identified their Jewishness as the source of the energy which motivated their battle for universal ideals. Such a notion, which asserts that being Jewish does not necessarily lead to Jewish nationalism, Scholem denied on the basis of the first principle: an individual is authentically himself only if he maintains a basic, living connection to his natural community. Such connection to their Jewish identity was weakening among Jewish intellectuals, and so Scholem concluded his comments in 1963 on the Diaspora in great pain. "I think that anyone who comes to New York and takes a serious look at what is happening there must inevitably conclude that it is a *Galut*—but it is a *Galut* the existence of which is denied by those who live there. . . . Many years ago Ahad Ha-Am wrote his famous essay, 'Slavery in the Midst of Freedom,' which was directed against the assimilationists in Germany, France, Italy. What would he write today against the second and third generation of immigrants from Russia, and elsewhere, who came to the United States and have explained their historic experience in all its importance, as they have, for their own purposes: finding innumerable reasons with which to assert that they are totally at home in this land of many peoples and to deny any consciousness of being in *Galut*? And we are as yet only at the beginning of this road!"[12]

In the light of this compound of sorrow and disdain, why did Scholem spend so much of his later years writing in English and in German and attending innumerable scholarly and intellectual conferences all over the Western world and especially in North America? It was not because he had a passionate desire to teach his chosen subject, the Kabbalah and Jewish mysticism, but because he wanted to suggest something to the intelligentsia as a whole and especially to its Jewish component. A Jew in the *Galut* might need to spend his time painfully balancing out the relationship between his Jewish and his Western identities. Scholem, the Zionist, had left that situation behind in order to express his Jewishness primarily through a lifelong preoccupation with Jewish mysticism. This tradition, as understood from within Judaism, shed its own light on such universal themes as that of order versus creativity in human life. Precisely because he had early chosen to be only a Jew, without hyphen or adjective, not a Western Jew or a German Jew or an American Jew, Scholem felt himself free to speak to Western culture unapologetically and very directly. He was particularly firm in that role because he was supported by, so he believed, a creative new Jewish culture which had been freed to change and to experiment because Jews were now in their own land. There the clash of various contrasting and even inimical ideologies and factions was welcome, because out of these battles a new formulation of modern Jewish existence would arise. To speak for such a world being born, to represent as scholar a neglected area of past Jewish experience of universal interest, Jewish mysticism, the study of which he single-handedly revived in the Land of Israel, was to be at once intensely Jewish and movingly contemporary.

The study of Kabbalah became Scholem's life work and, as Buber once said about him, other scholars have made major contributions to learning but Scholem alone created a new field, both in his historiographic interpretations and in his untiring research, which he conducted with the energy and the brilliance of genius. In his reading of the Kabbalah and Jewish mysticism, Scholem's relationship to the founders of the *Wissenschaft des Judentums* was more complicated than he ever admitted to himself. In 1945 he published an essay under the title of "Reflections on *Wissenschaft des Judentums*" in which he denounced Abraham Geiger with particular passion. Geiger had been not only a great scholar but also one of the founders of Reform Judaism. Scholem denounced him for "clerical hypocrisy," and yet he admired Geiger for "the sovereign power which animates a great historian, to force the facts into his own construction and to explain relationships on the basis of historical intuition, a dangerous and creative power that Graetz also possessed."[13] What precisely did Abraham Geiger do with this "sovereign power"? He assessed Talmudic Judaism as having once been a live and creative period in Jewish history, a reform of the Bible, an adaptation of it to new circumstances and a break with those elements within it which were no longer of living value. In Geiger's view rabbinic Judaism fitted that stage of Jewish history in which the Jews were involved in their own specific national identity. In the era of the emancipation, when Judaism was not becoming a universal religion, Reform was setting out to do in its day something comparable to what the Talmud had done before, that is, to revise Judaism for its newest stage. Therefore the Ritual Law was now superseded and there remained only the mission of Israel to represent universal moral categories.

Scholem has said comparable things about the Kabbalah. He made it very clear in several of his essays that the Kabbalah was no longer alive. The last representatives of any authentic kind of Kabbalism were older contemporaries of his in Jerusalem in the 1920s, such as Rabbi Abraham Isaac Kook and the Hassidic Rebbe Arele Roth.[14] No contemporary Jewish life can be made out of the Kabbalah. On the contrary, the Kabbalah itself can lead directly and logically to total religious anarchy. Once it is accepted that the text of the Torah has deeper meanings than its literal ones, and that its meanings are many, anything that a Kabbalist would like to imagine, including point-by-point destruction of the literal Torah, in order to free the "spiritual Torah," becomes possible.[15] Scholem rang the changes on all of this in perhaps his single most famous essay, published in 1937 under the title "The Holiness of Sin," in which he summarized the ideas which underlie his work on Shabtai Zvi and his followers, including the explanation of the apostasy of the messiah and the breaking of every commandment by some of his most extreme followers as, in their view, religious necessity.[16]

In Scholem's own religious outlook he was frightened of anarchic values, religious or secular, for he kept insisting that he believed in God and that only in the belief in God was there any grounding for morality. Without a social order based on morality as an absolute, everything was possible, precisely because "God was dead." The writing of the history of the Kabbalah is then an act of telling the past correctly and even a way of suggesting that the present Jewish era, which was inevitably different from both the immediate and, even more, from the distant past, had to take account of mystical experience and learn from it as a model, but the present did not, and could not, directly continue the Kabbalah. The grandeur of Scholem's writing, the passion with which he invested his scholarship, and the empathy with which he brings to life a whole host of strange figures has tended to obscure the fact that his writing is an act of magic. Scholem was quite clearly reevoking these fascinating shades but ultimately, to use the language of his charge against the scholars of the *Wissenschaft* school, in order to bury them with due respect. It was part of the Jewish past; the present was Zionism.

To the degree to which the Kabbalah was alive for him, Scholem used it as a model for a new secular mysticism which had some subterranean links, perhaps, to the believing past. In 1964 he wrote an essay under the title "Reflections on the Possibility of Jewish

Mysticism in Our Day." At the end of those reflections Scholem once again raised the issue with which he had dealt as a historian in 1937, that mysticism leads inevitably to anarchic individualism. Jewish continuity has depended, so Scholem asserted very flatly, upon the belief in revealed religion; since that belief is no longer held by many Jews, what can ensure both continuity and community? Ongoing secularization has posed a new question: Can secular life in any sense be regarded as sacred? He finally concluded that "there are those who see in the secularism of our lives and in the building of the Zionist state the expression of the mystical meaning of the secret of the Universe."[17]

Geiger, committed to Jewish universalism in the era of Reform, had asserted that his Judaism was a call to act in the manner of the Talmud, as he identified it, in a new day. So Scholem—committed more deeply to Zionism than to anything else—asserted that the passion for re-creating Israel, the very secular Israel of modern twentieth-century men and women, is the ladder on which Jews in this time can ascend to the *Ein-Sof*.

Scholem had a comparable relationship to Leopold Zunz, the founder of the scientific studies of Judaism, whom he had attacked with great vehemence, along with Geiger. If Geiger's scholarship was "theological," an apologia for reforming Judaism, Zunz's was "political": he wanted to describe Judaism in such fashion as to further the cause of the emancipation of Jews. The charge was true. The political purpose of modern Jewish studies was to establish that Jews had made major contributions to the founding of Western culture, and that they had not spent their time throughout all the centuries simply studying the Talmud and pilpulistic commentaries to it. Behold, Zunz proved, there had been Jewish philosophers in the Middle Ages, and physicians such as Maimonides, and a whole host of mathematicians and grammarians—in short, Jews who were prominent in every aspect of general culture. Such a people had a right to demand, now, in the modern era, all the benefits of legal equality that the state extends to its citizens, for the Jews could not be considered alien to Western culture.

Zunz's aim was radically denied by Scholem, who knew that, after legal equality had already been achieved, the Jews were not living happily ever after in Germany. Nonetheless, Scholem admired Zunz for his demonic power as historian, for his capacity to rescue from oblivion neglected parts of the Jewish past and make them available for those who would make use of this past in the present. Scholem's work on the Kabbalah had, of course, been described by himself in the same way: it was a way of making available for use in the present a neglected part of the Jewish past. The parallelism with Zunz is, however, even deeper. Scholem's "political" purpose was different, to serve the Jewish national revival, but it was just as political. In the service of that ideal, Scholem presented his studies of the Kabbalah not only to Jews but to the learned world as a whole, to suggest that the wide interest in mysticism could profit from encountering its Jewish expressions, and that Jewish culture and spirituality included not only the essentially rational rabbinic law but also, like the other great traditions, it included profound constructions of the human spirit based on the mysterious and nonrational.

In the essay in 1964 that was his final assessment of the relevance of mysticism to contemporary Jewish life, Scholem ended a discussion that was obviously very difficult for him to write, as follows:

> For our new life (unless the teaching of A. D. Gordon is to be mentioned here) those of us who are laboring as Jews in the Land of Israel have an interest in the poetry of Walt Whitman. In his *Leaves of Grass*, in which he sang the song of America one hundred years ago, he projected a feeling of the absolute holiness of absolute secularity. . . .
>
> In the coming generations such mysticism is destined to take the form of naturalist, secular ways of thinking, which will have on their surface no trace of traditional religious concepts, even though the substance of the mystical experience will be perceived and continue to grow beneath the surface.

Scholem concluded by suggesting that the future of secular mysticism is in the expansion of the human mind.[18] In context, the clear implication of this last comment is that Jewish man will experience such a possibility in its highest within the Zionist community.

Perhaps the most astonishing of Scholem's final hints in the last decade or two of his life about his own views is to be found in the lecture that he gave in Santa Barbara in 1973 on "Jewish theology today." There at the very end Scholem, the lifelong exponent of the

significance of the Kabbalah, said the following: "I am convinced that
... Zionism contains within it religious content and a religious potential that is far more fundamental than anything that is expressed
by the existing 'religious parties of the State of Israel.' In the dialectic
of Jewish life, the religious tradition continues to be the challenge,
and the fundamental element in that tradition is the Halacha."[19] The
circle that began in his youth was thus closed in his later years. Halacha
is no longer, as he sometimes said in his earlier years, a fossil; it is
now the central element of religious continuity. Mysticism is the
refresher and corrective, but one can detect a progression in Scholem's
years of growing worry about its anarchic tendencies. The combat of
law and mysticism will take place in the new secular Zionist community within which a new Jewish culture is arising. Despite Scholem's past emphasis on the secularity of the Zionist culture, he remained convinced that the religious elements in Judaism were so
powerful that "so long as the belief in God is a fundamental phenomenon among all beings created in His image, a faith which cannot
be destroyed by any ideology, it appears to me that the absolute
secularization of Israel is inconceivable. The continued wrestling with
this process of secularization, with both its positives and its limitations,
seems to me to be creative and determining."[20]

The issue of religion, of Scholem's abiding faith in God, was the
reason for his eventual break with Ahad Ha'am, the central figure of
cultural Zionism. Ahad Ha'am had proposed at the turn of the century
the creation in Palestine of a "spiritual center," a Jewish community
of high quality which, though not necessarily of large size, would
create a modern Jewish culture that in the very process of encountering modernity in a deeply Jewish way, would invigorate the whole
of the Jewish world and act as a model for it. Ahad Ha'am had a
profoundly Jewish education of the kind imparted to rabbis in Eastern
Europe in the mid-nineteenth century, but he was an agnostic, and
his vision of the new Jewish culture was secular. All his life this Russian
Jewish positivist tried to find a way of defining the Jewish national
genius as particularly suited to producing a unique morality, but he
never found the way to do much more than simply assert this proposition as an undoubted truth. The young Scholem had been attracted
to Zionism by East Europeans who were largely followers of Ahad

Ha'am; they saw themselves as on the way, as many of them indeed were, to the Land of Israel, to help create there an elite community which would be Jewish in its sense of historical continuity and morality, and contemporary in its intellectual freedom.

Scholem's journey to Jerusalem was spiritually and even physically in the company of these men, almost all of whom remained his lifelong friends. A good number of his East European contemporaries were in the Labor movement and Scholem, even though he did not belong to that party, maintained connection all his life with its intelligentsia. Nonetheless, what ultimately divided Scholem from Ahad Ha'am and even from some of his friends in Labor was that he was a believer and that he could not imagine the new Zionist creation in Israel as breaking with faith in God.[21]

Scholem was thus both a mystic and humanist. He had chosen, early, his own authentic people and their land and he wanted that place not to be "a light unto nations," because the term itself had been vulgarized by its use in modern Jewish apologetics, but certainly a model community. He demanded of it seriousness and absence of militarism and an austere national morality, bordering on pacifism. He thus did indeed belong to such Russian Jewish intellectuals as A. D. Gordon, the rebbe of the Labor movement, who brought with him from Russia a Narodnik kind of desire to return to the land; and to the scholars who founded the Hebrew University and who, at their best, were trying to continue Jewish religious piety with a secular high-mindedness rooted in history and national consciousness, and, often, an untraditional religious piety.

It was a noble effort. Why was it not joined by large elements of the Jewish intelligentsia in the last two generations? Why did Scholem leave this world in tragedy, with a sense of fulfillment as a scholar but with the feeling that his work as a Zionist was unfinished, and perhaps even impossible? The simplest answer is that throughout the ages, including the last century of modern Zionism, only a minority of Jewish intelligentsia has gone to the Land of Israel, even when they could. Only in their minority, and a very small one at that, did West European Jewish intellectuals come to Palestine before 1933. The bulk of the secularized Jewish intelligentsia has for the last two centuries, in situation after situation, preferred to believe that a significant role existed for it in the larger culture, either as critics in unfriendly places or as culture-bearers in good times. The probability that after several generations such an intelligentsia will cease being Jewish, except perhaps in some remaining indefinable aroma, is of concern only to those who, like the young Scholem, have made a deep prior commitment to Jewish particularism. That is an act of faith. It cannot be compelled by argument; it can only be given life by the example of individuals such as Scholem. In Israel he was a scholar and a spiritual teacher within a society that both gave him room to be his idiosyncratic self and that cared about him. It is this sense of both protecting context and utter freedom which Scholem insisted does not exist for the Jewish intellectual outside Israel; even at his freest, a Jew in the Diaspora is within a culture that others not of his kind largely created.

The bulk of Jewish intelligentsia, especially in America today, rejects the notion of Jewish alienation in any sense. Jewish experience, so we have been assured, is now one of the regions of America, like William Faulkner's South or Duke Ellington's Harlem. Perhaps it is. Scholem did not believe it, and he kept insisting that the increasing number of Jewish intellectuals from abroad who had become his friends, or his semidisciples, in recent decades needed to think again. In this dialogue Scholem and those whom he addressed came from quite different situations. His family in Berlin had already traversed the journey from a village, and near poverty, to bourgeois comfort, and from isolation in the ghetto to assimilation. His auditors among the Jewish intelligentsia in America were at least a generation behind him, for they were mostly the grandchildren of immigrants from Eastern Europe and they were still engaged in completing the journey from their grandparents' memories of pogroms and their parents' experience of the depression and substantial exclusion even in America to the center of a culture that was increasingly large, plural, and chaotic.

To be sure, in the last fifteen years American culture has developed major interests in Eastern religion and in mysticism, in general. This development parallels what was happening in Europe in Scholem's youth, and it is largely because of these interests that Scholem's work has become popular in recent years. Few of the Jewish intelligentsia have, as yet, read him the way he wanted to be read. It is useful to quote here the remarks of Harold Bloom in his recent book *Agon* in the essay entitled "Free and Broken Tablets: The Cultural Prospects of American Jewry." Bloom is not very hopeful about the cultural prospects of American Jewry, because he finds this community is not at all oriented to classic texts. The baggage of Jewish learning of the American Jewish intelligentsia is very skimpy. Bloom therefore invokes Scholem, as the contemporary moral prophet in Jewry, in his insistence on Jewish primary sources and in his regarding nothing Jewish as alien. Even so careful a reader as Bloom has, however, misread Scholem. Bloom declares that "Scholem has never made the mistake of analogizing German and American Jewry."[22] This is simply not true, for, as I proved at the beginning of this essay, Scholem did exactly that. Any Jewry that had fallen away from text was for Scholem on the way out of its Jewishness; a serious return to text led inevitably away from the wider culture to the Jewish life being created by Zionism. In his own mind, Scholem had not spent his life trying to purvey knowledge of the Kabbalah even to those lovers of the occult who wanted exact information. His work was his contribution to the sum total of the Jewish national revival; it was part of his Zionist demand on the lives of his Jewish readers.

Scholem's relationship to contemporary Israel had in it, at the end of his days, an element of great sorrow. He often charged the contemporary rabbis with narrowness, for they restricted themselves to ritual matters and were uninterested in the life of the community. In his last years he was witness to a new breed of rabbi, the leaders of Gush Emunim who fulfilled his expectation, at least in its verbal formulation: they and their followers have become vitally involved in public questions in the name of a religious ideal, as they define it. It is no secret that Scholem did not look upon this particular combination of religion and public policy with great joy. He had once declared that the new Jewish settlement in the Land of Israel was the place where all the clashing elements and schools of thought within Jewry would encounter each other and even quarrel, and that what would result from this process and be accepted by a majority would be the new Judaism. Clearly he imagined that such a result would occur within the bounds set by a liberal, humanitarian tradition.

And yet, for all his unhappiness in much of Israel's current life, Scholem remained unshakably a Zionist. The issues that the modern age had raised in relationship to the Jewish heritage, the question of what was to be retained or rebuilt and what was to be destroyed, remained in Zion "as yet entirely unsolved, and everything is still open." Scholem continued to believe that Zionism was "a great experiment in human alchemy; through its agency hatred and enmity would be changed at some future time into understanding, respect and fraternity."[23]

1982

FIVE

Contemplating America,
Without Illusions

The power and influence of the
American Jewish community crested in the early 1960s. The last
presidential election to which the Jewish vote made a critical difference was the contest between John F. Kennedy and Richard Nixon
in 1960. Jews voted overwhelmingly for Kennedy; if they had split
more evenly Nixon would have been elected. The Kennedy cabinet
contained two Jews. There were many Jews in the intelligentsia that
surrounded the new young president. For the community as a whole,
the economic and social barriers of the 1930s had largely fallen.
Hundreds of thousands of middle-aged Jews, who had grown up
during the Depression, now migrated to suburbia. It was an age of
confidence.

I doubted the confidence, even then. The inner life of the Jewish
community seemed to me to be shallow. It consisted of immigrant
memory, and it contained very little Jewish learning. In the 1960s
the Jewish community was very activist, as it still is. I did not believe
that activism without learning would be enough to create continuity.
In an essay published in 1963, when only one in eight Jews were
finding non-Jewish marriage partners, I predicted that the number
would soon reach at least one in three. Eventually, in 1989, I published

a book of history, *The Jews in America: Four Centuries of an Uneasy Encounter,* in which I attempted to explain the whole course of American Jewish experience as leading naturally, and inevitably, to these contemporary problems.

13. Why Did the East European Jews Come to America?

I return again to Ahad Ha'am. He suggested a fundamental distinction between the "problem of Judaism" and the "problem of the Jews." The "problem of Judaism" was the question of redefining the tradition in the contemporary age. The "problem of the Jews" was how to escape anti-Semitism and find a society within which Jews could make a living. Ahad Ha'am suggested that the "problem of Judaism" was best solved by members in a small elite community who had decided to make these spiritual problems their primary concern. He proposed that such individuals join in creating a "spiritual center" in the land of Israel. The "problem of the Jews" could best be solved by immigration to the United States. In the paper below I suggested that the American Jewish community, which was conceived in economic need, had not yet faced the question of its cultural and spiritual content.

▼

This year, 1980, is an appropriate one for rethinking the meaning of the American Jewish experience. Next year, in 1981, we shall be marking the one hundredth anniversary of a great turning point in American Jewish history, the pogroms in Russia. The great wave of East European migration that brought something approaching two and a half million Jews to the United States came in the quarter of a century between 1881 and the outbreak of the First World War in 1914. This migration transformed the Jews of America from a small, largely inconspicuous and essentially exotic community into a visible and large group. Jews crowded into the ten largest cities; by 1914 they had become more than one-tenth of the population of these major cities. In New York, the most important American city, the proportion exceeded one in four.

The historian who looks back upon that era is reasonably secure in his assessment of the forces that pushed Jews out of tsarist Russia: economic discrimination and pogroms which resulted in an ever-greater impoverishment of the large masses of Russian Jewry. We even know that the pogroms alone were not the central issue, for there was an equally large immigration, proportionately, from the Hapsburg empire. There were no pogroms in Austria-Hungary, but there was, there too, great impoverishment. Historians are even beginning to know which elements came from Eastern Europe. The migration did not represent, at least not until after the Kisheneff program in 1903, the intelligentsia, both traditional and secularized, or the bourgeois. These could still hold on in Russia (the overwhelming majority did), and they never emigrated. Indeed, though reemigration among Jews was lower than that of any other ethnic group, those who did leave to go back to their country of origin were, in outsize proportions, intellectuals and middle-class people. The great majority of those who came and remained was, thus, overwhelmingly petty bourgeois and proletarian. Such people had little or nothing left in Russia, and even less to which to return, after the pogroms and exclusionary laws pushed them. They traveled the most lightly.

What did these masses expect to find in the new land? What was on their minds when they undertook the journey? On what scale did they weigh what they were to gain by migrating and what they were willing to discard on the way, or soon after arrival? Or were they simply running away, without plan?

There is a famous sentence in the Talmud that when in doubt, even about the law, "Go and see what the people are doing in the streets." I think that the answers to the questions just posed are to be found in the rhetoric of those migrants at the very time of the mass movement to these shores. Two phrases recur in all the accounts. America is called over and over again, "di goldene medina" (the golden land) and "di treifene medina" (the irreligious land). Those who got on the ships and were willing to sleep on deck or in steerage all the way from Hamburg to New York, having already negotiated the dangerous journey from some small village in Russia to the exit port, were lured by the beckoning vision of "streets paved with gold"; they knew that some radical surrender of their Jewishness, and not only in its traditional religious version, would be demanded of them in the new land. They did not imagine that they would pick gold off the streets of New York, for the very first arrivals sent letters home to make it clear that hard, even tragically hard, work was required in sweatshop conditions, and that only a few would break through to riches. They also knew, for that matter, that no one would present them with roast pork at Ellis Island, to make the eating of it a precondition for being allowed into the country, but everyone was soon aware that economic pressure would make many work on the Sabbath and otherwise disregard the tradition. Most of the immigrants knew that survival in America would leave them little time for Jewish culture, in any version, and that their children would become "Yankees."

Exaggerated though the phrases were, even consciously exaggerated, they nonetheless were the fundamental estimate of the new land as held by the mass of migrants. Perhaps the most precise statement of both themes is to be found in the great contemporary novel by Abraham Cahan, *The Rise of David Levinsky*. The young hero, as a teenage immigrant, speaks of his coming to the United States as a "second birth" and of himself as a "newborn babe." Soon, as he struggles his way to economic success in the garment district, he knows how large is the price that one must pay for success. One of his competitors addresses him as follows:

> "The world is not a wedding feast, Levinsky. It is a big barnyard full of chickens and they are scratching one another and scrambling over one another. Why? Because there are little heaps of grain in the yard and each chicken wants to get as much of it as possible."

At the very end of the novel, the successful Levinsky, who has abandoned his early Jewishness and yet yearns for it, surveys his own life and asks, and answers, the critical question: "Am I happy? No."

We must trust this account of Cahan's because it is confirmed by the whole of contemporary literature. For example, the great Zionist theoretician who never came to the United States, A. D. Gordon, writing in 1911, about the time when Cahan was drafting his novel, addressed himself in an essay in Hebrew to those then going at the rate of 100,000 or more a year to the United States. He counterposed the economic drives that were propelling the masses to the United States to the ideological ones that were bringing handfuls to Zionism. Gordon insisted that those looking for success did not know how tremendous its cost would be, and they were not aware that, for their ultimate happiness and that of their children, they would be better off helping him found a new life for Jews in Palestine.

The theme of the "treifene medina" is just as pronounced. The jeremiads of rabbis, both in America and especially abroad, were without number, and they began long before the East European migration. It was already well established in earlier decades that the United States was not a place for piety. The young Isaac Mayer Wise, arriving in 1846, took one look at the Spanish-Portuguese congregation in New York and decided that a regeneration of the Jewish population in New York was necessary, for the older Spanish-Portuguese, except for a few formalistic purposes, had abandoned the faith.

One of the earliest Orthodox rabbis in the United States was Bernard Illowy. Preaching the eulogy in Baltimore in November 1862, of his predecessor Abraham Rice, the very first Orthodox rabbi to serve in the United States (he arrived in 1840), Illowy said:

> "We must acknowledge to our own shame that since the downfall of the Jewish monarchy there has been no age and no country in which the Israelites were more degenerated and more indifferent towards their religion than in our own age and in our own country."

Why then, did a generation of Jews, many of whom (the Austrian-Hungarians) were not even chased by pogroms, prefer to struggle and be poor in the United States, at substantial cost to their Jewish identity, when they could have elected to have struggled and be poor, with little cost to their Jewish identity, back home? The answer is to be found in a third and most critical phrase of the emigrants. They came not for themselves, but for "die kinder."

What made it possible for hundreds of thousands of men and women to come to spend their lives in sweatshops was not the illusion that they might personally succeed and achieve economic ease. They knew, most of them, that this would never happen. So they said in countless letters written at the time, or in memoirs that some of them deposited in such places as YIVO Institute for Jewish Research in their old age. There are still some aged remnants of the last of this migration, still living in poverty in the old neighborhoods, surviving mostly on Social Security payments.

The critical difference, the main reason for migrating, was to find opportunity for the young. The battle to get into the *gymnasium* in tsarist Russia ceased when the ship arrived at the port of New York, for the high schools were free and open, and so was City College of New York. The parents might, and mostly did, accept the fact that their own lives would probably be no easier in America, but at least their children would have it better, radically better. The children of the bourgeois (the young Chaim Weizmann, for example) could, at very worst, if no place was open in Russia, go on to a university in Germany or Switzerland. The poor could harbor such hopes only if they came as far as America.

Parenthetically, concern for the future of children as the main driving force of migration of Jews from Russia has appeared again in our own days among those who have been fighting their way out of the Soviet Union. Today, the Jewish immigrants from Russia are different from those of a century ago, for they are overwhelmingly middle class, with a high proportion of academically trained professionals. They say over and over again that their own careers in the Soviet Union were satisfactory, but that rising anti-Semitism made it impossible for their children to enter good universities. Almost everyone who is at all involved in Jewish life knows at least one former professor in Russia, now either in Israel or in America, who says, with some sadness, that he is willing to drive a taxi for the rest of his life, if he must, so that his children may freely enter the professions.

The statistics of the mass migration from 1881 to 1914 confirm what we derive from letters, memoirs, and contemporary literature as a whole. An astonishingly high proportion of this migration, 44 percent, were women, and 20 percent were children. This is the profile of whole families on the move. To be sure, many were left behind. There were nearly 100,000 cases of family desertion, by husbands who came to the United States and did not send for their wives and children. Most of the migrating families, however, remained united.

The promise of America was, indeed, realized. The children of the immigrants traveled very quickly the extraordinarily long journey from the East Side to middle-class suburbia. Not primarily for the first generation but rather for its children, America was indeed the answer to "the problem of the Jews." They have achieved, in large numbers, their individual success.

But what has happened to Judaism? Here the story is much less happy. From the very beginnings of the mass migration, the leaders of the older, resident Jewish community, and those of the new arrivals themselves, were aware of the spiritual dislocation that the move to the new country, under near panic conditions, represented. An older leadership of people already well established in the United States tried to help. They summoned Solomon Schechter to New York at the turn of the century to create, primarily for the new arrivals, a traditional religious leadership indigenous to the United States. Older and newer forces joined in trying to found in New York and Philadelphia a *Kehillah*—that is, an overarching Jewish communal structure which would care for the spiritual and educational needs of the Jews, as well as provide the necessary social services. Nonetheless, despite all the efforts, many of them heroic, that have gone into the battle for the survival of Judaism in the United States, there is today among Jews, even more than at the very beginning of the mass migration, an enormous amount of marginality and even total alienation. Some of the direst of pessimists are beginning to predict the disappearance from Jewish life, in a generation or two, of a large majority of the Jewish population.

We are now nearing the beginning of the second century of mass Jewish presence in the United States; we are no nearer solving the problem of the survival of Judaism in the open, success-oriented American society, the very one that Jews have helped to create in the last century. Out of the experience of our failures, and of our partial successes, we know one simple truth: Jewish commitment based on knowledge, learning, and piety has a longer life span in America than Jewish activism without knowledge, learning, or piety.

1980

14. The Graying of American Jewry

The argument about the origins and caused of the mass migrations to the United States occupied me in the 1980s not only because I was writing a book about the history of American Jews, but, even more, because I kept asking the question: what of the future? In the summer of 1982 I lectured on the question of origins of the mass migration at the plenum of the World Union of Jewish Studies in Jerusalem. That paper was published in 1984, in the proceedings of that conference, under the title *Treifene Medina* (Land that is not Kosher). In this heavily footnoted essay, I established that rabbis and secular intellectuals had consistently opposed emigration to the United States. This attitude was well defined by beginning of the 1830s, and it did not begin to change until the Nazis came to power in 1933. The intelligentsia had therefore been underrepresented among the founding fathers of American Jewry.

In the early 1980s American Jewish confidence was beginning to ebb. The community was beginning to worry not only about its inner content, but also about its influence in America. How much power did the Jewish minority really have in American society and politics? The maximalists in Israel believed that this power was well-nigh unlimited; it was a blank check with which to pay for anything that Israel might want to do. Some American Jews were beginning to fear that the ultranationalists in Israel were pushing Jewish power beyond its limits.

▼

For American Jews the year 1982 was a watershed. This community had emerged from World War II intact and optimistic and in possession of rapidly expanding opportunity and power. Its inner morale was high, and for the next three decades, as Jews rose to high estate in America, the sense of confidence kept growing. This era of pride and innocence has ended now. The American Jewish community is troubled about its future and about its connection with Israel.

These are worries that had not existed for the last generation, not since the 1930s. With the impact of the Nazi example, anti-Semitism was a real and present threat even in the United States, then in the grip of the great economic Depression. Despite the liberal policies of the Roosevelt administration, Jews remained excluded from many parts of the economy, and there were quotas against them in most of the colleges and universities. Jewish talent and verve expressed itself before World War II primarily in new endeavors such as motion pictures and in a variety of middlemen occupations. The needle trades were the one area of primary production that remained in Jewish hands, but this was more true of the entrepreneurs and the managers of the unions who were still almost all Jews in the 1930s; it was ever less true of the labor force, for Italians were becoming the workers, as Jews moved out to open small businesses of their own.

Jews were active in politics in the 1930s; they were a major element in the coalition of the dispossessed (labor, the Negroes, and the other ethnic minorities) that formed the New Deal majority. Their immediate reward was jobs, for many thousands of Jewish professionals were hired, on a plane of equality, to work in the vastly increased governmental bureaucracy of the welfare state.

The entry of the United States as a belligerent in World War II in December 1941 made anti-Semitism unfashionable, though slurs were still voiced by former isolationists or Nazi sympathizers that it was a "Jewish war." The pursuit of the war required the entire labor force and all the talent that America could muster. Jewish graduates from colleges and universities who had had trouble in the late 1930s finding jobs commensurate with their training were now broadly welcomed in civilian production and in the military. American Jews thus came out of the war with far broader economic access for their professionals and technocrats than ever before and with far wider social acceptability. American Jewish businessmen who had been mostly lower bourgeois as late as 1939 were now, in the booming postwar economy, well on the way to substantial affluence.

Two transcendent events of Jewish history in those years added to this mood of American Jewish confidence. There was briefly horror, and even shame and fear, in the mid-1940s when the death camps of Nazi Germany were opened. Nevertheless, American Jewry soon reacted in a very American way, pragmatically, with a desire to do whatever was necessary to help the survivors without dwelling much on the sorrow and the pity of the events in Europe. In America as a whole, in a booming economy, Jews could find a place, as never before, in American society. The creation of the State of Israel added to this confidence. To be sure, even in the early years all was not necessarily smooth in the relationship between the new state and the American government. American support for the United Nations resolution in November 1947 that created the State of Israel was lukewarm, and there was no American military aid for Israel in its own War of Independence struggle. In 1956, in the aftermath of the campaign that brought Israel's troops to the Suez Canal, the American reaction was severely negative. For the first twenty years of the life of the State of Israel, until after the Six Day War of June 1967, Israel received relatively negligible financial or military support even indirectly from the United States government. Nonetheless, Israel was extremely popular in American public opinion. It was a shining example of courage and democratic life. It was seen as a great act of rebuilding after the horrors of World War II. A successful American Jewish community thus added to its pride through its connection with an admired, young State of Israel.

Since the security of American Jews and even of Israel could be taken for granted by the mid-1950s, large elements of American Jewry devoted their energies to the battle for the rights of blacks. These endeavors involved both those organizations that were interested in domestic affairs and younger liberals who were not part of the organized Jewish community. In the next decade, such younger elements, including an ever more crystallized New Left, were increasingly involved in the effort to end the war in Vietnam. The prominence of Jews in both these endeavors betokened a high watermark of their at-homeness in American society. Jews could now, with hardly a second thought, dare to challenge the American establishment on two most sensitive and divisive issues, race relations and the war in Vietnam. The seal had been set on this new confidence in the presidential election of 1960. John F. Kennedy, the first and so far the only Catholic to become president, had reached the White House through the votes of four-fifths or more of four minorities— labor, Catholics, blacks, and Jews—which combined together against the other half of American society, those who were, or thought they were, the descendants of the earliest American settlers.

The days before and during the Six Day War were a historic turning point in American Jewish consciousness. Almost all elements of American Jewry, including those that had been indifferent or even estranged earlier, turned overwhelmingly toward Israel, and all their other concerns became secondary. Fears engendered by the memory of the Hitler years (it could not be allowed to happen again—and not to Israel), and the confidence that derived from a quarter of a century of American Jewish success, acted together to evoke an unprecedented response. Most striking in those days was the freedom with which Jews of all persuasions were willing to break with some of their comrades in other causes who remained "universalists" and could not fathom the peculiar passion of Jews for Israel. Even among the young, the New Left split as many Jews opted for Israel despite third world slogans that were pro-Arab. The great victory in June 1967 made Israel immensely popular and admired, and the American Jewish community thus rode at the very crest of a historic tide of self-confidence. The residue of that great moment has been that in the last fifteen years American Jewry has not hesitated to put the political battle for Israel at the center of its concerns and to continue to display this passion for Israel, even in the face of governmental opposition.

If in 1967 Israel was at the very height of its prestige, it began to be reduced from mythic and heroic stature to the grayer place of human fallibility during the Yom Kippur War. That near disaster created doubt in the Diaspora about the wisdom of Israel's most charismatic leaders. Golda Meir and Moshe Dayan were held responsible in the public mind for failing to foresee the Egyptian and Syrian attacks and to prevent them, either by diplomacy or by adequate preparation for war. The Rabin government that followed in the mid-1970s lacked charisma, and it was dogged by a succession of scandals that finally brought it down. Menachem Begin came to power in 1977 as the last of the heroic figures from the days of Israel's struggle for its independence. The American Jewish community knew very little about him from his twenty-nine years in opposition. It was aware that he had once commanded the Irgun, which had engaged in guerrilla warfare against the British, and that after the declaration of the state, Begin had disbanded his forces and joined the parliamentary system. American Jews preferred to believe that this doughty "freedom fighter" was a tough representative of Israel's national pride and will, a man whose style spoke without inhibition of the pain of the Holocaust, and of the right of a people which had been powerless for too many centuries to use power in defense of its interests. The American Jewish community chose to believe that Menachem Begin would compromise with the Arabs for the sake of peace, but that he would make his compromise at a point far more advantageous to Israel than could be achieved by a less tough-minded negotiator.

This opinion was in the ascendant in American Jewry in the first years of the Begin government. It fostered a return to the mood in relation to Israel to which American Jews had become accustomed. They wanted very much to look with respect, tinged with awe and even with a quasi-religious reverence, to a charismatic figure, Israel's prime minister, who spoke for the deepest emotions of world Jewry. This respect for a prime minister of Israel of the proportions of David Ben-Gurion and Golda Meir became all the stronger in the light of the moderation with which Menachem Begin governed in his first years in office. He made no radical changes in the bureaucracy, which was a creation of the twenty-nine years of Labor-dominated governments. He did accelerate the creation of settlements on the West Bank, and he gave free rein to ultranationalist forces that insisted on such actions. At the distance of six thousand miles, and with the desire to believe in the prime minister of Israel as ultimately beyond faction, as an Olympian, wise, and a uniting figure, American Jews simply preferred not to understand the distinction, to the degree to which there is any, between settlements in the Jordan Valley or on top of the Judean hills for "defensive purposes" and settlements near Hebron to assert the right of the Jewish people to the "undivided land of their ancestors."

The desired, and desirable, image of Israel's prime minister as a hero of peace and reasonableness, of statesmanship on a grand scale, reached its peak in 1978, when Menachem Begin was the host to Anwar Sadat on his historic journey to Jerusalem, and (after a somewhat prolonged haggle in the ensuing months) when Jimmy Carter engineered the peace treaty between Israel and Egypt at Camp David. Begin then took a step that no other leader in Israel could possibly have taken, to agree to return the whole of the Sinai to Egypt, in exchange for peace and mutual recognition. This involved a commitment to give up some Jewish settlements in the northeastern Sinai that Begin himself, when in opposition, had sworn never to abandon and which his foreign minister, Moshe Dayan, who had been part of the previous Labor governments, had helped establish. The signing of the Camp David accords on the White House lawn in July 1979, and the awarding of the Nobel Peace Prize to Begin and Sadat soon after this, were climactic moments for American Jewry. Israel's leader was seen as capable of large and heroic reassessments, on the scale of Charles de Gaulle's withdrawal from Algeria fifteen years before for the sake of peace, despite the objection of the *pieds-noirs* and of his own generals. In the summer of 1979, the American Jewish community in its vast majority thus looked forward to more years of Menachem Begin's leadership in which he would ultimately display equal diplomatic daring to drive a hard bargain—but to make a bargain—with the Arab world as a whole and thus make an end, on a worldwide scale, of Jewish-Arab confrontation.

Internally, the American Jewish community was being made somewhat uncomfortable, then, by the activities of the oil lobby, and by increasing propaganda of the political left. These disparate forces agreed together that America had an interest in the Arab world that required a solution to the Palestinian question in terms that at least the "moderates" among the Arab states and the Palestinians themselves would accept. Jimmy Carter himself was pushing Begin, after the high point of Camp David, to get on with negotiations about the West Bank, and there was an immediate falling out between the two leaders over the establishment of new settlements. Carter insisted that the meaning of the Camp David agreements included an acceptance by Israel of an indefinite freeze on future settlements on the West Bank until the issue of its future was decided by the end of the five-year period. Begin publicly and forcefully disagreed. He insisted that he had promised only a three-month freeze, and he proceeded to demonstrate that he meant what he said by moving forward immediately, after the ninety-day period, to establish more and more new centers for Jews beyond the 1967 borders of Israel.

A certain amount of discomfort began, then, to grow within the American Jewish community. Publicly, Begin was supported by all the organizations and almost all the recognized leaders in and out of office, though some were supporting him by silence rather than by overt enthusiasm. American Jews still preferred to believe, or, to be more exact, to hope that this Israeli tough-mindedness which led to the confrontation with an incumbent president of the United States would be seen, finally, to be tough-mindedness on a way to a compromise in the grand manner, but quiet doubts had begun to intrude on this perception.

It became more apparent in the American presidential campaign of 1980 that something had gone awry. The Israeli government maintained a correct public distance from involvement in the recurrent domestic drama of a presidential election every four years. It may even have been true that the leaders of the Israeli government were realistic enough, even in private, to suspect that, as far as their interests were concerned, it would probably not make great deal of difference who won the American presidential election. Nonetheless, public perceptions are themselves a fact, even if they are based on little or no reality. "Everyone" in America believed that Israel's Likud-led government preferred Reagan to Carter. This was based on, at the very least, two facts: some of Menachem Begin's most fervent ideological supporters in American Jewry were also leaders in American domestic politics and active in the Republican party campaign. Second, in the course of the election campaign, Ronald Reagan had used, by design, such Begin code words as "the settlements are not illegal," and he had accepted the Jewish claim, supported by all the parties in Israel, of the indivisibility of Jerusalem. Menachem Begin had already intervened overtly in domestic American affairs in a seemingly nonpolitical area, but one that had important political weight. He had moved closer to the "Moral Majority" led by Jerry Falwell, a group of Fundamentalist Christians who believed in the God-given right of Israel to its biblical boundaries. In American domestic politics, the "Moral Majority" was very much on the right; it was opposed to liberal views on abortion and prayer in public schools, and it wanted generally to increase the role of Fundamentalist Christianity in American public life. The bulk of organized Jewry and of its constituents remained frontally opposed to this agenda.

On a more sophisticated level, the neoconservatives, who were largely led by Jewish intellectuals such as Irving Kristol, the central figure of this movement, were now moving vocally against the welfare state and against most of the results of the New Deal of the 1930s. These individuals turned away from earlier hopes of détente with the Soviet Union to the most vigorous anti-Soviet posture being expressed in America in the mid- and late 1970s. Most of the neoconservatives had not been Zionists before 1967; they now cast Israel for the role of the doughtiest of defenders of American and Western interests against Soviet encroachment in the Middle East. The neoconservatives had no hesitancy about seeing Israel as an important military power, at least in regional terms, and of its need for arms and for space, with American help and consent, to fulfill its mission. The debacle in Iran strengthened the arguments for this view. This was also, and not entirely by accident, the rhetoric with which the Begin government was defining itself ever more publicly after the Camp David accords, especially as the presence of General Sharon in the Begin government became an ever larger factor. Israel kept insisting, over and over again, that its strength was not merely good for itself but that it was a vital necessity to the United States, which therefore ought to see that, in its own interest, its wisest option was the most generous economic, military, and political support of Israel. This would spare the United States the far more expensive alternative of policing the Middle East itself. In the light of the congruence of such grand designs, so the argument went, the issue of the West Bank could only be regarded as a minor footnote, best solved in ways that Israel's reigning government could accept.

This more or less acknowledged "coalition" between Israel's government and a collection of old-line Republican conservatives, ideological neoconservatives, and the "Moral Majority" caused some rift in American Jewry. In the election of 1980, Ronald Reagan won at least 40 percent of the Jewish vote, a figure that had been matched in recent years only once before, by the universally popular Eisenhower in 1952 against Adlai Stevenson, who was suspected then of being less than enthusiastic about Israel, as Jimmy Carter was depicted in 1980 as being more ready to pressure Israel than Ronald Reagan was likely to be. Nonetheless, the majority of the American Jewish community, despite its bourgeois affluence and despite the suspected wish of the leaders of Israel's government, voted in its majority for the Democrats. The liberal wing in domestic affairs of the American Jewish establishment (notably the American Jewish Congress and the Union of American Hebrew Congregations) distanced itself from the "Moral Majority" and declared its continued support for the welfare state.

American Jews continued to cling to the vision of a hardheaded Begin who would ultimately compromise and whose toughness was tactical, but some doubts began appearing in public even among some of his supporters. One of the signals came from a former chairman of the Conference of Presidents of Major Jewish Organizations, Theodore Mann. This body had, and has, as its raison d'être the defense and support of Israel in American public opinion, and it has performed this function through all the changes in Israeli governments. Theodore Mann left office in 1979, and he soon thereafter expressed his public disagreement with the policy of Israel's government of continuing settlements on the West Bank. The conflict become most overt in the public expressions by leading intellectuals such as the novelist Saul Bellow and a host of prominent Jewish liberal academics. The conflict was increasingly apparent in the years 1979 to 1981, as advertisements were taken out by both sides in major organs of the press such as the *New York Times*, that there was some ideological disagreement within the American Jewish community. It was widely, and correctly, perceived that vocal elements on both the right and the left, both the annexationists and the dissenters, spoke then for minority opinions. The bulk of the American Jewish community, probably three-quarters of it on the basis of poll evidence, wanted to support Israel and to avoid this controversy, in the hope that it would somehow or other go away.

The turn toward polarization came in 1982 with the war in Lebanon. The announced objective of the war was the "peace of the Galilee," which meant the cleaning up of PLO bases in southern Lebanon in order to be sure that there would be no possibility of bombardments or incursions into northern Israel. This objective was achieved in the early days of the war, but it soon became apparent, in Israel and in the United States, that the objective of the war was geopolitical, and on a much grander scale. Opinion in Israel was divided by the war, and this division was reflected almost immediately in the United States as well. The first overt expression came from the circles of the liberal intelligentsia, but the media coverage of the war soon added to the discomforts of American Jewry. The accounts from Lebanon in June and from Beirut in July—as the siege of the PLO-dominated West Beirut wore on—emphasized, and often exaggerated, the extent of the destruction of property and the numbers of civilian casualties. Television pictures that juxtaposed clips of Yasser Arafat fondling babies with the images of Israeli tanks pounding apartment houses were not pleasant for American Jews to watch, especially since the major newspapers of the United States were in the main critical of Israel's venture northward. Jews in the United States reacted with anger and disbelief at the news from the media, with some fear that such accounts might be prejudicial not only to Israel but even to them, and with the wish that if there were any grain of truth in these stories, Israel should take note of the criticism and act more moderately.

On the immediate issue of the extent of the destruction inflicted by the Lebanese war, the situation was calmed by midsummer. The several bombardments of West Beirut, and especially an all-day aerial attack in mid-August, gave a setback to the effort to improve the image of Israel, but enough had been reported by then about the large-scale murders that the Palestinians, the Phalangists, and various smaller factions had been inflicting on each other for years to make American opinion feel that the whole issue of Lebanon was far more complicated than had first appeared. The long-term facts about Lebanon did not allow a simple and unjust conclusion that Israel was merely the unprovoked aggressor. It was, however, a sustainable judgment that Israel had entered Lebanon in its own interest to displace the PLO permanently, to force out the Syrians by some combination of military pressure and diplomacy, and to make it possible for a Lebanon friendly to Israel to be created. Optimism reigned briefly as the PLO finally left West Beirut under the pressure of Israeli guns, and especially as Bashir Gemayel, who was known to have long association with Israel, was elected president of Lebanon. At that moment, the war in Lebanon seemed to have been won. American Jews generally began to feel good about the image of Lebanon being ushered by Israel to its new freedom. The more hardheaded thinkers in American Jewry were in agreement with Israel's government that the victory in Lebanon had increased America's influence in the region and that Israel had thus won a victory not only for itself but for its great friend, the United States.

This comforting assessment of the war in Lebanon was abandoned by many within several days, with the announcement of the Reagan plan for the settlement of the Palestinian question on September 1. This was followed by the assassination of Bashir Gemayel and by the Israeli move into West Beirut, which soon brought with it peripheral involvement and responsibility for the murders in the Palestinian camps of Sabra and Shattila on the weekend of September 16–18.

The immediate reaction of the Israeli government was to oppose an independent inquiry. The public unity of the Jewish establishment in the United States had already been frayed in response to the Reagan proposals on how to resolve the issue of the West Bank. Thomas Dine, the executive director of the pro-Israel lobby, the American Israel Public Affairs Committee, had publicly endorsed the Reagan plan as at least a basis for negotiation, and he had deplored Menachem Begin's out-of-hand rejection of the plan. A few other figures in the American Jewish establishment went so far as to regret publicly the Begin response, but most took refuge in pronouncements about their procedural disagreements with the American president. They added their criticism of the supposedly undue pressure that the announcement of an American peace plan by the president was putting on Israel.

As the days went by, the response of the American Jewish establishment became ever more "regular." The organizational leaders did what they had done for years; they quieted down the critics and defended the Israeli government's outright rejectionism. It was no secret that in private there was deep division among the leadership, for the Israeli Labor party, the official opposition with which most American Jewish establishment figures had historic ties, had accepted the Reagan proposal.

The division of opinion boiled over two weeks later in the aftermath of the massacre in Beirut. Menachem Begin's opposition to an independent juridical inquiry failed to silence two of his most highly placed supporters in American Jewish officialdom. The two immediate past chairmen of the Conference of Presidents of Major Jewish Organizations, Howard Squadron and Alexander Schindler, called publicly for such an inquiry, even as the organization they once headed asserted that though it was shocked by the massacre, Israel could not possibly bear any responsibility for it. The outcry in Israel itself was so vast that the Begin government reversed itself in a matter of days and appointed an independent high-level commission which satisfied the demands of the critics. This action restored the unity of the American Jewish establishment, but only on the surface. The cumulative effect of the disagreements over the Reagan plan and over the response to the Beirut massacre was to fray the fundamental relationship between organized American Jewry and the Israeli government. A distinction had now to be made, at least by some, within the establishment between supporting Israel, which remained a strong commitment, and supporting the policies of its incumbent government, which now was no longer an automatic certainty, at least not among all the leaders of the Jewish organizations.

The events of the Lebanese war accentuated another trend that had been becoming more marked after the mid-1970s, but which now assumed serious significance. The American Jewish organizations represent in their overlapping memberships perhaps half of the American Jews. Those Jews who belong to these organizations are overwhelmingly older and more nearly likely to be in business than in the professions. These organizations also have a significant element of that smallest proportion of the American Jewish population, those who arrived from Europe, North Africa, or Israel after World War II. The other half of American Jews who are not formally affiliated tends to be heavily weighted with the academic intelligentsia and with younger people whose families have been in the United States for at least three generations.

For a generation after 1945, this other, unorganized Jewish community allowed the organizations to speak for American Jewry's pro-Israel emotions. A large consensus existed, especially after the Six Day War of 1967, in admiration both of Israel's internal virtue as the only democracy in the Middle East and of its announced foreign policy of waiting for intransigent Arabs to exhibit their readiness to make generous peace with it. By the mid-1970s, even before the

Likud victory in the election of 1977, some liberal elements in American Jewry, including the very ones that had become pro-Israel for the first time in 1967, began to wonder out loud whether the Israeli government really wanted to return the West Bank, or even substantially all of it, to Arab rule. As these doubts were being expressed, three kinds of counterattack were mounted by the defenders of Israel's policies. First, the critics were widely accused of helping the enemies of Israel. The public demonstrations of Jewish disunity, which often followed such criticism, was alleged to weaken the impact of the pressures then being applied by pro-Israel groups in Washington for aid to Israel. A second line of criticism insisted that those Jews who did not live in Israel had no moral right to voice critical opinions of Israel, for their lives and the lives of their children were not surety for their views. Perhaps the most pointed attack came from the partisans of the Likud view, which included an alliance of largely Orthodox Jews and the most vocal neoconservatives, who argued that control of the West Bank by Israel was both proper in international law and a defense of Western interests; Israel was keeping strategically sensitive territory from probable Soviet penetration.

This argument prevailed in the 1970s among the great majority of American Jews, who preferred to leave Israel to the Israelis and not to be troubled by disagreements over its policies. In 1982 such avoidance became less possible. Cumulatively, the events of the Lebanese war and the debates that attended it established beyond any doubt that the policy of the Israeli government on the West Bank was not a negotiating counter; it was an ideological position to which Menachem Begin held with unapologetic consistency. On this issue, one could either support Begin or disagree with him, but the issue of the preparation by Israel to annex the West Bank could no longer be avoided, especially since the whole world was aware that the disagreements over this question cut across Israel itself. Those who supported opposition views in the United States kept saying that to agree in the Diaspora with Israel's opposition parties could hardly be denounced as sinful.

Some of the ultimate results of these difficulties between Israel's government and significant elements in American Jewry began to surface toward the end of the year. Here again, Rabbi Alexander

Schindler was the most representative figure. In 1977, when Begin came to power, Schindler was the chairman of the Conference of Presidents of Major Jewish Organizations, and he had led the American Jewish establishment to move toward unfailing loyalty to the policies of the new premier. In early December 1982, Schindler finally moved to a total break with Menachem Begin. In an address to the body of which he is the professional head, the Union of Hebrew Congregations (the synagogues of Reform Judaism), Rabbi Schindler announced his opposition to the policy of annexing the West Bank, and he made the distinction between loyalty to Israel and support of its incumbent government. But he went far beyond these two assertions. Schindler now joined a small group of leaders that included Rabbi Gerson Cohen, chancellor of the Jewish Theological Seminary (the rabbinic school of Conservative Judaism), who had been arguing that American Jewry as a whole, while maintaining its concern for Israel, needed not to fashion its own destiny, without accepting the centrality of Israel in the life of the Diaspora. The final push for such "heresy" had no doubt come from the passionate disagreements over the events in Lebanon, but these were merely the trigger mechanisms.

A largely unnoticed disenchantment had been growing for years in several aspects of the "marriage" between American Jewry and Israel. Conservative and Reform Jews had consistently had trouble with Israel, which still continues, over the issue of "who is a Jew." These liberal rabbinates have remained unrecognized in Israel by the Orthodox, the governmentally established religious authorities, and there was a constant threat to lighten the restrictions against them. This quarrel has erupted several times in recent years, and twice again in 1982. Conservative and Reform Jews in the United States criticized Israel's governing coalition, which includes a powerful Orthodox bloc, for not extending equality to the non-Orthodox elements within Jewry. More fundamentally, the American Jewish connection with Israel had been for a generation a generally outspoken but nonetheless very real "social compact." The effort for Israel was accepted joyously as the central endeavor for American Jewry, on the presumption that these labors were not only good for Israel; they would act to preserve the American Jewish community and provide it with the inner verve necessary for its continuity. This theory broke down visibly in 1982.

The evidence kept mounting in the 1970s of deep inner trouble for American Jews. The rate of intermarriage is, at the very least, one in three among those American Jews being married today. The younger generation of American Jews is very much less affiliated with any organized Jewish endeavor than was its parents. All the demographic indexes show a disastrously small birthrate and an ever-aging population, probably the oldest of any group in the United States. To be sure, caring Jews of all kinds have Israel at the center of their concern, but unconcerned Jews are drifting away at an alarming rate. Increasingly through the years there has been much talk, and even some action, by the organized American Jewish community toward greater effort in the field of Jewish education. The Jewish day-school population has grown to perhaps one-quarter of all the Jewish children now receiving some kind of Jewish education, but the total number in all the schools has fallen by half in the last two decades. There is in the whole of American Jewry a minority element that is becoming more intensely Jewish, but this group represents perhaps one-tenth of all American Jews. Of the funds raised by the central appeals of the organized Jewish community, the percentage that goes to Israel has fallen from very nearly two-thirds a decade ago to perhaps one-half now. There is as yet no consensus, and certainly no strategy, as to what the American Jewish community ought to do about the dire threat of rapid assimilation. The central question before the organized Jewish community is still the day-to-day relationship with Israel through fund-raising and political activity, but the grave danger to American Jewry's inner survival has now been posed as a separate question that must be dealt with in its own right. The confidence of earlier years that this situation will somehow or other take care of itself has vanished.

Through the years, even in the best of times, the American Jewish community has often remeasured the temperature of anti-Semitism, if only because so much of its organized life was constructed to do battle against this threat. In the winter of 1973–74, during the Arab oil embargo in the aftermath of the Yom Kippur War, it was widely reported that bumper stickers had been seen on automobiles in the United States saying "Burn Jews, not oil." Despite the pervasiveness of this story, no one could be found who had actually seen such a sticker. It was remarkable that the oil embargo failed totally to foster any anti-Semitism in the United States. Jewish fears imagined something that simply did not happen. There has been a repetition of this phenomenon in 1982. Recent public opinion polls have shown that the support for Israel remains strong among the American people, and that the PLO continues to be held in low regard. Swastika daubings on synagogues and Jewish buildings have, however, increased in recent years, but the polls show anti-Semitism has not increased. Indeed, in the congressional election of November 1982, Jews were elected in substantial numbers to both houses of Congress, where Jews now represent roughly 8 percent of the total. This is very nearly four times the proportion of Jews to the total population.

This quite unalarming overall picture has nonetheless given rise to vastly increased apprehension by American Jews, the majority of whom believe that anti-Semitism is more menacing today than it has been ever before in the post–World War II era. Most troubling to American Jews is something as yet almost totally unexpressed, their situation within the total economy of the United States. In a year of growing depression and misery, the American Jews remain a striking and important element among the "haves." Certainly some Jewish businesses have gone bankrupt and not all is well even in the most elegant suburbs, but, by and large, the Jewish community is weathering the economic crisis reasonably well. The deep, gnawing fear in American Jewry is that further social tension, fed by the increasing anger of the poor, who are finding Ronald Reagan's "safety net" not very safe at all, might indeed become grounds for more virulent anti-Semitism. American Jews are uncomfortable that Israel is constantly in the headlines, and therefore the continual struggle of American Jews for the support of Israel, both economically and politically, is emphasized—and sometimes criticized. American Jews today could define their public policy in the language of a Franco-Jewish worthy during the Dreyfus Affair. He wished profoundly for a return to a situation where whatever was striking about Jews would be ignored ("faites-vous oublier"), lest harm come to the Jewish community in a tempestuous time. Such a wish is not likely to be fulfilled in the United States in 1983. The comforting probability is that the institutions of American democracy will withstand future shocks, and that anti-Semitism, despite Jewish fears, is not likely to burgeon in the United States. American Jews will nonetheless keep worrying. They are now returning to the Democratic party and to the welfare state, not because they think the Democrats would be better for Israel but because they prefer to pay the price in high taxes for a dampening of social angers.

The year 1982 has thus forced on the American Jewish community a new maturity, which it probably did not desire. The Jewish community in the United States has preferred to let Israel determine its own policy and provide the Jewish community with pride and hope for its own American future. The mood is now far more sober. The classic problems of the Diaspora have now recurred. American Jewry must now fight its own battles against assimilation and anti-Semitism and work out its destiny in relationship to the rest of American society, mindful of Israel and passionately concerned about it, but without the illusion that Israel is the answer to all its problems. American Jews have now to be called to statesmanship of their own, to the making of policy that reflects an independent assessment of their own needs and wants, while remaining indissolubly bound to Israel. This redefinition will not become easier, even after the war in Lebanon finally ends. The deeper problems of American Jews, and their disagreements with Israel, will remain and become sharper.

1983

15. *"The Triumph of the Jews"*: A Critique of Charles Silberman's Optimism

The journalist Charles Silberman published a book in 1985 entitled *A Certain People; the Triumph of the Jews.* His thesis was, at the time, the high-water mark of expressed published optimism: in his view, not only had the Jews arrived permanently as equals in America, but they had defined an American Judaism that was now secure for the future. Silberman even predicted that the rate of intermarriage, which he undercounted then at less than 30 percent, had become stable and might even soon decline. I disagreed with his optimism, and not only on factual grounds. In the years since the review-essay below was written, his prediction about intermarriage has been totally disproved. In 1990 the Council of Jewish Federations, the coordinating body of the major Jewish fund-raising bodies in the United States, published the results of a comprehensive study of the American Jewish population. A slight majority of all the marriages now being contracted by Jews are with non-Jews. Less than one-third of the non-Jewish spouses convert to Judaism. But my basic quarrel with the optimists, such as Charles Silberman, has concerned not the statistics about intermarriage, but the quality of the ethnicity which they have been hailing as the "new Judaism."

▼

For at least a century, Jews in America have worried about three main issues: their success in establishing themselves in American society; their continuity as a community; and their legitimacy, that is, their justification to themselves of the value of being Jews. Their concerns about worldly success were always connected with the fear of anti-Semitism. Hatred of Jews did not have economic effects until the mass immigration of the 1880s. The German Jews who arrived before then had often been subjected to social discrimination, but this did not prevent them from doing well in business. Roughly half of the German Jewish immigrants settled in the rapidly expanding cities of the West and South, where their skills as middlemen were welcome.

The situation was quite different for the approximately two million Eastern European Jews who arrived between 1880 and 1914. Their children had great difficulty entering the professions and getting good jobs in many established businesses. These barriers began to break down during and after the Second World War; by now the economic exclusion of Jews has become rare. It is, therefore, possible to imagine that the clock will now stop, that this success will not undergo any further change, and that the large and seemingly untroubled status of Jews in the American economy can thus be celebrated as the end of a process, an unprecedented achievement in the history of the Jewish Diaspora.

The question of the continuity of the Jewish community has been equally troubling, at least to the majority that has continued to prefer being Jewish. Here, too, fear predominated for several generations. Among the intellectuals in the immigrant generation, some of the most influential were antireligious universalists of one kind or another. In the next generation, socialism of several kinds, and not Judaism in any form, was the faith of many Jewish writers and political activists. Almost without exception, those who were seriously concerned about the survival of Judaism in America wrote and spoke, during the first half of the twentieth century, as if they were fighting a rearguard action against inevitable attrition. They were not cheered by the attention that the immigrant generation and its children were paying to bar-mitzvah celebrations and Jewish cooking. This was widely regarded as vulgar folk-Jewishness, which might last a while or even for a long time, but could not be regarded as a substitute for the knowledge of sacred texts and adherence to Jewish practices. Even in the heyday of the Catskill resorts, those who enjoyed vacationing at Grossinger's knew that such a place was neither the heir of the European synagogue nor a substitute for it.

Now, in the third and fourth generations of the descendants of East European immigrants, the popular Jewish culture seems to continue. Fewer Jews today observe the High Holy Days than their parents did, but many pay dues to synagogues, turn up for the Passover Seder, light candles for Hanukkah, and are overwhelmingly pro-Israel, willing to give and raise money in its behalf. Some assume that "American Jewry"—the Americans who identify themselves as Jews—has become a stable community, one firmly based on the new Judaism. If one believes this, one may even dare to predict that this consolidated community will eventually even acquire a deeper sense of Jewish values. It follows that Jews no longer have cause to feel guilty of deserting their heritage, or to feel somehow inferior to their forebears.

Taken together, these arguments have a deeper purpose. If American Jews have now achieved lasting, unprecedented success in preserving Judaism in the open society, and if America is now the secure place in which the Jews can be as rich as anyone else—and be widely praised for it—then the deepest question of American Jewish life from its very beginnings, the issue of legitimacy, is solved. American Jewry today can accept itself as it is.

More than that, it can make its wealth legitimate through good deeds, domestic and foreign. This too has happened before. The German Jews, "our crowd," had some conscience about their success. The more radical among them, such as Felix Adler and Lillian Wald, insisted on the moral obligation to help the needy whether they were Jewish or not. The more conservative German Jewish leaders worried about poor Jews, especially among the newest immigrants, and about the troubles of Jews abroad. Similarly, today, the efforts of the Jewish community are largely devoted to raising money for Israel, and to alleviate misery in America. Those who take the lead in these activities are rewarded with honors in the organized community as pious Jews used to be honored in the synagogue in recognition of their learning and their high dedication to the love and fear of God. The "giver" and the "activist" are seen as heirs of the scholars and pietists of old.

In summary, this is the argument of Charles Silberman's A Certain People (1985). He leaves us in no doubt about his intentions. He calls the first section of his book "An American Success Story," and the second "A Jewish Success Story." Whatever successes and disasters might have happened elsewhere are for him irrelevant. Only in America could a Jew have become president of Du Pont and only in America is there a fourth generation of Jews who still attend a seder. The United States has provided the setting for the climactic moment of the Jewish Diaspora—America is, therefore, the best of all possible Jewish worlds.

It is instructive to list the subjects that Charles Silberman avoids in making this case. He is bold enough to talk about Jewish crime in the immigrant generation, as one of the forms of upward mobility; he does not bring himself to discuss Jewish communism, which was, until the 1950s, one of the major expressions of Jewish idealism. The trial and death of the Rosenbergs, for example, is simply not mentioned. Accused of being only two of a circle of leftist Jews who were loyal to the Soviet Union, they were prosecuted and defended mainly by Jews and were sentenced to death by a Jewish judge. The controversy over whether they were victims of fears of anti-Semitism or martyrs by choice to the cause of communism has been conducted in large part by Jews. Any serious assessment of contemporary American Jewish life cannot avoid this drama, whatever its meaning. For Silberman to have dealt with it, however, would have involved him in a question that he must avoid if he is to sustain the thesis of his book. He cannot allow his readers to start considering the evidence for the proposition that Jews, at least some significant elements among them, have had other things on their minds than making successful lives for themselves in the American suburbs.

Silberman cites the contribution of Jews for the last several generations to art and literature in America as further proof of the rise of Jews to a place in society, but he mutes the fact that most of the Jewish writers and artists worth mentioning have been critical of conventional bourgeois America, and of American Jewish values. The dominant tradition of the modern Jewish intelligentsia, since Spinoza and certainly since Marx and Freud, has been to express its Jewishness by standing apart from society and asking secular, prophetic questions about justice and morality. This is not to be confused with the alien feelings of immigrants who could hardly wait to "make it" in America, or even with some continuing sense of displacement felt by their children in a still anti-Semitic country. The young Jews who were so prominent in the civil rights struggle of the 1950s and the 1960s, and those who tried to end the war in Vietnam in the 1970s, are as much a part of the American Jewish culture as the members of the Jewish country clubs, but they hardly appear in Silberman's book.

Silberman disagrees with an essay I wrote in 1963 about assimilation. The rate of intermarriage of Jews in the United States was then one in twelve. I predicted that it would rise, as the grandchildren of the immigrants began to marry, to one in three. I suggested then, and later, that the American Jewish community was in danger of gradually disappearing. Silberman deplores such forebodings. Against them, he cites his impressions from his own talks with American Jews—mainly activists in Jewish organizations, it appears—and he draws on two recent statistical studies of American Jewish life.

Silberman admits that one out of four Jews now marries a partner who was not born Jewish, but he insists that this figure has now stabilized and is perhaps decreasing. To support this view he cites as typical the rate of intermarriage in Boston, where it is estimated at under 20 percent; but he does not find equally or more significant the 39 percent rate of intermarriage in Los Angeles, the second largest Jewish community in the United States. But the truth about most statistical estimates of the behavior of American Jews is that they are based on limited samples, are of varying reliability, and are subject, as Silberman himself tells us, to widely different interpretations. The most famous, the Jewish population study of 1971, in which the largest number of American Jews were surveyed, was inconclusive. The two principal authors each arrived at a different estimate of intermarriage from the same statistics. The United States Census Bureau does not ask about religious affiliation. In Canada, however, where the government compiles such information, the rate of Jewish intermarriage has already risen to over 20 percent in a community that is more than a generation closer to its European origins than the Jews of the United States. What cannot be doubted about most such marriages is that the children they produce, even if the originally non-Jewish parent converts, have, on the whole, a less secure sense of their Jewishness than the children of marriages in which both partners were born Jews. Silberman's conviction that intermarriage is probably strengthening the American Jewish community, or, at the very least, that it is a matter of no consequence for group survival, is simply unbelievable.

In recounting his impressions of Jewish attitudes, Silberman has much to say about the young Jews who are returning in some fashion to the established Jewish community, but we hear very little from him about an equally significant number who have turned to teachers such as Ram Dass, himself of Jewish origin, in search of enlightenment. Silberman makes much of the Jewish Studies courses in American colleges and universities. I have taught such courses for twenty-five years, at Columbia and, now, at Dartmouth, and I have not observed that a rebirth of Jewish consciousness has become pervasive. On the campuses I know well, I find that roughly 10 or 15 percent of the Jewish students, some of them children of Holocaust survivors (and thus different from their third- and fourth-generation peers), have become more intensely Jewish. But most Jewish students are less involved in Jewish life than college students were a generation ago. Ask any Hillel director anywhere in the country, as I have asked many of them in recent years, and he or she will tell you that the number of Jewish students who do not want to be considered as Jews is at least as large as the faithful minority that turns up fairly regularly at the campus Hillel House. The High Holy Days have become everywhere on campus a demonstration of active Jewish identity; thousands come to services, but thousands more go to class.

Silberman seems to have talked to many leaders of the various federations of Jewish charitable organizations. These represent today about 45 percent of American Jewry, the part that belongs to the organized Jewish community. As Silberman barely mentions, there is substantial evidence that these numbers have been dropping. A decade or so ago the consensus among Jewish leaders, based on surveys by Jewish organizations, was that something over half of American Jews belonged to such organizations. Silberman accounts for this apparent decline by arguing at several points that younger Jews tend to "join" after marriage or, at the latest, when they have children. Therefore the statistical drop in membership is more apparent than real. I do not believe this theory. Silberman writes that he has talked with many rabbis, but they do not seem to be the ones I have known during forty years as a rabbi. The more thoughtful among them, including some of those who are prominent in the supposedly reviving Orthodox community, could have told him that they contemplate the Jewishness of the third and fourth generations with more bleakness than hope. Practically every rabbi knows dozens of Jews who have hardly any Jewish life at all except perhaps at funerals. More important, a Jewish life that is passive before the birth of children tends to become passive again after the bar-mitzvah or bat-mitzvah ceremonies are over.

Silberman could even have documented such concerns about the Jewish community from the very statistics that he quotes to bolster his case. He makes considerable use of a study commissioned by the Federation of Jewish Philanthropies of New York, directed by Steven M. Cohen and Paul Ritterband, which will be published in 1986 as *Family, Community, and Identity: The Jews of Greater New York*. In their draft text, Cohen and Ritterband argue, along with Silberman, for the view that a new kind of American Jewish survivalism has now appeared: practically all American Jews, they find, now care about Israel and Soviet Jews while, at the same time, relatively few obey the dietary laws or follow other traditional practices. The most persuasive interpretation of such statistical evidence was made, I think, by Donald Feldstein, the former executive vice president of the American Jewish Committee. In 1984, in a pamphlet commissioned by the American Jewish Congress ("The American Jewish Community in the 21st Century: A Projection"), he gave a much less sanguine account of recent trends toward Jewish activism:

> One group, the smaller, will be more Jewishly educated, more involved in Jewish matters. The other group, the larger, will be largely uneducated Jewishly, less involved, and less identified and dependent upon their stores of Jewish "capital" for their survival as Jews. They will be vulnerable to being lost from the Jewish people, but still Jewish enough to have their attention captured in a crisis, and to be worked on towards winning over their sons and daughters to the other group.

The fundamental issue, as Cohen and Ritterband acknowledge more clearly than Silberman does, is how one chooses to interpret the statistical surveys. No doubt the fewer than 10 percent of American Jews who live with the "thou shalt nots" of the religious tradition are far more securely tied to their Jewishness. The rest have for the most part worked out a version of Jewishness that is pleasant for them and acceptable to Gentiles (as the advertising slogan proclaimed, "you don't have to be Jewish to like Levy's rye bread"); but they do not recognize the force of biblical injunction as a presence in their lives. This is not the faith of prophets and martyrs.

Two questions that should be asked are whether the new Jewishness is unprecedented, as Cohen, Ritterband, and Silberman would have it, and whether it has staying power. The two questions are in fact interrelated. If contemporary American Jewishness, of the kind that these writers describe, is indeed a new phenomenon in modern Jewish experience, then it might be argued that its future is unpredictable, and that this unprecedented community might enjoy a future all its own.

The truth is that the same kinds of claims have been made before, and the results are known. During the French Revolution, when the

Jews were first emancipated in Europe, the first group to be given equality were the Sephardim of southern France. After their representatives returned from Paris in February 1790 bearing the decree that gave them equality, the leaders of the community met and disbanded as a separate entity. They then reorganized themselves at that very same meeting as a "committee for welfare." The prosperous Jews of Bordeaux had for the most part ceased believing in the Jewish God, but they continued to worry about poor Jews, at home and in other parts of Europe. Three generations later, at least half the descendants of the Jews who had been in Bordeaux before the revolution had left the Jewish community.

Another striking example occurred in the United States. By the turn of the century, the German Jews were into their second and third generations. Their relationship to the synagogue, even at its most reformed, was vestigial and sentimental, and, as I noted above, they expressed their Jewishness through deeds of charity. These were the founders of the federations of Jewish philanthropy throughout the country and of many Jewish hospitals. They supported the American Jewish Committee in order to protect Jewish rights everywhere, at home and abroad, and the Joint Distribution Committee in order to help poor Jews abroad. Today one could not fill the boards of directors of either organization with the descendants of its founders. Many of their great-grandchildren simply do not want to be considered as Jews.

The historic evidence suggests, contrary to Silberman and to the sociologists whom he quotes (and who quote him in turn), that activism can work as a substitute for faith for no more than one or two generations. The causes of Israel, of Jewish social service, and of antidefamation clearly seem to serve the same purpose today: ultimately, the result seems likely to be the same. Silberman cites the rise in Jewish charitable contributions as evidence of a Jewish revival. It is true that the money raised by Jewish charities has risen in dollar amounts, but the number of givers is static at best, or, more probably, declining. Such statistics are known to the Jewish federations, but are not much talked about. Sources in the national office of the United Jewish Appeal have recently revealed, however, that the organization estimates that no rise in income will take place during the next few years, and some of its officials fear that receipts will drop before the year 2000. Silberman himself mentions that the Jewish fund-raising establishment is perturbed by the increasing prominence of the "big givers" on the boards of museums and symphony orchestras. They are making princely gifts to these institutions because status in American life is much more easily bought by contributing to them than to Jewish charities. These facts should have caused even the optimistic Silberman to wonder whether the American open society is the place where Jewish loyalty is solidly secure.

The momentum of ethnic Jewishness that Silberman describes cannot last, in my view, for reasons that I suggested a few years ago in the Israeli newspaper *Ha'aretz*. I was, I wrote, plagued by a nightmare about American Jewry: the day might come when Israel would strike oil, and thus no longer be dependent on money from abroad; on that day, the Arabs might make peace, and so Israel would no longer need a lobby in Washington; the Soviet Union might open its doors wide for all Jews who wanted to leave; and anti-Semitism in America would disappear. At that point, the Jewish activism that Charles Silberman, along with Cohen and Ritterband, suggests is the basis for a new American Judaism would have to disband. Even if the Jewish charitable organizations tried to continue (like the March of Dimes after the cure for polio was found), the attempt would fail. The "new Jewishness" thus seems to me founded on two very questionable, even frightening, assumptions: that peace will never come in the Middle East, or, at the very least, that Israel's situation will never become that of a normally independent nation; and second, that successive generations of the Jewish bourgeoisie will not find other causes to engage their attention.

Charles Silberman's most hopeful assertion is that the Jewishness he has described is moving toward religious and cultural revival. He claims that what is happening now in America is unprecedented. This, too, seems to me untrue: every postemancipation Jewish community, even as it moved from faith to activism to large-scale assimilation, has cast up some remarkable leaders and thinkers who have returned at the last moment to their Jewish origins. Among the German Jews in America Ludwig Lewisohn was such a figure, although his audience consisted of the most recent immigrants from Eastern Europe. The same was true in Germany in the early years of the century. Although they had the help of the popular sage Martin Buber, Franz Rosenzweig and Gershom Scholem persuaded very few of their German Jewish contemporaries to take part in the revival of Jewish learning they hoped for. They found their allies among Eastern Europeans who had been brought up on traditional Judaism. What is different about America is both the size of the American Jewish community and, at least in Silberman's view, the unique hospitality of America to ethnic variation. He simply rejects out of hand the possibility that this unique hospitality makes relatively painless assimilation an even easier choice for many Jews than the choice to engage in separatist activism within the Jewish community.

The issues raised by Charles Silberman's book turn on the question of what it is to be authentically Jewish. From the beginning of Jewish history there have been those who have wanted to be at ease with themselves and with their neighbors. Destroying idols is an unpleasant and usually dangerous activity, as Abraham once discovered. Silberman claims, and plausibly so, that his approach was influenced by the views of Rabbi Mordecai Kaplan, the leader of the Reconstructionist movement. Although he does not mention him, I find his views are also close to those of the philosopher Horace Kallen. Both arrived in the United States during the 1880s as the children of East European immigrants. In the early years of the century they defined their own idea of "cultural pluralism." They set themselves against the idea of America as a "melting pot," wanting Jews to find a niche as equals, not simply in the day-to-day contest for fair treatment but in creating American history itself. The climactic statement of this view was Oscar Handlin's assertion, in his book *The Uprooted,* in 1952, that American history is in fact the story of a country constructed through the efforts of immigrants. Handlin, in effect, confirmed that the great hope of Kallen and Kaplan was becoming a reality—that those who came from Minsk and Prague in the 1880s could now be regarded as just as legitimate in America as those who came from England during the 1620s.

Kallen was an entirely secular Jew who disliked religion. Kaplan was a rabbi who moved away from Orthodoxy to "reconstruct" Judaism as ethnic loyalty and practical ethics. Both of them, however, denied with great vehemence the fundamental religious doctrine the

Jews have held about themselves, that they are "a chosen people" who must fulfill unique God-given obligations. If Jews were to be defined as one of the many groups that were trying to be at home in America, then the claim of any of these communities to be carrying out a special, divinely appointed mission has to be modified or abandoned. This position implied a deep religious reform for American Jews, one far more fundamental than the Reform Judaism of the earlier German Jewish immigrants, who abandoned the Jewish rituals for the sake of Western respectability but who continued to conceive themselves as having theological claims to be "a chosen people."

Kallen and Kaplan, for all the differences between them, essentially asserted that being Jewish was to be defined in America less according to the light of the past than as a description of what Jews were doing together as a community. There was no reason to be Jewish out of theological guilt or to continue to cower before the God who had thundered on Sinai. Jews in the open society would remain Jews only because their activities together could be more moving and more morally and aesthetically satisfying to the individual Jew than any other way of life that might be available. Kallen and Kaplan were both political liberals and even flirted with socialism. (Kallen was a progressive and Kaplan sympathized with Labor Zionism.) They largely appealed to their own generation, the children of immigrants who wanted to find a solid place in American middle-class society. Kallen and Kaplan did not abandon classic Jewish religion in order to substitute for it the kind of political and cultural radicalism that would put them and their disciples outside the American social structure.

Silberman has now written a book which essentially asserts that the dream of Kaplan and Kallen has come true. Whether or not the organized Jewish life Silberman describes as stable and flourishing turns out to be a transient phenomenon, as I have argued it probably will, we must ask a deeper question. Is this Judaism? The authority of Mordecai Kaplan and Horace Kallen will not help (and not only because the Orthodox rabbis become incensed at the very mention of their names). The liberal American rabbis, both Conservative and Reform—the rabbis who lead four-fifths of the American Jews belonging to synagogues—essentially follow Kaplan in practice while they overwhelmingly reject his theology. They insist on affirming the doctrine of the "chosen people," the central concept Kaplan wanted to replace. Whether these rabbis can produce a cogent theological defense of their view is not the point here. What is important is that their rejection of Kaplan on this question is a way of asserting that Jews are different. Apart from this, what remains of Jewish ethnic difference "beyond the melting pot," to use the phrase of Nathan Glazer and Daniel Patrick Moynihan? As Silberman describes that difference, it hardly seems one worth suffering for or even that it will cause much inconvenience.

When Silberman considers the concept of the Jews as "chosen," he defines it as a feeling of being somewhat on the margins of society, a feeling that acts as a stimulus to success. He gives no hint that the Jews he describes as undergoing a "revival" have any sense of the deep religious meaning of "chosenness" as the source of moral and social conscience. What Silberman cannot see is that authentic Jewish teaching has always demanded a willingness to stand apart, to risk being contrary. I suggest that Philip Roth's Mrs. Portnoy, even as she is happy in her house in suburban New Jersey, and probably now also in West Palm Beach, knows this to be true. She remembers from her childhood that her mother or her grandmother told her that "you should remember to be good to Jews," but she also heard, over and over again, that "the other person is also a human being," and that "a Jew is different; he does not do such things." This is the source of the lasting Jewish political liberalism in America. The neoconservatives are right: if Jews really feel themselves to be like all other Americans, as "haves" they ought to turn to the right wing in their politics. No doubt, as I once argued in an essay in the *New York Review of Books* (see essay 18) there is a component of enlightened self-interest in Jewish liberalism, a concern to avoid the animosity of the poor and the blacks. This, for Silberman, entirely explains the Jewish vote for the Democrats in recent elections. What he misses in his characteristic concentration on the tactics of success is the echo of a unique moral sensibility, a willingness to act in disregard of economic interest when the cause seems just.

Sophie Portnoy and her son Alexander, the heroes of Philip Roth's famous 1969 novel *Portnoy's Complaint* (Alexander has now perhaps found a place within the Jewish fund-raising establishment), will probably read Charles Silberman's book with some pleasure, for it assures them that all is well with them, and that they deserve unqualified admiration. And yet, after Mrs. Portnoy has savored this pastry, I believe she will feel vaguely hungry, perhaps for the truth. Judaism is neither authentic, nor can it survive, if it amounts to no more than a triumph of adjustment to suburban life. In all its authentic versions, even at its most secular, Judaism is the faith of those who are dissatisfied with the society around them and have a critical sense of the hollowness of worldly success—and only through such people can Judaism survive, or have reason for survival.

1985

16. *Sharing Culture: Learning to Talk Together as Jews*

The critical pessimism that I had been expressing in the essays above, and especially in my book *The Jews in America*, caused the leaders of the Council of Jewish Federations to challenge me. They invited me to lecture to a meeting of their national board in New York in early September 1990. In this talk, published here for the first time, I attempted to answer the question: what do you propose as cultural policy for this generation of American Jews?

▼

In the 1930s, the Jewish world had at least as many problems as it has today. I was then in my teens and so I went avidly to hear every visiting lecturer who came to Baltimore. Without exception, they delivered eloquent and searing analyses of the problems of our people. We were then being abandoned by most of the world. We were poor in the Great Depression, and many were unhappy in their Jewishness.

One day, Hayim Greenberg, the leading intellectual figure among the Labor Zionists in America, came to town. His speech mocked all the others, and even his own. Jewish speakers, Greenberg said, came visiting, as he was doing, to analyze our "tsores" (problems) for the better part of an hour: they then reached a climax by shouting thunderously "m'darf, m'muz, m'zol" (one ought to do something, one must do something, one should do something). The speaker then sat down to large applause, leaving us in the dark as to what we ought to be doing. Greenberg went on that night to suggest that Jewish life in the Diaspora had little future and that all Jews should head for Palestine. He was too clearheaded even then, in the midst of the Arab riots of the mid-1930s, to imagine that all would be peaceful forever in the land of Israel. Zionism did not offer the end of conflict, but the ingathered Jewish people would at least be saved from assimilation.

In the half century since I heard Hayim Greenberg, the experience of our tribe has been both unutterably tragic and gloriously creative— but some of the problems are the same. The Jewish people, especially its near-majority which lives in the United States, is more troubled by assimilation now than it was in the 1930s. The British no longer bar the door to Palestine; those who fear assimilation—and who does not?—can now move to Israel, but very few have. American Jews are not behaving "according to plan." In the fifth decade of the existence of the State of Israel, it is clear that they care deeply about Israel but most intend to stay in America. In their large majority, they have decided not to assimilate. And so, the basic question is before us: What is the content of this American Jewishness?

A younger school of Jewish sociologists has been asserting that American Jews have evolved a culture of their own. This American Jewishness has been called their "civil religion" whose "commandments" can be enumerated: a majority takes note of the High Holy Days, observes Passover and Hanukkah, cares deeply about Israel, and has a more liberal conscience than other Americans of the same socioeconomic class. The new sociologists make us feel better by offering proof that this American Jewishness is stable into the third and fourth generation, and beyond, of the descendants of the immigrants. Thus we can sleep at peace in the certainty that, in its own fashion, American Jewish life will continue.

This optimistic assessment is not shared universally. Some of the leading Jewish sociologists are worried by low fertility rates in Jewish

America (the Orthodox are the only exception), by a rising rate of divorce, by the dispersion of families in a very mobile society, and by a rate of intermarriage among the young of 40 percent.

But the fundamental issue is not this quarrel among Jewish sociologists whether the rate of assimilation is stable. Let us agree that caring Jews of this day are indeed practicing the "civil religion" of a few holiday events, and of involvement in Israel and in social liberalism. Where is this "civil religion" leading? Does it have the power to last indefinitely?

One of the keys to answering this question is in an unpublished piece of research that was done a few years ago for the Federation of Jewish Philanthropies in New York. The attempt was made to find out what determines how much money people give to Jewish causes. The study showed that in each economic class the variables were additional years of intensive Jewish education and the number of religious practices observed by each individual. Synagogue members were twice as likely to give money as nonmembers. The conclusion was inescapable: Jewish "tsores" (problems) do not create a giving community; those who, to begin with, care deeply as Jews, respond to Jewish "tsores" much more generously than those who do not. Everyone knows, especially the leaders of the Jewish fund-raising community, that all too many younger people, including those who still show up for their parents' Passover feast, are less deeply involved in their Jewishness—and give less. The key to Jewish continuity is thus not in the problems of the Jews, but in how those problems are perceived and felt by every individual.

My experience as a teacher, and especially in recent years at Dartmouth College, has provided another insight into the meaning of American Jewry's "civil religion." In a recent study of the Jewish students at Dartmouth, we found that a majority of the students did drop in at one point or another during the day, between classes, on the morning services of the High Holy Days, but most of their parents, during their days at college, had absented themselves from school entirely. Statistically it can be maintained that the rate of observance has hardly fallen off, but such statistics slide over the question of the intensity of commitment. Most pointedly, the Dartmouth students (they are third- and fourth-generation Americans) told that their grandparents would be terribly upset by intermarriage in the family, their parents would not like it but would accept it, and they themselves preferred not to intermarry—but the large majority saw no reason to avoid such a possibility by dating only Jews.

There is, of course, one dimension of Jewish ethnic experience that is unique: anti-Semitism. Every American minority has been under some attack, but the Jews are different. We have been, until almost yesterday, the only non-Christians in an overwhelmingly Christian society. Jews are the bearers of a tradition that has been the object of calumny for three millennia. The battle against anti-Semitism has been at the core of American Jewish ethnicity. Indeed, for the last two centuries of Jewish history, as the Jewish community has become ever more plural and divided, it has asserted its unity because the anti-Semites make no distinction between Jewish believers in all their varieties and Jews who would prefer to disappear. It is an open secret that if anti-Semitism could be made to disappear, they and their children would at last become unlabeled individuals, free of any responsibility toward the group into which they were born.

Anti-Semitism does, alas, continue to exist, even in America, at a time when Jews are freer and more equal than they have ever been anywhere in the Diaspora. Nonetheless, I do not believe that opposing anti-Semitism even can remain that basis of Jewish continuity. On the contrary, some Jews will be tempted—if anti-Semitism is their only concern—to abandon their Jewishness altogether. No less a figure than Theodor Herzl played with the idea of mass conversion of Jews to Christianity to evade anti-Semitism as an alternative to creating a Zionist state. My own research on college students has shown that those of the young whose Jewishness is primarily a fear of anti-Semitism are significantly more likely to want to intermarry—to live permanently among the anti-Semites! What explains this paradox is that such young people really want to "pass" into a society in which there is neither Jew nor Gentile. Nor does the memory of the Holocaust act decisively to keep all Jews from assimilating. On the contrary, from the day that the death camps were opened, some of the very survivors (there is no way of estimating their number) simply disappeared as Jews. Younger students of today ask: If being Jewish means that I remain, uniquely, a candidate for the gas chambers, why should I live in that danger? Should I not strive to save my descendants from such a destiny by making an end of this dangerous identity? Anti-Semitism may drive many Jews toward their Jewishness; it has given some others, who have no other reason for caring, the impetus to leave us. Anti-Semitism needs to be fought, but it is not the tie that binds Jews together.

Inevitably, therefore, one turns to religion—but the situation of Judaism in our century, like that of Christianity, and even of Islam, is one of increasing fragmentation. The wars of religion are becoming sharper within each of these communities, not least our own. More fundamentally, American Jews have been socialized by American culture as a whole to express their being by solving problems rather than by looking inward to their soul or outward toward the meaning and purpose of creation. The commandments of the "civil religion" of American Jews express togetherness; they leave the soul alone— and lonely—in the universe, with only activism to light the way.

One revealing piece of evidence, from the very circles of Jewish activist leadership, suggests that the ultimate source of Jewish continuity is not in activism but in the religious tradition. A few years ago some of the leaders of the fund-raising bodies were asked whether they believed in the chosenness of Israel. Seventy percent said they did. These were not Orthodox believers; they were overwhelmingly the kind of people to whom the rhetoric of cultural pluralism is almost second nature. The answer one would expect from this circle is that Jews are, in America, one ethnic group among the many. But those who were surveyed knew better than their surface rhetoric. They knew that the irreducible premise on which Jewish continuity rests is the faith that it makes a profound and transcendent difference whether Jews exist as a distinct and affirming community. Those surveyed were willing, as liberals, to grant Italians and Irish in America the right to disappear quietly in an open society, but they regarded it as a tragedy if Jews followed suit and opted out en masse. Indeed, it is the paradoxical function of Jewish leadership to work for an American society in which everyone can choose without any fear or coercion to abandon his past and be who he wants to be—and to convince Jews that abandoning their Jewishness is profoundly wrong.

Ethnicity is not forever; anti-Semitism can, at least in logic, chase

Jews out of their Judaism rather than make them rally together, and our deepest-held religious convictions are ill-defined and splintered. So how can we accomplish our Jewish purpose?

I propose that the only realm to which we are the heirs, together, are Jewish texts and the Hebrew language. We can no longer agree to study the Mishnah or the writings of Maimonides from the same perspective, and we are even less likely to find common ground on the question of how obedient we are to the injunctions in these texts, but the Mishnah and Maimonides, and all the texts of the classic tradition which belong with them, are ours in a way in which they do not belong even to the most learned scholars among the non-Jews.

The Jewish community must transform itself from being primarily a reacting, problem-solving community into one that stresses the joy, and the intellectual and moral depth, of being Jewish. Such an outlook requires a shared rhetoric based on shared learning. The basic pragmatism of American culture stands in the way, and so does the plural, even fragmented nature of the Jewish community. But American society as a whole is moving toward refurbishing education by insisting that there is some central body of learning that everyone must know. To be sure, there are battles about what should be included in such a "core curriculum," but there is fast-growing assent to the idea that cultural fragmentation has gone so far as to threaten the coherence of America.

I propose a Jewish "core curriculum" for adults. Simply put, every Jew—and especially those in leadership positions—should know some basic facts about Jewish history and Jewish religion, and have some sense of the ideas and values that are part of our heritage. It is certainly wrong to presume that they have such knowledge by osmosis, or from Sunday school and Hebrew school. My own experience—teaching basic Judaism on a college level to large classes which include even graduates of day schools—is that an adult awareness of Jewish history and thought is radically different from what one has learned in bits and pieces when very young.

There is precedent for such an endeavor, and not merely in the injunction in the Shema to study. At various points in Jewish history, when "learning was in danger of being forgotten," texts were constructed to act as the summary for the mass of Jews. Maimonides' summary of Jewish thought and law in his Mishnah Torah is a prime model. It was a very conscious attempt to provide a compendium, in clear and accessible Hebrew, of what all Jews needed to know. Contrary to what later scholars have made of this book, it was written for the adult layman who had not the time to immerse himself in the vast "sea of the Talmud."

I propose nothing as elaborate as Maimonides' compendium. The Council of Jewish Federations, in broad cooperation with other agencies, should commission a small group of laymen as well as scholars and rabbis, to do a set of readings in "basic Jewishness." We—all the organizations of American Jewry, lay and rabbinic—must work together, and very hard, that these texts be taught, read, and discussed. I am thinking of the equivalent of no more than three to five normal-length books. Obviously, such a project is open-ended. More might and should be published in the future. Right now we need basic, accessible material which provides some common Jewish rhetoric and knowledge. In preparing such material, the committee should be sensitive to the plural nature of the Jewish community. The protagonists of all the various ideologies, religious and political, must simply agree to hear each other fairly in a work for the general knowledge of all Jews.

The last time such an endeavor was attempted was in Frankfurt in the 1920s. Franz Rosenzweig created a nondenominational "house of study" for adult Jews, people who were thoroughly modern and well-educated, but who knew very little about their tradition, history, and culture. Rosenzweig's adult school saved a significant element of German Jewry from assimilation. It is time now in America to follow the Rosenzweig model on a national scale, with all the resources and all the passion for the continuity that we can command.

Such an endeavor cannot be conducted without Israel. Those who begin to appreciate Jewish texts will want to study them further in Israel, the place in which they are most natural. I have a dream that the myriads of groups which travel to Israel today will study not only the problems of Israel but the sources of the values which bind all Jews together. Many people are taking to attending summer sessions given by the colleges and universities of which they are alumni. Is it not the essence of our sense of ourselves as Jews that we are "alumni" of the Holy Land?

In recent conversation, one of the most sensitive minds and spirits among the leaders of the Jewish community in America told, in my hearing, that one of his children is deeply involved in his Jewishness and the other seems to care much less. One had spent a year in Israel and the other had not; that was the only discernible difference. This story is consonant with my own experiences as rabbi, college teacher, and parent. Those who get to know Israel well enough to be at home in its culture, especially if they have stayed long enough to be able to communicate in Hebrew, are markedly different from those young people who have, at most, experienced Israel as tourists.

The evidence is beyond doubt, and we must act on it. The organized community as a whole should make a study year in Israel, or at the very least a semester, during the high school or early college years an accepted mitzvah—and a possibility, regardless of financial circumstance—for the mass of the Jewish young. This suggestion is an evocation of a classic Jewish practice: teenage boys went away from home to study in a yeshiva before they went to work. Programs of learning in Israel, for young men and women alike, is the way we can apply this wisdom of our ancestors to our own needs and sensibilities.

We must reach out to the unaffiliated; we dare not write them off because they will cost us scarce money and even scarcer time, and we might fail more often than we will succeed. A recent such effort in St. Louis was welcomed by almost everyone contacted. In Denver, a comparable outreach to the intermarried evoked wide gratitude. In both communities, the common response by those who were contacted—it was almost a refrain—was: "I did not know that anyone cared." We must, all of us, begin caring much more than we have. The unaffiliated half of the American Jewish community does not consist of vast masses who want out of their Jewishness on ideological grounds. They are adrift, but not irrevocably.

Many of those who are adrift are people who really care, who want to be part of the Jewish community. Their particular difficulty is that some are individuals and not families; they are one-parent families.

Others are too poor to afford the ever-growing costs of belonging to our institutions, and they are too ashamed to come and ask for special consideration. Abraham did not wait for the needy and the poor to come into his tent; he rushed forward to embrace them. Our contemporary community must be one of outreach. We must use every technique, including the most advanced technology, to keep track of Jewish individuals and to make sure that no individual Jew is neglected or allowed to feel friendless. We need a national computer bank—and much old-fashioned human personal warmth. Above all, we must suggest that Jews do not exist to help us balance our budgets; we exist to serve them. If a hard and expensive effort succeeds in reaching only one in five, hundreds of thousands would thus be added to committed Jewish life; they would refresh the community.

Perhaps the most difficult of all the problems, most difficult because it is the most tangible, is the question of money. The cost for a family of belonging to the organized community, especially if it includes day-school tuition for children, is now such that anyone with a medium, white-collar income is hard-pressed. I have no idea what it would cost in budgetary deficits to make the services of the Jewish community truly available on a "need-blind" basis. The very best colleges in America pride themselves on the policy. They cannot let talent be lost because their parents have no money. Can we afford—and never mind the cost—to run a Jewish community that lets so many of its potential leaders and scholars disappear because their parents were too poor, in money or commitment, to raise them within our circle of caring and learning?

These reflections lead almost inevitably to one simple and, I believe, transforming proposal. The organized Jewish community is accustomed to ringing every doorbell, or telephone, once a year to ask everyone we can find for money. Could we not organize once a year to ask Jews to affiliate with some purpose—any that they might choose—within the Jewish community? Surely such an endeavor would be supported by all the Jewish persuasions.

Let us imagine an interviewer who asks an individual Jew, or a family, to check off what kind of affiliation they might want to pursue. The results of such a census would give us the happy problems of making room for new people who will, at first, strain budget and resources, for they will probably be poorer or less interested (or both) than those who already belong to the organized community.

But we must go out into America to find our silent brothers. Such an endeavor would have immediate ' transforming value even before the first doorbell is rung. Hundreds of volunteers would have to be trained to do this task. Here time and enthusiasm will be demanded, and these can be given by rich and poor alike. Those who work at this census will themselves increase in pride as "owners." They will have become part of the management of the Jewish community, and they will be going to other Jews not to demand money, but to offer help.

I am very much aware that the effort I am proposing is difficult to mount, especially in the larger communities. I am sure that the ringing of all the doorbells of New York, Chicago, or Los Angeles is a few years off, but can we not begin by ringing the doorbells of a selected neighborhood in each of these cities? The effort should be coordinated centrally by the Conference of Jewish Federations, so that what is learned in several places can be refined and become the pattern for future large-scale endeavor. We must begin to retrieve Jews who are adrift, and the time is now.

This generation of American Jews has a choice to make. We can bet our future on the essentially pragmatic, problem-solving Jewish life that exists today. It is a fair guess that there will be problems for the future generations, but adversities do not secure the unity of a family. They are sometimes the cause of divorce. Families remain united in the worst and the best of times because they share a unique heritage of love, values, and memories.

The distance that is undeniably growing between Israel and the American Jewish community is not the result of politics, of differences between "hawks" and "doves," or liberals and conservatives: it is the result of growing cultural estrangement. The loosening of ties within American Jewry is the result of the erosion of a shared culture. We are, too many of us, middle-class Americans who differ from all the others only because we harbor Jewish fears.

For the last century or so, the American Jewish community has tried every mode in securing its Jewish life, except the mass cultivation of Jewish culture. We have done the same in our relationship to Israel. The connection is intense on every level, but we do not share the riches which are to be found in Hebrew. The earliest of all commandments given to Jews was to learn and to teach. The time has come, in this day of anxiety, for us to return to basics.

1990

SIX

In Debate with American Jews

The American Jewish community's attitude toward Israel is, supposedly, expressed by the leaders of the Jewish organizations. I argued in the first two chapters of this book that the statements of this leadership very often did not even reflect their own real views, and that they did not speak for the continuing "dovish" majority of American Jews. The situation has been very nearly the same on the domestic front. A small but very vocal group of intellectuals had turned neoconservative in domestic affairs, some in the 1950s and more by the late 1960s. Most of these men and women had also become supporters of the ultranationalists in Israel. A major issue on which the domestic debate turned was "affirmative action." Here the neoconservatives were the most clearly victorious, because they persuaded almost all the national Jewish organizations to part company with the blacks on this issue. The neoconservatives were much less successful in trying to persuade Jews that their class interests should propel them to the Republican party. The large majority of American Jews have remained liberals; they keep voting for the Democrats. In the three essays in this section I confronted the neoconservative positions and found them morally unacceptable and politically sterile. Those who had been spending millions to promote neoconservative views in the Jewish community had largely failed. I continue to take pride in the fact that American

Jews are the only major community of "haves" that keeps voting its concern for the "have-nots."

17. *In Support of Affirmative Action*

Most of the major national American Jewish organizations have moved away from commitments to affirmative action in the last decade—and thus some of the seeds of the present quarrel between blacks and Jews were planted.

The tough-minded have spoken of "merit" as the only standard for preferment, especially in education and employment in the United States. Every time I hear the rhetoric with which "merit" is defended, I remember the anti-Semites who dominated the professions and the academic world in the 1920s and 1930s. They maintained that American society required social peace—that it needed to be defended against bright young Jewish intellectuals who wanted to "change the rules." Lionel Trilling of Columbia University and Bryllion Fagin of Johns Hopkins, for example, were among many excluded from tenure until World War II on the grounds that no Jew could possibly represent the true spirit of the English language and culture. The academic anti-Semites argued that unless social peace could be enforced, American power in the world would be weakened. Such arguments against change were not true then, when they were advanced against young Jewish intellectuals by middle-aged Gentile reactionaries. They are no more true today, when they are advanced by middle-aged Jewish conservatives who look fearfully behind their own backs at those bidding for places in society.

The half-hidden Jewish premise in defense of meritocracy is that "It is good for Jews." Is it really? The answer must be qualified. It may indeed be good for some Jews in the short run, but in the long run it is not likely to work even for the present meritocratic elite. An elite that is totally inflexible is more likely to be swept away than to survive. The wisest, longest-lasting elitists in the Western world, the aristocratic British Tories, have survived many changes because they learned early "how to dish the Whigs"—that is, how to move over sufficiently to keep the tensions between themselves and new people bidding for a share in power from becoming explosive confrontations. The present American meritocracy, in which some Jews are prominent, will survive only if it learns some flexibility.

Fortunately, the American Jewish community has not totally followed its right-wingers on the range of issues symbolized by the conflict between "merit" and "affirmative action." One national organization, the Anti-Defamation League, has entered every case on the side of "merit." Practically all the others have waffled somewhere in the middle. One, the National Council of Jewish Women, took its stand firmly on the side of the University of California Medical School in the famous Bakke case, arguing for affirmative action in admission and even accepting race as one consideration. Its action was particularly significant because the council represents the top of the socioeconomic pyramid in the American Jewish community. Its members are the mothers (sometimes the grandmothers) of many of the young Jews who apply first to Ivy League undergraduate colleges and then to medical, law, and other professional schools. The members of the council knew that "affirmative action" could adversely affect their own children and their families, yet they were prepared to pay a personal price for the sake of justice and social peace in this country.

On occasion through the years I have served on admissions committees, or have been asked to write letters of support for young people who are the children of friends or congregants. Often the request from a parent goes like this: My son is really a better student than his grades show, because he had emotional problems this year over a girl-friend. He "freezes" in exams and thus has not done as well in the S.A.T. college entrance exams as he should have. But concerned teaching will bring him to his full potential and he will do brilliantly at Harvard or Yale, if only you will persuade one of them to accept him out of regard for his particular abilities.

These of course are perfectly valid requests, and I am sensitive to them. What I find incredible is that some of the people who make such requests, and add letters from psychiatrists to prove that the claims are true, will not listen to very much less verbal black or Puerto Rican dayworkers who may say (in poor English): My daughter is far better than her grades or S.A.T. scores show—but she's handicapped because we live on a block where there are drug pushers, and she has to study in a noisy, two-room apartment. Suddenly the great god "merit" is invoked—and its definition is that only test-scores may determine preferment.

The issue is moral. There are concrete, aching, suffering, trapped, enraged human beings out there, in the ghettos and in the barrios, in the hundreds of thousands. They are not intellectuals who know how to use sociological jargon, to argue and confute. They know, in their own bodies and in the marrow of their bones, that a ruling elite structures the system to protect its privileges, and that the elite must be persuaded—or pressured—to move over.

The ultimate constitutional authority in the United States is the Supreme Court. Even in its present conservative composition, the Court has twice voted in recent cases, Bakke and Weber, for some form of affirmative action; in the latter case, it took race into some account for the sake of social peace. The Supreme Court is right and the proponents of "merit" are wrong. The Court knows very well what time it is in America. The Court is saying, in various ways, that social peace must be constructed out of different building blocks in these times than those of the early 1960s.

Jewish historical experience points to the path in the political spectrum of America that is occupied by moderate reformers. Their views, and the actions to accompany them, are the true public interest of all America.

1980

18. *Reagan and the Jews*

During the national election of 1984, the Republican party spent at least $2 million to directly influence the Jewish vote. This effort failed. Jews are the only white "have" group in America to withstand the Reagan landslide: they voted two to one for the Democrats and are, with blacks, the last members of the old New Deal coalition to support the party as strongly as they did in the past.

Some Republicans have argued that the Jewish vote for Reagan has been underestimated; others are trying to explain this "aberration" as having been caused by last-minute switches over the issue of separation of church and state. Many leaders of Jewish organizations thought they could deliver an unusually high Jewish vote to Reagan, and now they are trying to account for their failure to do so. During the campaign, a number of Orthodox, Conservative, and Reform rabbis, speaking for themselves, came out for Mondale, but figures of much heavier weight in the Jewish community asked Jews to support Reagan. They included Max Fisher, the honorary chairman of the United Jewish Appeal and the Jewish Agency for Israel; Jacques Torczyner, a past president of the Zionist Organization of America; and George Klein, a major builder in New York and a central figure in the Orthodox community. In conversations with well-placed Jews, the argument was made that a large Jewish vote for Reagan was necessary in order for the Jews to influence government policy on behalf of Israel. This argument, so far as I know, never made its way into print in any of the publications of the Republican National Committee, but it was very much at the center of the appeal to Jews. Toward the end of the campaign it was published, I noticed, in a mailing piece sent to Jews in Bergen County, New Jersey, where I live, by the local branch of the "Jewish Republican Coalition."

That this argument was on the minds of important Jewish leaders is beyond doubt. On the morning after the election *Ma'ariv*, one of Israel's two large afternoon newspapers, interviewed a number of them to get their reaction to the election. Yehuda Helman, the executive vice president of the Conference of Presidents of Major American Jewish Organizations, the central representative body of the Jewish establishment, told *Ma'ariv*'s New York correspondent: "We now will have a very hard task to repair the damage that the Jewish vote has caused; the Jewish organizations will have to struggle to restore their influence in the American establishment."

The same theme was stated more openly and with greater passion by Abraham Foxman, the second-ranking professional staff member of the Anti-Defamation League. Foxman insisted that the exit polls taken by the press and television, which showed Jewish support for Mondale by two to one, were wrong, and that the vote was actually

53 percent for Mondale and 47 percent for Reagan, a bare majority. (He attributed these figures to Republican sources.) Thus, Foxman asserted, Reagan indeed had advanced substantially beyond the 40 percent that he had received in 1980 against Carter. Foxman said that the Republicans had made a serious effort to influence the Jewish vote and they had spent large sums to do so. "If the results of the polls will not change, and if the facts as given by the Reagan Election Committee will not be proved; then the Jews will have a very great problem with the Republican party. . . . The Republicans might then say, we have no interest in the Jewish minority."[24]

Foxman softened his analysis at the end of the interview, as did Helman, by emphasizing that on the issue of Israel there was no difference between the two parties; support for Israel was a bipartisan matter in American politics. The same theme was elaborated a few days later by the American Israel Political Action Committee (AI-PAC), the group that lobbies on behalf of Israel in Washington. In the November 26 issue of AIPAC'S weekly *Near East Report*, its editor, M. J. Rosenberg, wrote that "some people are uncomfortable with the very noticeable Jewish vote for Mondale. They fear that the Reagan administration will 'take it out' on Israel." Rosenberg denied that this was so. "That mentality," he wrote, "is rooted in the diaspora experience." It has "no relevance today." It was "certain," he wrote, that "the President is not going to determine the U.S. course in the Middle East with a copy of the election returns from Great Neck and the San Fernando Valley in his hand."

The connection between the Jewish vote and Jewish influence in the White House was so much on Rosenberg's mind, however, that he returned to it at the end of the column. "It is insulting to the President—and to the American Jewish community—to suggest that when casting their votes on November 6, 1984, Jews should also have cast fearful glances at the White House. That was once our way. It is not any more."

The forces in the Jewish establishment that were disappointed by the vote thus moved back to asserting the bipartisan nature of American support for Israel. Rosenberg himself seemed to be getting ready for disputes with the administration over the export of sophisticated weapons to some of the Arab states and a revived Reagan plan for the Middle East. He predicted that Reagan's policies will not always be acceptable to pro-Israel forces. Perhaps he was taking account of the fact that the Democrats continue to control the Congress, and had gained two seats in the Senate, while Democrats are still governors of thirty-four states and mayors of most of the large U.S. cities.

This year's Jewish vote has also posed a problem for the Jewish intellectuals who call themselves neoconservative. Leading the Jews away from liberalism and the Democratic party has, of course, not been the only or even the main purpose of the neoconservatives. Their influence among Jews, however, became an issue of some interest during the 1984 election. *Commentary*, published by the American Jewish Committee and closely identified with the neoconservative viewpoint, printed an article by Irving Kristol in its July issue with the title, "The Political Dilemma of American Jews." He advised the Jewish community to take Jesse Jackson seriously as a continuing threat to its interests:

> In foreign policy he is pro-Third World and anti-American, pro-PLO and anti-Israel—and he is on the way to making this the quasi-official foreign policy of the black community. . . . He has already indicated that he will be coming to New York in 1985 to back and stump for a properly militant black candidate against Mayor Koch in the Democratic primaries. The black-Jewish polarization that would ensue is almost too scary to contemplate.

Jesse Jackson was firmly hung around the neck of the Democratic party.

On the other hand, Kristol argued that the commitment of the Moral Majority "to a set of 'social issues'—school prayer, anti-abortion, the relation of church and state in general that tend to evoke a hostile reaction among most (though not all) American Jews" should not be taken as threatening. The campaign of the Moral Majority on these issues "is meeting with practically no success" and "the Reagan administration has got absolutely nowhere in its espousal of these issues." What is important is that the "Moral Majority is unequivocally pro-Israel."

Kristol argued at some length that the support of Jewish interests, both domestic and in relation to Israel, required Jews to move to the right, away from their old Democratic associates whose foreign policy was still influenced by soft-minded internationalism, muddled liberalism, and an increasing tendency toward a foreign policy excessively sympathetic to the Third World and hostile to Israel. He ended his article by asserting that it is not even any longer in question that the American Jewish community and its "traditional allies"—whether among blacks, liberal intellectuals, or the leaders of organized labor—are moving away from one another. "That is an established fact—and one that American Jews must candidly confront."

This plea to support Reagan failed. The Republican Campaign Committee itself has claimed for Reagan some 40 percent of the Jewish vote, hardly more than he received in 1980. In a postelection interview with the *New York Times* (December 18, 1984), Kristol simply observed that about a third of the Jewish vote had been voting Republican in recent elections.

In the weeks since the national election, much more information about the Jewish vote has become available through exit polls taken on the day of the election. The American Jewish Committee recently published a pamphlet on the results of a national survey done by Steven M. Cohen, a sociologist at Queens College, on "The Political Attitudes of American Jews in 1984." This was based on a random sample of 996 Jews who were questioned between April and August 1984, that is, when the controversy over Jesse Jackson was at its height. More significant still are two major, as yet unpublished, studies of the Jewish vote in the election. The Jewish Community Relations Council in New York has analyzed the figures for seventeen election districts in the five boroughs of New York, most of which have Jewish populations of at least 70 percent. For the country as a whole, the American Jewish Congress did an exit poll of 2,700 Jewish voters in fourteen cities, including all those with sizable Jewish populations.[25] Taken together these three studies give an informative picture of Jewish political opinions and voting behavior.

In 1936, 11 percent of the Jews who voted supported the Republican candidate, Alfred Landon. In the American Jewish Congress exit poll on November 6, 1984, 79 percent of the Jews identified themselves as liberal or moderate, 10 percent as conservative. When asked their party allegiance, only 12 percent said they were Republican. It seems clear that about one-tenth of Jewish votes have been unshakably Republican since the days of the Great Depression. No generalization will apply precisely to the views of all of them or indeed to any of the other voting groups I shall discuss. I think, however, that most close observers of Jewish life will agree that for the most part this group is made up of descendants of the Jews, largely from Germany and Central Europe, who came to America before the mass migration from Eastern Europe that began around 1881. Many members of this group see themselves as belonging to the American business elite and have long wanted to believe that they are part of the old America, which they take to be represented by the Republican party.

Another group with a pronounced tendency to vote Republican consists of Orthodox Jews, most of whom arrived in the United States after World War II. In Hassidic communities of Boro Park and Williamsburg in New York City, Reagan beat Mondale four to one. This was not an unprecedented victory: in 1972, Nixon beat McGovern in these same election districts by the same margin. For these Jews parochial issues count heavily. Nearly all ultra-Orthodox Jews, for example, send their children to religious day schools and they want state aid for such education. This community is also the most hawkish in its position on Israel, and it prefers Republican tough-mindedness, real or verbal, toward the Russians.

The Orthodox community, however, also includes a less traditional group which votes Republican far less heavily. In the Midwood election district in Brooklyn, which contains a diverse Jewish population, including a large proportion of modern Orthodox Jews, Mondale won two to one. Among the relatively poor elderly Jews who live largely on pensions, at least half of whom probably identify themselves as Orthodox, a major concern is for sustained Social Security benefits, and on this issue Mondale's position would have had strong appeal. In Brighton, the Brooklyn election district with the largest proportion of such people, McGovern, who seemed to many people soft on Israel, lost to Nixon by 43 percent to 54 percent. In 1984, however, Reagan got only 26 percent of the vote in Brighton.

It has been argued, and not only by Republicans, that the Orthodox, and especially the ultra-Orthodox, tend to be underrepresented in studies based on questionnaires, and perhaps even in exit polls.

(Yiddish-speaking neighborhoods are not congenial to pollsters.) This could be true even if the lopsided vote of elderly Jews for Mondale helps to cancel out, in part, the lopsidedness of the ultra-Orthodox vote for Reagan. It seems reasonable to believe that there is a normal, built-in Republican majority of nearly two to one in the Orthodox community, taken as a whole; for even in the Reagan-Carter election of 1980, and the Ford-Carter election of 1976, the ultra-Orthodox voted three to two for the Republicans. Orthodox Jews thus add perhaps another 10 percent to the irreducible Republican column.

The Republicans, according to this analysis, can bank on about 20 percent of the Jewish vote before a national campaign begins. A further question must then be answered: how large did the Jewish Republican vote really grow beyond this irreducible minimum in the last election? The analysis of the New York City vote by the Jewish Community Relations Council concluded that Reagan won 38 percent and Mondale 62 percent of the vote, a 2 percent gain for Reagan over 36 percent in the 1980 election. This difference is statistically insignificant. In fact the findings of the Jewish Community Relations Council, in view of the standard margins of error in sampling studies, are consonant with the *New York Times*–CBS News exit poll for New York state, which posited that 34 percent of the Jewish voters in New York City voted for Reagan. Nowhere else in the country is there a concentration of ultra-Orthodox Jews comparable to that in New York City; it is hardly likely, therefore, that the national result was as favorable to the Republicans.

The unanimous evidence of the national exit polls that the vote for Reagan in the Jewish community was less than a third thus seems undeniable. (Reagan's vote in New York City, moreover, was a few points *less* than Nixon got against McGovern in 1972.) The most comprehensive of the national exit polls, the American Jewish Congress survey, showed Reagan winning only 28 percent of the Jewish vote nationally. With further weighting to account for Orthodox opinion that is underrepresented in the polls, the results of the American Jewish Congress study show a national vote for Reagan among the Jews of about 30 percent. Reagan thus picked up only between 10 and 12 percent above the minimum he could expect from Jews who are committed to the Republican party. His 30 to 32 percent was nearly a quarter less than Nixon got nationally in 1972 and only a little more that Gerald Ford's 26 percent in 1976, and less than Reagan's own 40 percent in 1980.

Why have the Republicans lost ground in the Jewish community? Since the election, the favorite explanation has been that Jews were put off by Reagan's views on religion in public life. A rising tide of anger against the Republican positions in favor of outlawing abortion and allowing prayer in the public schools is supposed to have accounted for the Jewish vote, which otherwise was imagined to have been stampeding to the Republicans, in fear of Jesse Jackson. The turning points for Jews in this campaign are supposed to have been the President's remarks in the first days of September in Salt Lake City before the American Legion, where he insisted that one should not "twist the concept of freedom of religion to mean freedom against religion" and his failure to modify this view a few days later when he talked to the B'nai B'rith convention in Washington.

Reagan's position on the religious issue had already upset some Jews in August when his campaign manager, Senator Paul Laxalt, wrote a letter urging some 45,000 American Christian clergymen to support Reagan because "he has been faithful in his support of issues of concern to Christian citizens." At the Dallas convention, the Republican national platform affirmed its support "for the appointment of judges at all levels of the judiciary" who "support traditional family values and the sanctity of human life"—that is, who oppose abortion. The American Jewish Congress, the most politically liberal of all the Jewish organizations, campaigned vigorously against these views during the last days before the election. The other organizations of the Jewish establishment took a quieter position. They did not press Reagan to disavow his right-wing fundamentalist fellow travelers, as they had pursued Mondale to denounce Jesse Jackson and Jackson to denounce Louis Farrakhan.

In the American Jewish Congress exit poll, nearly half (44 percent) said that Reagan's stand on religion and state strongly influenced their vote. Only 20 percent said that Jesse Jackson's campaign had a comparable influence on them. Nonetheless, despite these answers, I believe the weight of the evidence suggests that the church-state issue was only marginally important in this election. The Jewish vote was determined by other, deeper tendencies.

The most apparent of these is the continuing perception of the character of the two major parties by a decisive majority of American Jews. The American Jewish Congress survey asked the question: which political party cares most about Jews? The answers were: Democrats, 61 percent; Republicans, 11 percent; 28 percent not sure. In 1983 the American Jewish Committee investigated the attitude of American Jews toward Israel. In its survey, one question asked which American groups were regarded as friendly or unfriendly to Israel. The Democrats, liberals, Congress, and the labor unions were all regarded as "very friendly," the Democrats most friendly of all. The attitudes of President Reagan, the Republicans, the military, conservatives, mainstream Protestants, and evangelical Protestants were seen as "mixed," and if their ratings had been a little lower, they would have been seen as "unfriendly." The State Department and the major corporations were very near the bottom of the list—"quite unfriendly." The nearly half of the Jewish voters who say they were influenced by concerns about demands for a "Christian America" were not discovering new threats, or moving in a new direction.

The more unexpected response was to the black issue. Here, the evidence is startling. In the American Jewish Committee study of 1983, Jews gave their lowest and most negative assessment to the attitudes of blacks, a majority of Jews seeing them as unfriendly to Israel. The same views were generally confirmed by the American Jewish Committee survey of 1984, which concerned domestic anti-Semitism. Fundamentalist Protestants were now seen by a majority of Jews as disposed to be unfriendly, and the blacks were regarded as the most hostile of all groups in America. Jesse Jackson was thought to be anti-Semitic by 78 percent of the respondents.

Nonetheless, on election day, the American Jewish Congress survey, in answer to a question about how the Jewish community should deal with black-Jewish tensions, found that 7 percent said to ignore such tensions; 10 percent did not know; and 25 percent said to wait for positive action by the black community. That left an astonishing 58 percent who supported the suggestion that it was up to Jews "to reach out to the black community." Most American Jews thus seemed quite as aware as Irving Kristol that their relations with blacks are a serious problem. A majority, however, made it clear that they were against confrontation and in favor of attempts to keep peace, even if special efforts have to be made by Jews.

This concern not to exacerbate conflicts also prevails in the Jewish community on most of the other issues on which the neoconservatives have been urging a position of confrontation and tough-mindedness. In his *Commentary* article, Irving Kristol criticized Jewish support for the United Nations. In the American Jewish Committee's survey of 1984 on Jewish political attitudes, the proposition that "the United States should leave the United Nations" was rejected by three to one, although practically all American Jews were aware of the consistent anti-Zionism of the UN's General Assembly. A main theme of the neoconservative position is that détente with the Soviet Union is very nearly a policy of surrender by America and that it is against the interests of Israel. The 1984 survey showed that 50 percent of the respondents believed President Reagan had been "basically accurate" in calling the Soviet Union an "evil empire." Nonetheless, by more than two to one, the same respondents asserted that the President had shown "poor judgment" when he made such claims.

Overwhelmingly, by 84 percent against 10, with 6 percent not sure, Jews are for a nuclear freeze with the USSR (as the neoconservatives are not); 29 percent favor a more forceful policy toward the Soviet Union, while 55 percent oppose this, and 17 percent are not sure. Virtually without exception, American Jews are for strong U.S. military support for Israel. So far as U.S. military spending in general is concerned, however, their views are mixed. A plurality tends to the "neoliberal" position that the United States could reduce its military spending and still retain a strong military defense.

Taken together, these views on foreign policy suggest that American Jews favor a variety of policies to reduce tension in the world. And while they do not want to sponsor policies that will make for more acute confrontation with the third world countries and the USSR, this is not because they fail to realize that Jews have enemies in the third world and in the Soviet Union. American Jews, moreover, certainly know that they have dangerous enemies in the Arab world, and yet every poll taken in the American Jewish community during the last five years shows that two-thirds of American Jews would trade territories for peace in the Middle East. A strong majority would even recognize a Palestinian state on the West Bank, provided it agreed to live in peace with Israel. As for domestic fears, at the very height of the Jewish reaction to Jesse Jackson and Louis Farrakhan last spring, over half the Jews surveyed said they were for affirmative action; another fifth even supported "benign" quotas. Here, too, a large majority of the Jewish community refused to go along with the policies against affirmative action that neoconservatives have been advocating.

The fundamental explanation for this political behavior is not, as Irving Kristol would have it in his *Commentary* essay, that the Jews are unaware of their own interests. Kristol was trying to convince the men and women of his own generation (the children and grandchildren of East European migration that ended with the First World War). I believe myself that these Jewish voters understood very well what they were doing. They were reflecting, as he was not, the inherited political experience of their grandparents. What these Jews knew, after the many centuries in which Jews have lived as minorities, was that at the times when the *muzhiks* became poorer and hungrier in Russia, they could all the more easily be incited to pogroms, and that when European monarchs fought one another, they tended to expropriate Jewish property in order to pay the costs of battle. Self-interest worked together with the ethics of compassion defined in the biblical and rabbinic traditions: even an unsatisfactory peace may be better than war, and social peace is worth even major costs.

As the national election campaign wore on, Jesse Jackson did not (despite Kristol's predictions) become a more acute problem for American Jews. He was careful to avoid attacking support for Israel. The black caucus in Congress was even more circumspect, and it has since made efforts to strengthen its alliance with the Jewish community. Blacks know that they really have nowhere else to go in American politics except to the Democratic party and that the party cannot be an effective political force without Jews. Jews have decided to stay with the Democrats in order, at the very least, to make sure that the alliance among ethnic groups that the party represents should continue to stand for an increasing measure of fairness in American life, however ineffectual and disappointing in efforts to improve fairness in the past have been. If this alliance breaks apart, and the poor have no hope of sharing in political power, an anger might be unleashed in America that would be truly explosive. The Jewish vote for Democrats has helped ensure that if not the White House, the Congress will remain sympathetic to social programs that benefit the poor.

Both morally and politically, the American Jewish voters, in my view, did better for themselves, and for social peace and justice in America and the world, than if they had followed the advice of some of their organizational leaders and of the neoconservative intellectuals. Relatively few of them may have read the Talmud, but a good many acted as if they were aware of its wisdom: "When in doubt, and the leaders confuse you by divided counsel, go out into the street and see what the people are doing."

1985

19. *The Illusion of Jewish Unity*

In the political drama playing on Israeli television, American Jews are shown as largely supporting Israel's hard line. During Yitzhak Shamir's visit to the United States in March, he addressed two national Jewish conferences: first, of the "young leaders" of the United Jewish Appeal in Washington, then of the leaders of the American Jewish organizations in New York. He was cheered at the first meeting, and there was only a scattering of opposition to his views at the second. American Jewish leaders were demonstrating their solidarity with Israel at the very moment, in fact, that polls were showing that most American Jews were critical of its policies. But that criticism was not perceived in Israel.

After the meetings with Shamir, Gideon Samet, a columnist for *Ha'aretz* who had been its Washington correspondent in the early 1980s, protested that American Jews had betrayed their liberal convictions and had let Israel down. Samet was upset because he knew that the film clips of those meetings on the Israeli nine o'clock news, which the entire country stops to watch, would be interpreted as a triumph for Shamir. He would be seen to have persuaded American Jews to support the position that it was better to remain at war with the Palestinians than to have to surrender any part of the "undivided Land of Israel." Since Israel itself is split between hawks and doves, the doves needed direct and unmistakable support from American Jews to help them influence opinion. At the very least, they hoped for television images that would show the average Israeli that a serious confrontation had taken place with Shamir.

Israel's left wing should not have been surprised: they have been disappointed before. In the years before he came to power in 1977, Begin used to argue that American Jews were capitalists, that they were, indeed, among the greatest beneficiaries of the free enterprise system. He appealed to the Jews in the Diaspora to put their weight on the side of capitalism in Israel, and thus create a world Jewish majority against the socialism of the Labor party. Begin even went so far as to propose a second chamber to advise the Knesset—he called it, with a dose of melodrama, a Jewish "House of Lords"—to which leading figures in the Diaspora would be appointed along with their peers in Israel. This body was to act as a brake on the leftist policies of the Israeli government and give it advice from on high. Of course, nothing ever came of Begin's suggestion. So long as Labor was in power, it did not want such highly placed kibitzers. When Begin himself became prime minister, he never said another word about the "House of Lords." He made it even clearer than Golda Meir had before him that what he expected of Jewish leaders of the Diaspora was not advice but agreement.

The truth is that Israelis do not understand American Jews. Most Israelis, including some of the most sophisticated, want to believe that American Jews think of themselves as managers of a large warehouse that furnishes political influence and money, and even people, to serve Israel. Israel persists in asking one basic question of the news from America: Is it "good or bad for Israel"? Is the news of yesterday's meetings of Jews in Washington or New York, reported on the front pages of Israel's newspapers, good for Shamir or good for Peres?

This is a grave misconception of American Jews. Most of them are committed to helping Israel, but this commitment does not dominate their lives in the way Israelis think it does. If that were so, hundreds of thousands of American Jews would have gone to settle in the Jewish state, to help build and defend it. Many Israelis I have talked to believe that most of the money that is raised by the annual Jewish appeals throughout America is given to Israel, but it is not. Less than twenty years ago, Israel received nearly two-thirds of the total, and it now receives less than half. The leaders who conduct these drives in the several hundred organized Jewish communities in America loudly proclaim their loyalty to Israel. One sees them on their annual "missions to Israel" shouting "We are one!" from their tour buses, but in committee meetings back home they have allocated funds to build community centers and hospitals and old-age homes and day schools for the benefit of Jews in America.

It is also not true, as most Israelis want to believe, that many American Jews support Israel as an "insurance policy" for themselves—that is, as a haven that they are keeping in reserve for the day when they might feel threatened by anti-Semitism in America. Jews in New York and Los Angeles may sometimes say such things, especially when raising money for Israel, but they do not mean them. American Jews simply cannot imagine a truly murderous anti-Semitism in the United States. If they could, they would be more circumspect than they have been in forcing the issue of Israel to the very center of American domestic politics.

American Jews have become a "one issue" lobby in Washington. In the climate of a strong pro-Israel opinion in America, they have succeeded in establishing Israel as the major recipient of American foreign aid, now some $3 billion a year. The public display of passion for Israel represents not the fear of anti-Semitism and the need to prepare a refuge from it, as many Israelis think, but, on the contrary, an almost complete denial of the possibility of such a backlash.

Israel is, indeed, the center of Jewish loyalty for most American Jews, but not in the way that the Israelis imagine. For many American Jews, Israel is not only a cause to be supported but a place whose existence helps to make them more comfortable and secure in America. Jews in America are the only ethnic minority that does not have a homeland, a country of origin to which they can trace their roots. On trips to Europe, John F. Kennedy and Ronald Reagan each made a sentimental journey to the village in Ireland from which his ancestors came. German-Americans claim the past of Goethe and Beethoven, and skip over the Nazi years. The Jews cannot claim as their homeland Tsarist Russia or the Poland of Colonel Beck in which they were persecuted, especially since most of these Jewish communities were destroyed by the Nazis; and those communities that still exist in the Soviet Union do not remind American Jews of the towns from which their grandparents came. After 1948, Israel became the homeland. The connection with Israel has been an important element in making Jews seem a "normal" part of the American scene.

The need for a homeland of which American Jews "could be proud" has had many consequences. In the earliest years of the State of Israel it was possible for American Jews to learn something about the moral ambiguities that came with power, but they preferred not to do so. Little notice was taken in the United States of a novel by S. Yizhar, *Khirbet Khiza*, written as the Israeli War of Independence was ending, which spoke with pain about Jews with machine guns lording it over Arabs, or of the poems by Nathan Alterman, in which he berated Israelis for their failure to behave decently toward the Arabs they had just conquered. American Jews preferred to see Israel as it was depicted by Leon Uris in *Exodus*, in which Israelis were painted as totally noble and Arabs were the Middle Eastern equivalent of the murderous Indians of Hollywood Westerns. American Jews preferred to see Israel as unquestionably good.

Therefore, through the years, most American Jews have not wanted to know what was really happening in Israel. They could take pride in the kibbutzim as a "great social experiment," and resolutely ignore the fact that fewer than 5 percent of Jews lived in them, while most of Israel was trying to become more bourgeois, "just like America." By definition, among American Jews the "homeland" was simply the one peace-loving state in the Middle East. If they heard echoes from Jerusalem of statements about the "undivided land of Israel," such remarks could be dismissed, in a very American way, by claiming that the Israelis who made them did not really mean them: they were only trying to stake out a hard bargaining position from which they could achieve the best deal.

So far I have used the phrases "most American Jews" or "many American Jews," and not the usual phrase "the American Jewish community," because there is no such thing as an American Jewish community. American Jews are divided into three unequal, sometimes overlapping, parts.

On the right, a minority of less than 15 percent of American Jews are convinced, undeviating hard-liners. Most are Orthodox in religion, and many come from the small element of American Jewry that arrived after World War II; they tend to be Holocaust survivors, or the children of survivors. The experience of ultimate powerlessness in the Nazi death camps has made the survivors particularly susceptible to the appeal that Menachem Begin made his own: "never again." Even among the American Jews who remember the death camps, there are some with moderate views. For example, Menachem Rosensaft, the founding chairman of the Children of Holocaust Survivors, is an outspoken dove, even though many of the most vocal people in his group are hawks. But for most of those whose lives were deeply affected by the Holocaust, the memory of powerlessness translates into the assertion that Jews cannot show any weakness to their enemies, that only power counts. And the major enemies of the Jews, now, are the Arabs.

The other component of the right-wing minority is the neoconservatives. This right-wing intelligentsia makes considerable noise, because it produces countless articles and makes many speeches; but it has no substantial number of foot soldiers. In a poll of American Jewish opinion by the *Los Angeles Times* (the results of which were reported on April 12 and 13, 1988), 56 percent described themselves as belonging to the Democratic party and 27 percent described themselves as political moderates. Only 17 percent described themselves as conservatives: not much more than the 10 percent of American Jews who were Republicans in the Roosevelt era. And many of today's Jewish Republicans are, as was said in an earlier essay, Orthodox believers, few of whom are subscribers to *Commentary* or the *Wall Street Journal*.

The largest group of American Jewish opinion is in some conflict with itself. According to the *Los Angeles Times* poll, American Jews, by a majority of at least four to one, want some formula that would quell the violence. Two-thirds of those polled favored some form of political accommodation with the Palestinians. In keeping with the result, 57 percent of the American Jews polled said they were favorably impressed by Shimon Peres, who endorsed the Shultz plan, while 49 percent said they were impressed by Yitzhak Shamir, even though Shamir now has the prestige that comes with being prime minister of Israel. Perhaps most striking of all is that more than a quarter of those polled were willing to say that the "foreign and domestic policies of the State of Israel have become less acceptable to them," while only 11 percent, the bedrock constituency in America of the Israeli right wing, found Israel's recent policies more acceptable.

As American Jews are losing some of their illusions about Israel and are being forced to think about the real Israel, and to begin to make hard choices from among the clashing political factions, they remain predictably committed to its security. The researchers for the *Los Angeles Times* found that 85 percent of American Jews continue to "favor strong United States support for the government of Israel"; only 3 percent were opposed, and 12 percent said they did not know— roughly the same results as in other polls of the last thirty years. But there is one radically new note: the respondents were evenly split over whether those who privately disagree with Israeli policies should nevertheless publicly express their support. Younger Jews, those under forty-one, by a margin of 60 percent favored public criticism of Israel. An Israeli government that continues to resist political compromise can therefore expect open disaffection to increase among American Jews, and especially among the younger generation.

If Yitzhak Shamir wins the Israeli election in November, as he very well may, he is likely to maintain a tough, repressive policy toward the Palestinians, while opposing any attempt by a new American president to revive the Shultz initiative. Since returning home from his visit to the United States in March, Yitzhak Shamir has left no doubt in Israel about his political intentions. On Sunday night, April 24, speaking to the Central Committee of the Likud party in Tel Aviv, he was cheered when he said that "the Arabs must understand that we will never part from Judea, Samaria and Gaza." He added that the Palestinians would have an autonomy plan under which they would be able to run their own lives. As Israelis know, this means, at most, the right of Palestinians to run the local fire departments and sanitation services, while the government of Israel controls the disposition of land, water, and virtually everything else of any consequence. Shamir announced this policy as his election platform against the Labor party, which has accepted Shultz's formula of "land for peace."

In Israel, Shamir's declarations are understood against the background of his repeated insistence that the riots and the continuing civil disobedience by the Palestinians can be suppressed. Shamir has called the rioters "grasshoppers" by comparison to the Israel Defense Force. Shamir's views are opposed by some of the country's leading generals. Perhaps the most striking of all such statements was reported on the front page of *Ha'aretz* on April 1. Eleven retired generals— among them Aharon Yariv, a former head of military intelligence, and Motti Hod, a past commander of the Air Force—insisted that the future of Israel requires withdrawal from the territories. The generals want the West Bank to become a demilitarized region under Palestinian control, with a few Israeli observation points on the highest ground. The declaration of these generals, most of whom have been lionized repeatedly on the platforms of the American Jewish organizations, was ignored in all the American Jewish establishment publications I have seen.

When the refusal of Israel's hard-liners to deal politically with the uprising can no longer be explained as the negotiating tactics of tough bargainers who really want to compromise, American Jews will find themselves facing wrenching choices.

A movement toward open disaffection with Israel's right wing seems all the more likely because of one seemingly strange result in the latest *Los Angeles Times* poll. Half of the American Jews surveyed report that their major concern as Jews is not support of Israel but "social justice." Support of Israel is the main issue for 17 percent, and another 17 percent give religion as their prime concern. At first glance these figures seem to contradict the overwhelming support for Israel (85 percent) that these same respondents demonstrated when asked if they would continue to press the American government to support Israel—but the two results are really not contradictory. Among American Jews, as I have noted, Israel is supported by the majority as a homeland in which Jews take pride; only a minority is undeviatingly devoted to Israel, "right or wrong." Therefore, the mainstream of American Jewish opinion, which is essentially identical with the third and fourth generations of Jews who descend from the mass migration that began in the 1880s (i.e., the most "Americanized" elements of the community), will struggle to depict the homeland as virtuous by the standards of liberal, democratic opinion that they share. The breaking point will come when they can no longer do so. That this moment may be arriving is worrying for most American Jews and especially for the young.

Why, then, was Shamir cheered in Washington this March before a large gathering of "young leaders" of the United Jewish Appeal? Some were, no doubt, really on his side, inspired by a defiant assertion of "Jewish power." Many wanted to imagine that the Israeli leader was acting like an American politician, posturing as intransigent as a way of preparing for an inevitable compromise with the Palestinians. Here the fundamental difference between Israeli and American Jewish perspectives was apparent. The same political performance had different meanings for two different audiences. In Washington younger American Jews were asserting their pride in their homeland. In Tel Aviv and Jerusalem the standing ovation they gave Shamir was seen as support for the tough ideologue known to the Israelis, not for the "reasonable" Shamir of the Americans' imagination.

The most visible representatives of American Jews are the leaders of the national organizations who gather together as a bloc in support of Israel in the Conference of Presidents of Major American Jewish Organizations, and the official lobby in Washington, the American Israel Public Affairs Committee (AIPAC). Both groups, and especially the "Presidents' Conference," are widely regarded as the elected spokesmen of the American Jewish community. This is to exaggerate their representative character.

To begin with, the Jewish organizations, including religious groups, have an enrollment of fewer than half of the Jews of America. Since Jews can leave or join these organizations as they please, those who become disaffected are more likely to drop out than to stay and fight for their views. When they leave the organizations, however, they do not leave Jewish life. Most of their children have bar-mitzvahs or bat-mitzvahs and are married as Jews, and most are deeply concerned about Israel, especially at moments of crisis. That few unaffiliated

Jews rejoin Jewish organizations to fight the hard-liners creates an anomaly: the Jewish establishment claims to speak for an American Jewish community, but the real opinions of American Jews can be discovered only through opinion polling, and not through the pronouncements of the presidents and executive directors of the national organizations. On the contrary, as moderates leave the establishment organizations, or do not join, or find no way to express their views, and the hard-liners remain, these organizations give a more and more false impression of American Jewish opinion.

This false impression is particularly damaging in Israel, where the pronouncements of the "Presidents' Conference," or the kind of reception that it gives an Israeli leader, are taken as a reliable measure of the mood of American Jewry. Israelis tend to think that American Jews have elected these leaders after vigorous public debate on policy, because they themselves come, most of them, from Europe and the Arab world, where Jews were organized in *kehillot* (that is, in community councils that held periodic, and usually hard-fought, elections). Most Israelis imagine that American Jews are organized in roughly the same way. The Jewish organizations are listened to in Israel as if they were the elected representatives of American Jewry, and as if they had deliberated on the differing party platforms in some kind of national referendum.

Nor are most of the "establishment" leaders in the drama of the relationship between Israel and American Jews unaware of the effect they create in Israel. The American managers of such events as Yitzhak Shamir's speech in March to the "Presidents' Conference" know that Israelis will interpret their cheers not as respect for the prime minister but as backing for the leader of the Likud party. Why are they willing and even eager these days, in the face of majority American Jewish opinion, to oblige Shamir?

Most of the leaders of Jewish organizations believe that such displays of unity are necessary in order to strengthen Israel's prestige and position in America. Many share the dominant American Jewish myth that even an ideologue like Shamir is a politician comparable to American political leaders, and that he will ultimately negotiate a compromise. The counterargument—that public support for other, more moderate Israeli politicians is of far greater help to Israel than supposed unity behind an intransigent ideologue—has in the past been silenced by a cadre of leaders of organizations and of professional managers. But the solid front of the Jewish establishment, which was briefly shaken by the events surrounding the invasion of Lebanon in 1982, was broken by the Palestinian uprising that began in December.

An important sign of a crack in the unity of Jewish opinion is the strange and continuing silence of AIPAC, an independent membership organization that claims to represent the interests of Israel in the United States and that is not directly controlled by the Jewish national organizations. In recent years, it has often been even more tough-minded and maximalist than the establishment organizations in the pressures it has mounted in Washington on behalf of Israel. The strategists of AIPAC differ from the other Jewish leaders in that they are in close touch with a great many politicians in Washington, and especially in Congress. AIPAC's lobbyists, therefore, know that support for Israel in American opinion has been decreasing. According to the *Los Angeles Times* poll, while Jews have remained overwhelmingly in favor of strong American support for the government of Israel, non-Jews were in favor of it by 27 percent, opposed by 23 percent, and 50 percent answered "don't know." For the AIPAC lobbyists such results would indicate that Israel should move quickly toward a negotiated political solution of the conflict with the Palestinians.

AIPAC has not dissented from the hard line by merely remaining silent. Its office in Washington has also acted, indirectly but with strong effect. The now famous letter sent in March by thirty senators to Secretary Shultz in support of his peace initiative could not have been written without the knowledge of AIPAC. The signers of the letter included five of the seven Jewish senators, and the majority of Israel's most vocal Senate supporters. It is even more striking that the thirty senators who signed the letter were those who have received most of the money allocated by the pro-Israel PACs. A letter of support for the Shultz plan could not have circulated in the Senate without most of the strongly pro-Israel senators sooner or later discussing the matter with AIPAC. That these men would have signed such a letter immediately before Prime Minister Shamir's visit to Washington if AIPAC had objected vigorously is very unlikely.

AIPAC has denied that the letter of the thirty senators was drafted somewhere within AIPAC itself, and there is no point in trying to disprove its claim. What is clear is that the signing of the letter—and AIPAC's apparent decision not to try to stop it—was an act against Yitzhak Shamir, and he understood it correctly as a warning of disaffection not only in Congress but within American Jewry itself.

Shamir came to the United States in March to silence such views, and he moved adroitly. He deplored the letter of the thirty senators, but rapidly changed the subject. It was best, from his point of view, to suggest that these great friends of Israel had simply made a mistake, for which he benignly forgave them. He did not confront AIPAC.[26]

The turning point came at the beginning of March. A "mission" of the "Presidents' Conference" went to Jerusalem to confer with the prime minister, before his visit to Washington. He told his guests that he had no intention of accepting the Shultz plan; in fact he had announced, in advance of their coming, that there was not a single line in it that he found true except the signature. The leaders of the American Jewish establishment returned from that meeting knowing that their urgings since December for Israel's right wing to be reasonable—that is, to behave like De Gaulle in Algiers, or Nixon in China, or Begin at Camp David—had not succeeded. The organization presidents heard Shamir out, and most of them chose to go along with him.

Shamir, in Washington, did not want any more expressions of public disagreement, and he could use the "Presidents' Conference" to create the image of a consensus backing him, even though the various organization leaders, when polled privately, have long shown a majority of somewhere between three and four to one on the side of moderation.

True, almost every one of these leaders tells stories of how firmly he has spoken, and continues to speak, to Israel's leading politicians of all shades of opinion about the need for political compromise with the Palestinians. The tales of these conversations are repeated in the United States, and not only "off the record," to Jewish groups. They sometimes leak, and not always by accident, to the press in Tel Aviv and even in New York. But these leaders protect their positions by being publicly circumspect. To be in open conflict with a sitting prime minister, even one of a divided government, is a disaster for any leader within the Jewish establishment. He will be treated coolly in Jerusalem. He will not be able to return home to tell his board of trustees of his intimate conversation with the prime minister in Jerusalem, or carry messages of supposed importance between Jerusalem and Washington.

What the prime minister requires in return for listening privately in his Jerusalem office to a polite, perhaps even pained, disagreement with his policies is the staging in America of public support. Both the prime minister and the Jewish organization officials who give him a standing ovation while the cameras roll know what the bargain is all about. Shamir's position is built up in America, and especially in Israel, not only as prime minister of all Israel but as the triumphant Likud party leader. At the same time, the Jewish organization leaders cheering Shamir are confirmed by the prime minister as the legitimate representatives of American Jewry—and never mind the polls or the other Jewish leaders who speak for the moderate opinion of most Jews.

And yet, despite this seeming unity in public, the opinions of American Jews are inherently unstable. Uneasiness is growing even within the organizations, as the quiet, though temporary, defection of AIPAC in the spring of 1988 from support of the hard line proved. So far, a few of the organizations within the "Presidents' Conference" have already dissented from Shamir's line. These include the American Jewish Congress and the Union of American Hebrew Congregations, as well as the American affiliates of Israel's Labor party. In mid-April there was a mass rally in New York of some five thousand people who wanted to show their solidarity with moderate policies in Israel and to protest the views of the Likud. This virtually unprecedented gathering was cosponsored by twenty of the American Jewish organizations to which political moderates belong, among them the Labor Zionist Alliance, the Progressive Zionists, and the Children of Holocaust Survivors.

Perhaps most significant, mainstream organization leaders, the very people who support the prime minister in public, have recently been returning from visits to Israel deeply concerned about what will happen after the Israeli and American elections this fall. They are fearful that a confrontation will take place between the right-wing majority in Israel and the United States government. In this case an open break with Israel's policies could occur even within the establishment organizations. That such a confrontation may well be coming was suggested by Reagan's praise of Shimon Peres on May 17 and his criticism directed at Shamir.

Most American Jews certainly remain loyal to the homeland in Israel, but they are less and less willing to allow the organization leaders who have been speaking for them to say what they will. A public debate has been taking place between the spokespersons of the organizations and the leaders who speak for those Jews—they are the majority—who hold moderate opinions. The claim that American Jewry is largely united behind, and controlled by, the organizations is becoming exposed as an illusion.

1988

SEVEN

In Debate with Christianity and Christians

The Jewish-Christian dialogue has concerned me, both as writer and as communal figure, for nearly fifty years. In 1969 several of the major international Jewish bodies founded a representative group, cumbersomely named the International Jewish Committee for Interreligious Consultation, to act as official representative of the world Jewry in formal conversations with the World Council of Churches and with the Vatican. I was elected its first chairman. After leaving office in 1973, I remained actively involved for a number of years in the negotiations between communities of the Jewish and Christian faiths. The issues always led back to basic differences over theology or history. Inevitably, I have kept thinking about the reasons why Jews and Christians, even when there is good-will, continued to disagree.

20. *Synagogue and Church in the Age of Revolution*

A fundamental, recurring issue between Jews and churchmen, and especially Catholic churchmen, has been the question of the French and, to a lesser degree, the American revolutions. For Roman Catholic thinkers, especially in France, the revolution of two hundred years ago is still a disaster, for it moved the Church away from the center of society. In 1963, in a book about church and state in America entitled *The Outbursts That Await Us,* I published an essay on American Judaism in which I argued that the faiths in America did not live together out of their own ethos. They were constrained to refashion themselves by the First Amendment to the Constitution of the United States, which mandated the separation of church and state. In the essay below, I argue this case in relation to European experience.

▼

In the latter half of the seventeenth century, during the 1660s, two great scholars lived in the city of Metz in Eastern France. The rabbi of the Jewish community was Jonah Cohen Narol, who was one of the great figures in rabbinic scholarship of that age; the canon of the cathedral was the famous Jacques Benigne Bossuet, who was the most important Christian theologian in France. There is no record in either Jewish or Christian sources that they ever met, though it is possible that they did, for Metz was in a border area, and it had very recently been acquired by the French. Jewish rights in the city were far from secure, and it is therefore possible that the rabbi did go as supplicant to the bishop on occasion. The greater likelihood is that the Jewish community conducted its business with the military governor of the city and that Jews lived in total isolation from the local Catholic hierarchy.

Even if Narol and Bossuet did meet, they had nothing to talk about. Benign intellectual and theological encounters between Jews and Christians had almost never occurred during the Middle Ages— and many attitudes from the Middle Ages were still alive in Eastern France in the seventeenth century, at least in relationship to Jews. When rabbis and prelates met in person to discuss religion, it was usually in the tragic high drama of theological disputations to which Jews were summoned, and in which they could only lose.

The converse is also true: Christianity as religion was not ever a major theological concern for medieval Judaism. If the Jews of the

West had been left to themselves, without the historic pressure of the Christian majority on them, Christianity would have been ignored. To the degree to which it was discussed by Jewish thinkers of the medieval era, such considerations arose out of the necessities of keeping Jews from converting under the pressure of persecution, and of providing some formulas of grudging respect which would satisfy Christian critics, who kept insisting that the essence of Judaism was its unrelieved hatred of Christianity.

At about the time that Bossuet and Narol were living in Metz, the most important divine in the New World was Cotton Mather. His contemporaries regarded him, correctly, as the greatest intellect to have appeared in the American colonies. Cotton Mather persuaded himself that he understood the Hebrew Bible better that the Jews, who had been engaged for many centuries in avoiding the "truth" that God's revelation to them prefigured and announced through His ultimate incarnation in Jesus. Mather was very much a millenarian; that is, he believed the end of days was near and that it could be brought nearer by the conversion of the Jews. He even wrote a book some years later, in 1697, to demonstrate the truth of Christianity from a "correct" interpretation of many verses of the Hebrew Bible, without invoking a single passage from the New Testament. Mather had heard that there were a few Jews in Carolina, and so he sent this book southward in order to convert them with incontrovertible arguments from their own Scripture. The effort failed, for the Jews in Carolina either remained obstinate, or, more probably, were simply not interested. And so, if Mather had ever traveled to Metz, there would nonetheless have been no meeting of Catholic-Protestant-Jew. Bossuet would have had no time for a Protestant, for this heresy was then proscribed in France, and both Bossuet and Mather would have seen Rabbi Narol as only the most obdurate of all possible candidates for conversion.

This centuries-old abyss between Judaism and Christianity was not bridged in the next three centuries, on either side, out of inner necessity, by theological developments that arose within each of the traditions. The Jewish-Christian dialogue was made necessary by the Enlightenment and by the French and American revolutions.

While Rabbi Narol and Bishop Bossuet were not talking to each other in Metz, an ex-student in the yeshiva, the school of Talmud, in Amsterdam named Baruch de Spinoza was writing one of the most revolutionary of all books, his *Theological-Political Tractate*. His essential assertion was that both Judaism and Christianity were, at their best, imperfect reflections of the truths that were available in their fullness only through universal reason. Within a century, this heresy had become the dominant opinion of the educated class in Europe and America. The result of this historic change in the climate of opinion was the separation of church and state. This profound reordering of society was enacted by both of the great political revolutions, in America and in France, which occurred at the end of the eighteenth century. The modern era which began, for state and society, with these two great cataclysms was to be marked everywhere by moving religion formally away from the center of society, from its previous role as organizing principle to the margin. Individuals were now free to believe or not to believe, to associate or not to associate with the institutions of any of the faiths, but the modern state exercised no pressure for religion or in behalf of any of the faiths.

It is within this new climate that Judaism and Christianity began their dialogue. Since the various faiths were now equal before the law, they were now lumped together by civic authority. In some of the early dramas of the French Revolution, priests, ministers, and rabbis marched together in parades to mark the adoption in 1791 of the first French constitution. Two years earlier, when the new republican government of the United States had begun, comparable scenes had been enacted. The rabbi in New York had even participated (according to some accounts), along with other clergy, in the ceremony in which George Washington was inaugurated President. Such a scene could never have happened at coronations of French kings or of English monarchs, while the older relations between the faiths still obtained.

I do not know what the clergy talked about at these unprecedented functions, as they marched together, but I suspect that they passed the time discussing the immediate political scene rather than in creating a new theology for the Jewish-Christian encounter. Parades hardly lend themselves to such deliberations, and especially not when such moments of drama occur in the midst of dangerous times. Nonetheless, these marches were important. The new, secular state was forcing the religions to encounter each other and to establish a new relationship, not only with the state but also among themselves.

I cannot leave these considerations of history without making one more observation: on balance, Jews liked the new regime; Christians did not. The triumph of the secular state radically lessened the role of Christianity in society. The established church was everywhere a major loser, and nowhere as dramatically, and even as tragically, as in France, the "home of the Revolution" in Europe. At least in its Catholic version, Christianity throughout the nineteenth century and into the twentieth remained opposed to "modernism"—that is, to the removal of the church from its centrality in society and to forcing it to behave as a mere equal to Christian heretics, Jews, and even unbelievers. For Jews, the new secularism did bring a major threat to the faith, for wherever they could, Jews rushed in their many thousands into the secular schools. Some Jews very rapidly became part of the most "advanced" intelligentsia. This danger to the faith was understood early; it was deplored and fought, but even the bulk of the Orthodox gladly accepted the new political era, for it brought Jews economic equality and it allowed them, for the first time since the Diaspora had begun some eighteen centuries earlier, to live in society and not on its margins.

So, Christianity, on the whole, confronted modernity with mixed feelings, more negative than positive, while Jews hailed the secular revolutions as times of liberation. Christianity as organized faith was the big loser in the French and American revolutions; Judaism was essentially the big winner, for it now was, for the first time in the West (at least in theory), no worse off than anyone else.

Jews were of no consequence among the makers of the American and French revolutions. Both of these cataclysms would have occurred in precisely the same form if there had not been a single Jew in either the American colonies or France. But, for reasons that are obvious in the light of what I have just said, Jews were almost instantly major partisans of these revolutions, and so they have remained to this very day. In America today, Jews are the only religious community that remains unwaveringly, and almost unanimously, devoted to strict construction of the First Amendment. The Christian majority in

American, in all its parts, is overwhelmingly for some form of prayer in the public schools; most Jews are against such prayers. Why? Because they find in the First Amendment protection of their equality—that is, of their right to live in society free of the pressure that is inevitably exerted on the minority by the religio-cultural traditions of the majority.

It is no accident that throughout the nineteenth century and into the twentieth some of the greatest minds of Jewish origin followed after Spinoza in being against tradition, in wanting to dynamite the Western past and to recreate society on a new foundation. Spinoza invoked universal reason; Karl Marx declared all men to be alike in their deepest relations which, as he insisted, were determined by economic concerns; in due course Freud declared that, in his interior history, man was a battleground between instinct and conscience, and that social clashes would disappear if the inner disorders were cured. The thread that runs through all these theories is one that each of these three seminal figures of modernity acknowledged in his work, and not even very obliquely: in the new world of messiah on this earth, the painful, continuing threat of anti-Semitism would disappear, for its basis in unreason, or class conflict, or religious mythmaking would have disappeared. The bulk of the Jewish community, and certainly the representatives of the Jewish religion, opposed all three of these heretics, but these names continue to be cited as a kind of litany of great "Jewish contributions to Western culture" by people who do not know much about either Judaism or Jewish history—but there is nonetheless some truth in the proposition that these thinkers arose in part out of the Jewish situation in the premodern world. All three were reacting to the persistence of Jew-hatred, and each was trying to find a cure to this disease of Western culture.

Having said all this, it is nonetheless true that the Enlightenment and what followed after in the political history of the West was far from an unmixed blessing for Jews. The obvious problem, of the survival of the faith in the new open society, has already been mentioned in passing, but it must now be dealt with more directly. At the very dawn of the French Revolution, when the *cahiers*, or statement of demands, were being prepared for the delegates to the Etats Généraux that Louis XVI had convoked, the Jews requested equality of economic rights, but they did not imagine the abolition of the

separate Jewish community. In France they came around to this view
only in the turmoil of the revolution, and not without some reluctance.
The issue was clearer still a few years later in Holland, when the
revolutionary Batavian Republic was being created. The leaders of
the organized Jewish community argued formally and publicly before
the Constitutional Assembly that the Jews be allowed to maintain
their separate existence and that they not be integrated totally into
the new political structure. It was better to forego the right to vote
and hold public office, if thereby the coercive power of the organized
Jewish community over individual Jews could be preserved. The faith
would be more secure. In mid-nineteenth-century central Europe,
Rabbi Moses Schreiber, who had come from Frankfurt to be the rabbi
in Bratislava (a town in easy distance of the ever more secular Vienna),
thundered that all innovations were forbidden by Scripture. By fiat
and will, he created a Jewish ghetto in which his community lived
as if they were still in the sixteenth century. These counterattacks on
modernity did not prevail, except among a minority, but they were
not as unimportant as so many of those who write about modern
Jewish history have made them out to be. Most Jews knew that
modernity was not good for the ancestral faith.

A more important threat came from the very equality among the
religions that the Enlightenment had defined. All religions had been
praised by Voltaire, amidst his repetitive loud damns, as being equally
valid paths to virtue. A much more proreligious figure of the Enlightenment in Germany, Ephraim Gotthold Lessing, had written a
play, *Nathan the Wise*, to make the same point through the parable
of three rings. Each of them was equally genuine, or equally contrived;
they were the inheritance that the ultimate Father had left to his
Catholic, Protestant, and Jewish sons, until He perhaps would tell
them at the end of time which of the three rings was the original. If
there was no substantial difference among religions, it was possible
for some Jews to argue that it would serve their purposes better to
find virtue through Christianity. If the symbols and rituals of the
various faiths were accidents of history, those who wanted to enter
the new age could move freely, and even in good conscience, to the
religious camp of the majority. The cost of avoiding anti-Semitism
was more than worth it. Therefore, throughout the nineteenth century
there were thousands of conversions from Judaism to Christianity by

Jews, such as Heinrich Marx (Karl Marx's father) and Heinrich Heine, who did not believe either religion very much. Many thousands more simply assimilated into the dominant culture without undergoing any conversion rituals. Political and economic equality did not come cheap.

This problem had been foreshadowed in the earliest days of the French Revolution. The more moderate side of the Enlightenment had offered the Jews equality but, in return, they had been asked to assimilate. In the first debate, in December of 1789, about the Jewish question in the Parliament that made the French Revolution, Count Stanislas de Clermont-Tonnerre had asserted that "one must refuse everything to the Jews as a nation, but one must give them everything as individuals. They must become citizens." In his view, there could not be "a nation within a nation." Clermont-Tonnerre went on to insist that the Jews must abandon their separatist traditions and melt into the majority; if they refuse to do so, then they should all be forced to move to Palestine. In actual practice, of course, and especially in more pragmatic, and untidy, English-speaking countries, the grant of legal equality did not come with any overt demands that Jews assimilate—but there was a suggestion that entering freedom required a Jew to rethink his identity even more fundamentally than Christians had to rethink their Christianity. No one ever suggested that Christian old-believers should be shipped to the Holy Land.

The far greater calamity for Jews was the other, more doctrinaire element of the Enlightenment, which wanted to remake society according to ideological plan. The dominant idea of the Enlightenment was that men could be remade, but, as some of the greatest figures of the eighteenth century insisted, some men were hopelessly flawed and beyond redemption. They were by nature incapable of being reformed, and indeed, if they are given equality and freedom, this would simply give unbridled scope to their obnoxious and destructive nature. The leader of this opinion was Voltaire. He thought that blacks were less than human, and he was particularly venomous in his assessment of Jews. They were the enemies of humankind: "they are born with fanaticism in their hearts as Bretons are born blond." Their "genetic nature" was both dangerous and irreversible. This opinion was the root of the most searing problem that the Enlightenment brought Jews; it ushered in a new form of anti-Semitism that was more ferocious and deadlier than the medieval Christian variety, because a new raison d'état had been constructed for Jew-hatred. The Jews were now defined as a threatening disease. No matter what they did, no matter how they might try to remake themselves, the bulk of the Jews, and probably all of them, would remain "enemies of the human race." This fateful declaration was a prime root of modern racism. If it was possible in the eighteenth century for civilized gentlemen to live off the misery of black slaves, while talking of the equality of all humankind, Nazis who played Bach would eventually talk of a new order while they burned Jews at Auschwitz.

The account of Jews and of Judaism in the Enlightenment is thus far more complicated that it appears to be at first glance. It is only at its least ideological, in the thinking of Montesquieu in France and of the British Whigs, that the Enlightenment has offered true and lasting hope for humanity. We should have learned by now, two centuries after the American and the French revolutions, and two generations after the Bolshevik Revolution, that ideologies which promise to bring the Messiah on this earth are false. The end of days will come in God's good time, when He chooses, and as an act of grace; those who would force His hand have invariably murdered men and women who do not fit their visions, and, what is worse, they have committed such crimes in good conscience. People should not be "regenerated" according to someone else's prescription of what is good for them, and group identities should not be reformed to be parallel to one another in some tidy structure that an ideologue imagines. Freedom and decency are safe only in an untidy society in which individuals and groups are pressured as little as possible by the absolutes of other people.

We sit together these days, Jews and Christians, because we have been forced together by the Enlightenment. It uttered the demand that made our ancient traditions reformulate their way of living in society, so that we each could accommodate to a world which neither Christianity nor Judaism had made. We are together because we are frightened of the Pandora's box that the most ideological element of the Enlightenment opened: unrestrainable racial hatred. We act together in hope of lessening hatreds and avoiding the overwhelming tragedies.

Let us return, therefore, to the imaginary conversation with which

I began these reflections. Let us imagine that Rabbi Narol, Bishop Bossuet, Dr. Mather, and Baruch Spinoza had sat down together, or are perhaps sitting down together now somewhere in the empyrean. What would they be saying to each other? I suspect that it would make a difference whether the conversation had been held in its own time, in the seventeenth century, or whether these men of great intellect and piety (each toward his own truth) were talking today, three hundred years later. In their own day, each would have argued that all of humankind would soon come to true enlightenment, that the scales would fall from all eyes, and that the truth of *his* own particular ideology would shine triumphant over all the world. Those were still optimistic times.

I suspect that if this conversation was going on now, the four protagonists would still remain convinced of their respective beliefs, but the sobering realities of the intervening years would have made a difference. They would know that the distance between the dream of perfection and achieving it in this world is far greater than they had imagined, and that in the wars of Gog and Magog the forces of darkness often triumph, and they remain in power for very long times. I suspect that our four scholars would be saying, today, that all we have to protect us is a fabric of civility, for which we are responsible together. That civility offers the only hope for the survival of society. The "City of Man" is gravely endangered by all the horrors that humanity has devised. If the "City of Man" destroys itself, God is homeless.

21. *Disagreeing with Friendly Catholics*

My involvement in the dialogue has convinced me that there are limits to understanding. Faiths cannot compromise their theologies. I have even thought that some Jewish political demands, especially for the recognition of the State of Israel, could not be met by the Vatican because of ancient theological taboos. Very recently, this wall seems to have begun to crumble. The issue of Israel has recently been redefined by the Vatican, in public statements, as political and not theological; formal recognition is now in the realm of the possible. The Jewish-Catholic dialogue has moved far, and constructively, from its gingerly beginnings. Has Jewish pressure made the difference? I think so.

▼

In the twenty years since the Declaration of the Vatican Council on the Jews, enormous progress has, of course, been made in the relationship between Catholics and Jews. Since then, Jews and Catholics have been meeting, on the very highest levels, as equals. This "diplomatic recognition" has filtered down to all countries in which there are substantial communities of believers in both these faiths. It has had a profound effect on the relationship of churches and synagogues, even in some places where the bishops have had to battle with encrusted traditions of anti-Semitism. There are still journeys to be completed in this joint pilgrimage. There are many pockets of resistance in the Roman Catholic Church and, it is true to say, there are significant residues of suspicion in parts of the Jewish community, but these are problems that one can believe will be overcome as the years go by.

I wish I could be as optimistic about two of the more fundamental issues that remain unresolved in the Catholic-Jewish relationship. I believe that the dialogue has already reached its theoretical limit and that no further change is possible. On the political level some movement may occur, at least in theory, but I do not believe that it is likely to happen in actual practice. These two propositions mean, together, that both Roman Catholics and Jews will continue to be disappointed in their deepest expectations of the dialogue. They will have to work very hard to hold fast to the gains that have already been made. It will seem to some that just to stand fast is too little, and thus there may soon be hard feelings.

Having proposed these two theses, let me define both the theoretical and the political issues. The text of *Nostra Aetate*, and even its more relaxed and more liberal interpretation in the Declaration of 1974, must be read as Catholic documents which speak the language of the Church stretching to its very limits. From the Catholic perspective, Judaism must be respected because it is part of the religious history of Christianity. To be sure, both documents make it clear that the Church condemns any undue pressure for conversion and that it respects those who are committed to the first biblical revelation. What is between the lines of these Catholic documents— and what has appeared again and again at discussion tables between leaders of the two faiths—has been the profound desire (I would even say need) of Catholics to have Jews agree that Jesus is part of their religious history and that Jewish theology must take account of him, no less seriously than Catholic theology takes account of the Patriarchs and of the revelation to Moses on Sinai. Every time I, for one (and I have, of course, not been alone), have said at such tables that Jesus is no more important to Judaism than Muhammad is to Christianity faces have fallen.

In my view, Christianity at its deepest level continues to grapple with the problem of the rejection of the New Dispensation by Jews when it first appeared among them. Even liberal Catholics regard the renewed dialogue with Judaism as a historic opportunity to find a way, with the help of Jews, to solve this problem—that is, to make some sense of what appears to Christians to be incomprehensible: that the people which best know Jesus ignored him when he appeared and continue to do so. In this expectation, the Catholics in dialogue with Jews will continue to be disappointed, and this despite the attempt to "solve" this problem through "two covenant" theology that was proposed by Franz Rosenzweig. The mainstream of both Judaism and Christianity will each continue to insist that it alone is in possession of the fullness of the biblical revelation for all humanity.

On the political level, the continuing disappointment is on the Jewish side. It is no secret from anyone, and least of all from the Catholic partners to the dialogue, that Jews have been pushing the Church for all these twenty years toward formal recognition of the State of Israel. In large part, the Jewish motivation has been the obvious purpose of all such Jewish efforts in our day: to secure the acceptance of Israel as legitimate by all the major powers of the world. More subtly, the Jews have wanted to move Catholics to think of the Jewish community in its own terms and not through the glasses of Catholic theology. Even for the Catholics of *Nostra Aetate*, Judaism is a religion, a kind of Christianity without Jesus. Even as Jesus is not formally avowed by Jews, Christians believe on faith that his presence hovers over his brethren, who did not acknowledge him, and thus Jews are legitimate. The dimensions of people, history, and land—all the factors that unite believing Jews with unbelieving ones far more deeply than believing Jews are united with believing Christians— simply escape through the lines of these Catholic documents.

Jews are bound to be disappointed by the Catholic response to their arguments. Individual thinkers within the Church are capable of understanding the "mystery of Israel" in Jewish terms, as individual thinkers within Judaism are capable of internal sympathy to the Christian belief in the mystery of the Incarnation. The Church and the Jewish people as a whole cannot, however, yield, at least not in any foreseeable future. More practically, it is abundantly clear, after twenty years of quiet and not-so-quiet diplomacy, that Rome has interests in the Middle East which, in its view, preclude the possibility of extending formal recognition to Israel. The Vatican will continue to welcome Israeli dignitaries—but it will make gestures to Yassir Arafat, or his successors, and it will then cover its flanks with Jews by repeating the Church's condemnations of anti-Semitism. What has been in recent years is what will be.

What remains on the agenda is the joint effort for peace and justice in the world. It remains important that Catholics and Jews talk together, to find the platforms on which they can stand as one. It remains important that we keep talking so that we can at least differ with civility. Further revolutionary advance in the relationship is now almost impossible. The historian within me is willing to wait patiently for another age; the theologian yearns for an act of divine grace, which will help us find soon a new way to transcend these ancient quarrels.

1985

22. John Paul II's Theology of Judaism

The most searing of all the divides between Jews and Christians is the memory of the murder of six million Jews in Europe between 1939 and 1945. The Jewish community cannot forget that the overwhelming bulk of the murderers were baptized Christians and that no Christian church ever excommunicated the Nazis. Christians remember the many thousands who risked their lives to save Jews, and they speak of the millions of non-Jews whom the Nazis murdered as part of the Holocaust. Pope John Paul II is himself an intellectual and a theologian, and a survivor of the Nazi rule of Poland. His thinking about the Holocaust must be taken seriously.

▼

Whatever may happen in the quarrel over the convent in Auschwitz, in relationship to Jews, as on many other matters, the era of John XXIII is essentially over. The issue is not "the church" or "the Vatican"; it is the theology and politics of John Paul II. There is a pattern to all his actions that involve Jews, from his repeated condemnations of anti-Semitism, to his beatification of Edith Stein, the convert from Judaism whom the Nazis killed because she was a Jew by birth, while John Paul II insists that she was a martyr to Christianity. He has canonized Father Maximilian Kolbe, who gave his life in Auschwitz for another Polish prisoner, even though the Pope knew that Kolbe had been a leading propagandist of anti-Semitism in prewar Poland; John Paul II received Kurt Waldheim in the Vatican, in defiance of Jewish opinion, and he has not lessened the diplomatic distance between the Vatican and the state of Israel.

What undergirds this record is a fundamental premise: the Church is not guilty in any way of the Holocaust of the Jews; on the contrary, especially through the Polish Catholics, of whom three million were killed by the Nazis, the Church was a principal victim.

In the light of this assertion, to condemn anti-Semitism has not only moral but also political importance. It is part of a reinterpretation of the past. Individual Catholics may have behaved badly during the Nazi years, so this historiography goes, but the Church was without error. Individual Jews, especially the converts to the Catholic faith, were protected, as best the Church could; the silence of Pius XII, and his refusal to excommunicate the Nazis, were part of his divine mission to protect those whom he could help. A pragmatic historian might defend Pius XII as having protected the institutional interests of the Church in the Nazi years. That Pope excommunicated the Communists, for wherever they took power, they destroyed the Church; he did not excommunicate the Nazis, for they left the Church alone, so long as the Church did not oppose them. But John Paul II is a theologian. He must fit the facts to the notion that the Church remained pure. He cannot allow himself to think that the Church might have done more in the Nazi era, that it was not enough to save an indeterminate number of Jews, at the time when other parts of the Church were actively anti-Semitic. The question of excommunicating the Nazis must be finessed by arguing that this would not have helped the Jews, and not by any breath of a suggestion that this might have cost the Church more than it was willing to risk. Jews and this Pope can, thus, never agree about the Holocaust. In the mind of John Paul II, the Church's record was pure, and some individual Catholics behaved badly; Jews remember that some individual Catholics behaved well, but that the Church as an institution behaved sinfully, and that it has not yet, to use Catholic terms, made an Act of Contrition.

In the argument about degrees of suffering, it is true that as many Polish Catholics as Polish Jews were murdered by the Nazis and so, on the surface, Catholics can argue that they were at least as much victims as were the Jews—but this is, of course, not true. Ten percent of the Catholics of Poland were killed; more than 90 percent of the Jews were killed. Catholic Poles were killed selectively and, if they lived inconspicuously (like the present Pope as a young man), they could survive; Jews were killed for the crime of being Jews. But John Paul II must obliterate this distinction. In Christian theological terms, Jesus himself was martyred again by the Nazis, but whom did they martyr? If Jews were the sufferers, while the Church stood by, then an orthodox theologian, like the Pope, must think the unthinkable, that the Jews remain God's people, suffering for Him on the "cross" that was Auschwitz. The division of the goods of the Jews among the Poles is reminiscent of what the Romans did with the few belongings of Jesus.

No, a believing Catholic must cry out, Auschwitz could not have carried such meaning. The Church is the faithful bride, the representative of Jesus on this earth. If there was martyrdom to be had, it happened to the Catholics whose patroness in Poland is the Virgin Mary herself. It is self-evident that, here too, Jews and orthodox Catholics like John Paul II can never agree.

The convent at Auschwitz is a visible symbol of this deep and unbridgeable confrontation. It is unrealistic, and even silly, for some Jews to ask and even entreat John Paul II to assert, in the language and spirit of John XXIII, that the Church is not the exclusive keeper of the keys to God's kingdom. From the Jewish point of view, it is demeaning and without dignity to ask the Pope for kinder theological definitions of the place of Jews in God's plans. It is not the business of the Catholic Church to tell Jews what they are to think about themselves.

The only thing that is left to negotiate is pragmatic policy. Jews and Catholics have a right to ask of each other that we try not to be needlessly offensive. Receiving Waldheim in state at the Vatican, or persisting in allowing a convent on the grounds of Auschwitz by saying that its existence is the sole business of the Church in Poland, are actions that are not necessary to even the most orthodox Catholic; they are simply offensive. Jewish-Catholic relations are not likely to return, any time soon, to a discussion of historical or theological issues. Better so, for the words and actions of this Pope make clear that the liberals do not deliver the Church—as the Jewish liberals do not deliver the synagogue. The choice now is between pragmatic decency and wrenching religious war. The Church should learn that "What is hateful to you, do not do to your fellow man."

1989

23. The Case for Untidiness: Another View of Church and State

I continue to believe that revealed religions remain in theological conflict, but they can live together. God's truth will be made manifest in the messianic era. Until then, the religious traditions can survive only if they act in the "City of Man" as if the existence of each was equally precious to all.

▼

In Khomeini's Iran, the state exists as an instrument of Islam: Christian and Jewish nonbelievers are tolerated and heretics from Islam, such as the gentle believers in the Baha'i faith, are murdered. In the United States, these days, several varieties of Christian fundamentalists are campaigning, with official support from the Republican party, to pass a constitutional amendment against abortion and to change the law so as to foster prayer in the public schools. In Israel, the ultranationalist Rabbi Meir Kahane regards it as his divinely appointed mission to push, or even shoot, Arabs out of the West Bank. The annexation of that territory is held to be a sacred purpose, and the government that stands in the way is itself "illegal."

Iran, Israel, and the United States are, of course, not the same. Nonetheless, there are at least two threads which tie together all these different events. The liberal Western state, with its commitment to individual human rights, is under attack in all three countries. Those who are attacking represent constituencies which have felt themselves outside the political process. The mullahs in Iran, the fundamentalist preachers in America, and the fundamentalist rabbis in Israel are, for the most part, the leaders of elements in their various countries of the lower bourgeoisie and the proletariat. The Western state has, historically, been run by the educated middle class which, in its majority, is everywhere, East and West, this-worldly and nonbelieving. To its present enemies the Western liberal state is not a neutral traffic cop trying to insure the maximum amount of rights and freedom for all its citizens. It is an instrument of domination by a secular humanist bourgeoisie, which imposes its nonbelief through its control of public life.

The problem of church and state is all the more difficult because, theologically speaking, the conservatives are right and the liberals are wrong. Biblical religion makes no distinction between the civil and religious order. In Judaism, Christianity, and Islam, society in all its parts must be ruled theocratically to enact the will of God. The modern Western state is not a creation of biblical religion but rather of the splintering of Christianity into many factions during the sixteenth and seventeenth centuries, and of the Enlightenment in the eighteenth century. To keep civil peace, a state had to arise in a Europe that did not foster Christianity as its avowed primary purpose.

It is that state which is now increasingly under attack, and the issues are not quite as clear-cut as the most passionate protagonists on both sides of the argument would have it. In favor of the secular state, one can indeed quote John Courtney Murray, that pluralism is against the will of God but that it is the only way to keep peace in the "City of Man." Against this dictum there stands the prospect, awful to many, that all the principles, including those of basic ethics, which bind a pluralist society together are based on consent alone, and that having been so made, they can, similarly, be unmade. In Western thought the Roman Catholic tradition has held fast to the notion that this cannot be so; there is "natural law" which obligates all people, believers and nonbelievers alike. This concept exists also in rabbinic Judaism. Maimonides, basing himself on Talmudic sources, defined the "seven commandments which were given to the children of Noah" as constituting a basic moral code for all humanity. (Jews are obligated to all of the 613 positive and negative commandments that the rabbis found in the Five Books of Moses.)

Even many heretics from biblical religion could not abandon the belief in a moral law that was true for all humans. In the history of Jewish theology and thought, Baruch de Spinoza was the arch-heretic. He was the first important figure within Jewry to assert that the Bible contained many historical errors, and that even its morality was human and imperfect. Nonetheless, Spinoza did not relativize ethics; even as he devastated biblical morality, Spinoza nonetheless insisted that there was an absolute ethic that could be demonstrated with the exactness of mathematical proof; there were rules of conduct that applied to everyone. Spinoza, the arch-heretic, thus remained within the biblical religious tradition in one fundamental respect: he refused to believe that ethics were simply a matter of consent. There was a "natural law" more certain even than any injunctions that could be derived from the Bible.

Those right-wingers in America today who are arguing for a constitutional amendment to outlaw abortion or to permit prayer in the public school, no matter what may be the merit of their arguments on specific issues, are not without a case. There is some truth to the assertion that the liberal state tends to teach nonbelief. The separation of religion and the state inevitably suggests that the nonreligious, public realm which all citizens hold in common is more important than the sectarian private differences that divide us from each other. Biblical religion, in all its forms, has indeed been removed from its centrality in America by the separation of church and state. Some unabashed right-wingers have, therefore, been arguing, baldly and boldly, that America must return to being a "Christian nation."

But that is not the way of the more sophisticated. The new archbishop in New York, the most pluralistic city in America, John J. O'Connor (clearly a man of goodwill, who wants good relations with all non-Catholics) invokes "natural law," which supposedly teaches what is good for everybody. President Reagan has produced a further permutation: he has based his support for a constitutional amendment to ban abortion under almost all circumstances not even on natural law, at least not directly; it is really, so he has told the country, a defense of the *constitutional* principle of the protection of all human beings.

But is there a natural law that defines truth for all people? Can it be invoked to command the assent of rabbis, and even of Buddhist monks? I think not.

On the vexed question of abortion, rabbinic Judaism teaches that the fetus is not a person until it is born. On the famous moral question of whether to save the mother or the child in the birth process, Jewish teaching is unequivocal: under such dire circumstances, one is commanded "to hack the fetus to pieces in the womb" to save the life of the mother. If the antiabortion amendment passes, in the name of natural law, I would therefore be in the position of having to give moral instruction to Jews which would be illegal in the law of America. As a rabbi, I am not prepared to believe that Catholic theologians, or fundamentalist Protestants, have superior understanding of the moral laws that derive from the Bible. Under analysis, "natural law" thus tends to become the teaching of an individual tradition, with some universalist face-lift.

Certainly I must confess, again as a rabbi and without any pretense that I am basing myself on some universal values, that I find wholesale abortions, in the hundreds of thousands, morally revolting; and that, as a child of the Jewish version of the biblical tradition, I find such action morally defensible only in specific cases when the reason is compelling and where the case has been decided on grounds other than the mother's subjectivity. What I cannot do is to battle for a law in which I universalize for everybody my own anguish both for thousands of fetuses whose right to be born should be protected and over the occasional one which should in fact be denied that privilege.

Jewish teaching is itself not exempt from the same criticism, that what it teaches as universal truth applicable to all is really a rarefied version of its own principles. So Maimonides' version of the "seven commandments given to the children of Noah" includes among them, as basic to all the rest, the belief in a God who rewards the righteous and punishes the sinners. Obviously, this rules out believers in non-theistic religions, and even the most virtuous of humanists, as well as most believers in philosophic ethics. Maimonides may indeed have been right in insisting there is no sure foundation for ethics unless they are grounded in the revelation of a personal God, but this issue has been argued for centuries, before and after his day, without ultimate resolution. He who would make laws for all of society on the basis of Maimonides' definition of what is true, even for non-Jews, should at least know that he is really enacting a version of Judaism.

Religious or ideological absolutists may sometimes succeed, even today, in imposing their wills on society in the name of their God. They must be reminded that this opens the door to having exactly that happen to them in places where someone else's absolute is in control. Those who would stop all abortions in the United States, where major traditions believe that abortion is at least occasionally permissible, must remember that they cannot complain of the basic outlook of Khomeini (even as they deplore his murderous tactics), of his belief that he must purge his society of harmful elements.

Is there a limit to tolerance and to relativism? This is not an easy question, and I know no clear-cut answer. There is, supposedly, agreement everywhere on such basics as the prohibition against stealing and murder but, even so, there are quarrels, and not only about abortion. Are some forms of passive euthanasia, where help is withheld in hopeless medical situations, to be regarded as murder? Is capitalism or communism (take your choice, depending on your ideology) to be defined as inherently a form of stealing by one class from another? There is, on the other hand, consensus in American society on matters which are not against "natural" or biblical law. We have, for example, outlawed polygamy, which flourished in the Bible and exists to this day in Muslim societies.

The Western liberal state is indeed more secularist than it perhaps need be. Its only rationale is the one that was given by the Founding Fathers of America: the government exists as a traffic cop so that we may do one another the minimum amount of injury, either physical or spiritual. This secular state can only protect our bodies. Any state that enters the realm of our souls had better be one that God himself makes at the end of days. If we attempt to make a godly kingdom, it always becomes an engine of oppression. What we have learned, painfully, in recent centuries is that we can live best only in untidiness, with a decent concern for the opinions of all people, even as this costs many of us as believers something very precious to our own souls. In the West, even in an unbelieving twentieth century, what we tend to define by consent does bear relationship to the biblical roots of our common culture, and yet we cannot stretch this too far. We must be wary of forcing someone else's conscience.

1984

EIGHT

The Jewishness of
Modern Jews

The great turning point into the modern era took place for Jews at the end of the eighteenth century. Intellectually, some Jews had begun to enter the age of religious doubt. Indeed, one of the founders of the new thinking was Baruch de Spinoza. His earliest training was that of a rabbinic scholar, but his *Theological-Political Tractate*, written in Holland in the 1650s, had more influence than any other book in creating doubt about the divine origin of the Bible. A century later, in the American Constitution of 1789 and in acts of the French Revolutionary Assembly of 1790 and 1791, Jews were made equal citizens. In the new situation how were they to redefine their identity? What role models were available from the Jewish past? Some Jewish voices were raised in those very years, and since then to this day, to regret the Emancipation of the Jews. The community would have been better off, so these arguments have gone, if it had retained its separateness and had remained in control of individual Jews.

I have always thought that these arguments are a form of baying at the moon. Even a legally separate Jewish community would have been subject to the solvents of modern thought. Nonetheless, the relationship between society as a whole and the various communities that exist within it remains a basic question. This issue is indeed becoming sharper and more serious before our eyes. How can the various communities maintain their traditions, and be at peace with all other groups? These problems were in view at the beginning of the modern era. They remain unresolved, and ever more troubling.

24. *The Return of Maimonides*

The headquarters of UNESCO in Paris was an improbable place at which to celebrate, in mid-December 1985, the 850th anniversary of the birth of Maimonides. The United States had formally withdrawn from UNESCO the year before, after charging the organization with being a center of anti-Western propaganda, of support for "guided democracy" and, especially, of a "third world"–style controlled press. Just a few days before the Maimonides conference was to convene, Great Britain had announced its decision to withdraw from UNESCO, for reasons almost identical to those given by the Americans. Both governments had attacked Amadou Mahtar M'Bow, the director general of UNESCO, for his third world proclivities and his extravagant budgets. Several people in Paris suggested to me that M'Bow might be helped by the appearance of fairness and reasonableness that this conference would give him.

It did not turn out that way. The staff of UNESCO was on strike against the director general that week. It sat downstairs in the lobby in protest against personnel cuts that M'Bow had announced to compensate for the revenue, one-fourth of the total, that was lost with the departure of the United States. It seemed clear that M'Bow's politics were seen to be the enemy of much of the UNESCO bureaucracy, of their jobs and of their programs. No late nod to the Jews could now make a difference to his survival, especially since it was being whispered in the corridors that the Russians had abandoned him.

The idea for the conference on Maimonides had come from the World Jewish Congress in 1983. This international Jewish group did not back away even after the Americans and British departed from

UNESCO, largely because the Israelis had chosen to support the conference despite their own grievances against the organization for repeatedly condemning Israel's archaeological efforts in Jerusalem as attacks on Islam. The Maimonides anniversary would serve to reduce Israel's isolation and turn attention at UNESCO to a Jewish topic for the first time in at least a decade. A strange assortment of countries, none of which had normal relations with Israel, were cosponsors of the conference: Pakistan, India, Cuba, Spain, and the Soviet Union. (Spain and Israel later announced in January 1986 their intention to exchange ambassadors.) The scholars who came to the meeting were an even more surprising assortment. They came from Algeria, Morocco, Senegal, and Nigeria—as well as from Saudi Arabia, Kuwait, and Iran.

When, European-style, the assembled scholars elected a presidium to conduct the sessions, three of the four vice presidents were chosen from countries that do not have diplomatic relations with Israel: Souleymane Bachir Diagne, from Senegal; Mohammed Arkoun, a Moroccan who lives in Paris; and Vitaly Naumkin, of the Academy of Sciences of the USSR. The fourth was M. H. Zafrani, a North African Jew who teaches in Paris. The officers were elected quickly by consensus and no one seemed to have any problem with designating me, an American and a Jew, as president of the body. M'Bow not only gave a reception for the visiting scholars on the first evening of the conference, but he opened the meeting that morning with a speech summarizing Maimonides' biography (which seemed to come straight out of an encyclopedia). This flat performance by a nonscholar nevertheless raised a series of basic issues: Why is Maimonides the only religious figure since the biblical prophets about whom such an international conference could have been convened? Why are there, and have there been, so many diverse, and often clashing, schools of thought claiming sole possession of Maimonides as their true ancestor?

The answer to the first question was given in M'Bow's opening remarks and was soon echoed by Vitaly Naumkin of the USSR. Maimonides stood at the confluence of four cultures: Arab, Christian, Greek, and Jewish. More than anyone else, this single mind carried the main intellectual currents of his time.

Moses, the son of Maimon, was born in 1135 in Córdoba, which had been the intellectual center of Muslim Spain for more than two centuries. There were Christians as well as Jews in the city, and they were not sealed off from one another. In this milieu Jews were even writing war poems and drinking songs in Hebrew that were based on Arab models. The young Maimonides preferred philosophy to poetry. He composed his first work, a treatise on logic, when he was perhaps no older than sixteen. The manner of its writing suggested that Maimonides regarded himself as capable of thinking about philosophy as a rationalist among rationalists. It is striking that the young author made not a single reference to a Jewish source.

Maimonides and his family did not live long in Córdoba; they were forced to leave by a fanatical sect of Muslims, the Almohads, who conquered the city in 1148. The next dozen years in Maimonides' life are obscure. We do not know exactly how long the family remained in Córdoba after the arrival of the Almohads, or where they went after they left the city. By 1160, however, when Maimonides was twenty-five, he had arrived in Fez, where he spent the next five years. The family then took to wandering again. After a brief stay in the Holy Land, Maimonides established his permanent residence in Fustat, a suburb of Cairo. For the first eight years he was supported by his brother, David, who traded with India.

When David drowned on one of his voyages, Maimonides had to earn a living. He became a physician in the court of al-Fadhil, the vizier of Egypt under Saladin. Maimonides also served as head of the Jewish community, receiving people at the end of the day when he returned from his medical duties. He also conducted a large correspondence. Questions of law and policy were sent to him from throughout the Jewish world, but most especially from Arabic-speaking Jews; he almost invariably replied, sometimes at length, and with an overt passion that was absent from his more formal writing. We know the details of his daily schedule from a letter that he wrote to Samuel ibn-Tibbon, the translator of *The Guide of the Perplexed* from Arabic to Hebrew. Ibn-Tibbon wanted to visit him in Egypt; Maimonides was discouraging because he was afraid that his excessively crowded days would allow no time for any intellectual encounter.

Most of Maimonides' literary work was devoted to Jewish law. He had been bred to the subject because his father was a *dayyan*, a Jewish religious judge, who saw to it that his son learned the whole of rabbinic literature. Maimonides turned his genius in this subject first to an interpretation of the Mishnah, which is the core text of the Talmud. The six volumes of the Mishnah are a code of Jewish law based on thousands of rabbinic interpretations of the Bible, and other rabbinic traditions. It was composed in the second century in Palestine by Rabbi Judah "the Prince," who was then the acknowledged head of Jewry. During the next nine centuries, in Babylonia and Palestine, the Mishnah was studied and interpreted by scholars who often disagreed among themselves. The discussions that took place in the major Jewish centers during the earlier three centuries were recorded in two collections, the Babylonian Talmud and the Palestinian Talmud. For the next six centuries scholars and religious judges studied these enormous commentaries, especially the Babylonian Talmud, and added to them.

By the time of Maimonides, this legal corpus had grown so large that only scholars could find their way through its labyrinths. The original meaning of the core text, the Mishnah, had thus been obscured by generations of interpretation. Maimonides wrote his commentary on the Mishnah in Arabic, and he consciously tried to recover the meaning as it was intended by Rabbi Judah.

Maimonides' interpretations for the most part tended to follow the explanations of the Mishnah that were recorded in the Babylonian Talmud. Occasionally he infuriated the traditionalists by interpreting passages of the Mishnah by his own lights, independent of earlier authorities. Thus, one of his first comments on the Tractate Sanhedrin, which deals with the judiciary, boldly contradicted what was written in the Babylonian Talmud. It was held there that an "expert,"who was authorized to sit as the sole judge in civil cases, was to be defined as someone whom the public had accepted or who had been authorized to act as judge by the exilarch, the lay head of Babylonian Jewry. Maimonides was emphatic in insisting that such an "expert" could exist only if he were ordained in the Holy Land by a Jewish religious court.

This dissent from the Babylonian Talmud's interpretation of the Mishnah was part of a continuing quarrel that Maimonides had with the lay and rabbinic leaders of Babylonian Jewry. He refused to accept their authority. Even though Maimonides had remained only briefly in the land of Israel, the ordained religious leaders in the Holy Land were the only people who, in his view, had any claim to ultimate authority in Judaism. Maimonides did not doubt for a moment that his own reason, and his own learning, were superior to what could be gleaned from the religious rulings of the Babylonians, the rabbis (they were called *geonim*) of his day, and of the recent past.

The commentary on the Mishnah foreshadowed Maimonides' majestic summation and reworking of all rabbinic literature in the book he boldly called *Mishneh Torah* (best translated, I think, as "The Teachings of the Tradition"), thus inviting comparison to the second-century Mishnah itself. In this long work, Maimonides codified all Jewish law in fourteen major sections, each with many subsections. He announced his purpose in the introduction: he intended a book that laymen could consult; it would no longer be necessary for anyone, except the occasional scholar, to study rabbinic literature, or to have recourse to the scholarly keepers of its mysteries. Maimonides opened his code not with ritual or civil rules but with a statement of which theological doctrines Jews must believe. He was particularly insistent that God was incorporeal and that all biblical references to Him as a person were concessions to human speech. This assertion enraged his literalist critics. Many of them were even angrier that one man, even though one of acknowledged genius, was setting himself up as the supreme arbiter of Jewish law.

The *Mishneh Torah* was the only major book that Maimonides wrote in Hebrew. It was, and remains, in addition to its legal importance, a classic composition in the sacred language. Nonetheless this most Jewish and rabbinic of Maimonides' works was not so self-contained as it appeared. It owed a deep debt to Islamic models. Islam, like Judaism, is a religion of commandment and of law. In the earliest centuries after the Koran was composed, precepts and decisions in every aspect of human life, from religious ritual to political conduct, were derived from its text, or from authoritative accounts of the life of the Prophet. During the ninth century two major collections of such traditions—called *hadith*—were published by the Islamic scholars al-Bukhari and al-Hajjaj (called "Muslim"). Such codes continued to be composed for the next three centuries, and some were produced during Maimonides' lifetime. These works contained not only rules about ritual, and civil and political conduct; they also set down firmly what a Muslim had to believe. Maimonides' approach to codifying Jewish law was thus in keeping with the "spirit of the age." Even though he nowhere mentions any of the Muslim codifiers, the structure and organization of the *Mishneh Torah* showed that Maimonides was more than aware of Islamic models.

Indeed, one of the greatest Arabists of this century, Franz Rosenthal, insisted that aside from Maimonides' comments in the opening section of the *Mishneh Torah* on relations with non-Jews, the rest of the introductory "Book of Knowledge" was a "summary in miniature" of the supreme philosophical-legal work of his older Muslim contemporary al-Ghazzali, the *Ihya'*. Rosenthal wrote that "Maimonides possessed an original and extremely fertile mind" and that "he did not have to have recourse to any conscious imitation of any model. However, it is obvious that his 'Book of Knowledge' occurring as it does at the beginning of the *Law Code*, owes its title, its being, and its place to the attitude of Muslim civilization toward 'knowledge.' "[27]

Maimonides was also the supreme theologian of medieval Jewry. In his theological work he was much more openly influenced by philosophical work that was current in Islam. His magnum opus, *The Guide of the Perplexed*, which he completed in Egypt in 1200, was an attempt to reconcile reason and revelation. It was cast in the form of an address to Joseph ibn Aknin, his favorite student and disciple. Ibn Aknin was representative of many Jews who had difficulty, especially, with the anthropomorphisms in the Bible, for their conception of God had been fashioned in the Aristotelian philosophical tradition. Maimonides boldly explained away all the anthropomorphic passages extraneous to the central religious meaning of the Bible.

Maimonides' fundamental observation about theology, both in the *Mishneh Torah* and *The Guide of the Perplexed*, is that, contrary to Aristotle, the world has not always existed; it was created by God. So he begins his code with the assertion that "the most basic of all principles and the pillar of all sciences is to realize that there is a First Being who brought every existing thing into being." Since God created the world, He is totally other from all His creations: "His real essence is unlike that of any of them." Therefore, Maimonides asserts again and again, in the many passages in both his major works devoted to anthropomorphism, all anthropomorphic expressions are adapted to the mental capacity of the majority of his mankind who have a physical perception of bodies only. The Torah speaks in the language of men. According to Maimonides, all these phrases are metaphorical: "like the sentence 'If I whet my glittering sword' (Deut. 32:41). Has God then a sword and does He slay with a sword? The term is used allegorically and all these phrases are to be understood in a similar sense. . . . But God's essence as it really is, the human mind does not understand and is incapable of grasping or investigating" (this passage, too, is from his code, the *Mishneh Torah*, the "Book of Knowledge").

Maimonides repeated in *The Guide of the Perplexed* what he had ruled earlier in his legal works, that he who believed in the plain text of the Bible held false doctrine.

The Guide of the Perplexed was written in Arabic, but it was soon translated into Hebrew and widely disseminated throughout the Jewish world. It created an immediate and continuing storm in Europe, where philosophical speculation barely existed among Jews. Some European rabbis refused to believe that the great Talmudist, Maimonides, could have written so heretical a book; they insisted that *The Guide of the Perplexed* was a forgery. Others, especially after Maimonides' death, simply excommunicated the book; they distinguished between Maimonides the Talmudist, whom the Orthodox revered, and Maimonides the philosopher, whom they abhorred.

There was reason for their fury, even though Maimonides was not the first Jew to attempt to harmonize revelation with reason. Maimonides hardly refers to any of his Jewish predecessors, not even to a very famous scholar, Saadya, who had written a book in Arabic entitled *Faith and Reason* two and a half centuries earlier. For Maimonides the important philosophers were a group of Arab interpreters of Aristotle, and especially al-Farabi, who died less than three decades before the birth of Maimonides. Al-Farabi had taught that reason was superior to revelation and that the true teachings of divine revelation could be reached, and thus confirmed, by philosophical speculation. At least on the surface of the texts in *The Guide of the Perplexed*,

Maimonides refused to go that far; he insisted that revelation was superior to reason and that revelation taught truths which God had left mysterious, their reasons unknowable, to be accepted on faith.

Whether Maimonides really meant this, or whether he wrote cryptograms beneath the surface of his text to suggest to the close reader that he was, like al-Farabi, more philosopher than believer, has been the subject of argument from his day to the present. That controversy was the subject of a series of exchanges in the *New York Review of Books*. In a review of the work of Leo Strauss, M. F. Burnyeat (in the issue of May 30, 1985) reminded us that Strauss argued repeatedly that Maimonides is the lineal ancestor of Spinoza's philosophical universalism, and that this was the "hidden teaching" of his work. Against this view a distinguished Conservative rabbi, Robert Gordis, has insisted that Maimonides was a rationalist rabbi, and that his life's work was devoted to proving that there is no contradiction between faith and reason. The notion that there is only one Maimonides, who is preeminently a rabbi, has been argued in recent books by Isadore Twersky of Harvard, and by David Hartman of the Hebrew University in Jerusalem, both of whom are Orthodox rabbis of the "enlightened" kind.

A passage in Gordis' second letter to the *New York Review of Books* (April 24, 1986) speaks for their viewpoint: "He was not a closet philosopher for whom self-expression was the ultimate goal. Maimonides was an active leader of the Jewish community; deeply involved in their problems and concerns. He was strongly committed to propagating the truth as he saw it, even among the broad sectors of the people."

Gordis argues that there is no hidden meaning to *The Guide of the Perplexed*. Maimonides' statements in the introduction that the contradictions in his text were intended to lead the attentive reader to meanings that were not immediately apparent were, according to Gordis, mere pedagogical devices. To this Burnyeat has most recently replied that Maimonides, beyond any reasonable doubt, indicated, to those capable of understanding his intentions, that his text had an esoteric meaning; the only question that can be argued, in Burnyeat's view, is what the nature of that meaning is.

Burnyeat is not a specialist on Maimonides (nor for that matter is

Gordis, who is mainly a Bible scholar), but Burnyeat's view is similar to that of Shlomo Pines, professor emeritus at the Hebrew University and the author of the most important contemporary translation of *The Guide of the Perplexed* (to which, not incidentally, Leo Strauss wrote a brilliant introductory essay). Pines was the star at the conference in Paris. His presence gave the meeting an intellectual and political distinction that it would not otherwise have had.

In his lecture to the conference, Pines repeated his view that Maimonides' philosophical theology worked on at least two levels of meaning. One striking example of his point was that Maimonides explicitly insisted that the doctrine of the resurrection of the dead is a central religious dogma; nonetheless, in the text of *The Guide of the Perplexed*, he dissented from one of his Arab sources, the philosopher Avicenna, and agreed with ibn Bajja, the founder of Aristotelean philosophy in Spain, that "not even the soul remains after death" (*Guide*, part I, ch. 74). Maimonides was not hesitant to say that the permanent existence of souls "is a thing of which it has been indubitably demonstrated that it is false."

Why then did Maimonides follow the twelfth-century Muslim thinker Averroes—both of them drawing on Aristotle—in requiring all members of a community to hold some religious beliefs in common? Pines argued: "Maimonides had very strong convictions concerning the utility and even necessity of an official system of religious beliefs for the preservation of communal obedience to the law. What is more, he lived up to his convictions by formulating in his commentary on the Mishnah the thirteen principal dogmas of Judaism." In the very next sentence, however, Pines wrote that "many of these dogmas ran counter to philosophical truth."[28] Pines made it clear that in saying this he was not putting forward his own analytical judgment but stating something he believed Maimonides knew very well. The drift of Pines' argument is to make the link between Maimonides, the philosopher, and Maimonides, the supreme codifier of the law, a matter not of faith but of politics: Maimonides, in Pines' view, felt compelled to insist on beliefs and practices that kept the Jewish community alive as a discrete entity, even as he "knew" that men were divided only by their specific histories—and thus that Jewish religious practices were not the ultimate content of revelation.

I doubt that such assertions about Maimonides lend themselves to proof either way. They have a familiar ring to someone like myself who spent his earliest years in scholarship attempting to understand the development of modern Zionist thought. The supreme admirer of Maimonides among Zionist ideologues was Ahad Ha'am, a turn-of-the-century Russian Jewish intellectual who was the founder of "cultural Zionism." Even as he followed Darwin and Spencer in becoming an agnostic—and thus asserted that there was no special religious revelation to the Jews—Ahad Ha'am insisted with great passion on the uniqueness of Jewish historical experience and on the need for it to continue in the form of cultural nationalism. For Ahad Ha'am, religious practices were not ultimately a problem of the belief in revelation; they were a tool of national survival. In the modern era, religious observances could and had to be replaced by the Zionist emphasis on land and language.

Shlomo Pines has depicted a Maimonides who saw Jewishness as an affirmation of community and who argued passionately that Judaism, as a faith for the masses, is superior to its competitors, Christianity and Islam, even though no particular religion is to be equated with philosophical truth, for such truth is available to men of intellect, of whatever origin. In entering a wider intellectual world, Maimonides and Ahad Ha'am, seven centuries apart, both surrendered much of their intellectual particularism, and yet remained Jews. I take this to be the "faith" of the Israeli universities today. They are secular and universalist in their scholarship and yet strongly nationalist. Shlomo Pines is a major figure in Israeli intellectual life not only for his superb scholarship but for the ways he has helped to formulate this position. Pines' vision of the twelfth-century sage is clearly autobiographical.

Rabbinic intellectuals, such as Twersky, Hartman, and Gordis, have a different problem. To be consistent, they need to maintain that university scholarship and the Talmud academy are not incompatible and that, indeed, these two cultures are one. They need an intellectual ancestor who united these two worlds in himself and even "proved" that, correctly understood, there is no tension between them—and so it is not at all surprising that their Maimonides is an uncontradictory figure, a majestic unifier of faith and reason.

Isadore Twersky, who is generally acknowledged to be the premier authority on Maimonides in the United States, is well aware of the history of Maimonides' life and work and of the contradictory inter-pretations of both that have emerged. A "second posthumous Mai-monides," Twersky writes, "has been continuously recreated and refashioned in successive generations." Through the ages he has been admired, and sometimes attacked, by a variety of opinions. Funda-mentalist Jews have hated him, and some mystics have tried to make this rationalist philosopher into one of their own. Twersky knows that the main problem is whether Maimonides is to be interpreted as "a multifaceted but essentially an harmonious personality" or whether he was "tense and complex, riddled, whether consciously or uncon-sciously, with paradox and inconsistency." Some pages later in the essay from which I am quoting, Twersky does not hesitate to endorse the first view: Maimonides "wanted to unify mood and medium, to integrate the thought of eternity with the life of temporality, to com-bine religious tradition with philosophical doctrine." The legalist and the philosopher are one, so Twersky insists, as he "warns against the widespread misleading tendency on the part of students to fragmentize Maimonides' works."[29] These "students" include Leo Strauss and clearly also Shlomo Pines.

Twersky was invited to Paris but was unable to come. His absence was regrettable for, without him, there was no counterweight to the tendency to see Maimonides as a fragmented thinker. As I have said, such views came primarily from Arab scholars, but, apart from Pines, who had given a paper about the esoteric meanings in *The Guide of the Perplexed*, the Arabs were joined by one of the Jewish scholars, M. H. Zafrani, who, as I noted above, is a Sephardi who was born in North Africa. Zafrani's Maimonides came very close to being a supreme intellectual within the mode of Arab culture, having followed "the same intellectual itinerary" as the leading Arab philosophers. What divided him from that culture was the "attitude of independence which Judaism preserved, in its contact with Islam, on the funda-mental question of religion."

The discussion of Zafrani's paper was the occasion for the most heated debate—it was very nearly an outburst—of the conference. Abderrahmane Badawi, a scholar from Kuwait, had earlier, in his own paper, gone much further than Zafrani. He had discussed a murky period in Maimonides' early life. After the fanatical Almohads had conquered his native Córdoba in 1148, Maimonides remained in the city for some years. Two medieval Arabic authors asserted that Maimonides, when trapped in Córdoba, had converted to Islam. Jewish scholars have generally denied that this was possible, since, they have argued, Maimonides was never attacked by his opponents for conversion.

Badawi made a reasonable case for the contrary view. He argued that Maimonides could not have survived under the Almohads for even a day without conversion, and that he was not criticized for this by his enemies because such conversion to save your life until you could revert to Judaism was not unusual in those terrible times. During the discussion that followed, Badawi went farther still, arguing that Maimonides' supposed forced conversion was not entirely insincere. Badawi had looked through the text of *The Guide of the Perplexed*, he said, and he had not found a single uncomplimentary reference to Muhammad. At this point Shlomo Pines intervened, with more than a bit of sarcasm, to remind Badawi that there were many dozens of references to "the prophet" and that in every one of them Maimonides had made clear his distaste for the teachings of the Koran.

The dispute became more tense after Zafrani gave his paper. Badawi wanted to claim Maimonides for the Mediterranean world and to take him away from the bellicose Ashkenazim, the Westernized politicians and intellectuals whom he saw as the leaders of contemporary Jewry. The Sephardim, the Jews who were in the tradition of Maimonides, he argued, had always lived comfortably in Islamic culture; the ferociously particularist Ashkenazim had no right to claim Maimonides for themselves.

Badawi's insistence on the glories of Jewish-Muslim cooperation evoked from Roland Goetschel of Strasbourg University an angry reminder that Maimonides had been persecuted for his faith. I reminded Badawi that his fundamental thesis about the present was wrong. Every analysis of the Jewish world, and especially of Israel, has shown that Sephardim, the Arabic-speaking Jews of today, take a much harder line in their politics than the Ashkenazim. The very

Jews whom Badawi liked the least, the Ashkenazi intelligentsia, were the ones who largely made up the moderate political forces in Israel or supported them.

This quarrel was the most vocal of the conference, but it was ultimately less important than the Arab-Jewish discussion provoked by the paper of Hassan Hanafi, a professor of philosophy at Cairo University, now on leave at the United Nations University in Tokyo. Hanafi has an excellent, and deserved, reputation as a leading exponent in contemporary Islam of the reconciliation between faith and reason. His doctoral dissertation for a French university was an attempt to reinterpret orthodox principles of Islamic jurisprudence in the terminology of modern Western philosophy. At the very beginning of his career, Hanafi had undertaken to show how a believing Muslim could live in some balance with twentieth-century intellectual developments. He could be seen as the contemporary equivalent in Islam of the enlightened traditionalism that Twersky, Hartman, and Gordis argue for in modern Judaism. Like them, he supported those who see no contradiction between Maimonides the believer and Maimonides the philosopher.

As it drew to a close, his learned paper reached a political conclusion. Hanafi had argued, convincingly, that as philosophers, medieval Muslims, Jews, and Christians shared the same philosophical premises, which ultimately derived from Aristotle. Without any further discussion of political and social issues in the twelfth century, Hanafi asserted: "Mankind can be unified through universalism not ethnocentrism, sectarianism, parochialism, and chauvinism. Universalism, longtime-defended by the prophets since Noah, Abraham, and Moses, reaffirmed by Christ in the name of the new covenant and realized in Islam, in the Andalusian model of Spain, is a permanent virtue in a Palestinian model in which Jews, Christians, and Muslims can live again and under its protection." For the first time, I suspect, the "posthumous Maimonides" was enlisted as an ancestor of the Palestinian National Covenant.

Hanafi was, of course, challenged. A state of Palestine that would supersede Israel based on a Muslim majority, with the promise of fairness for Jews and Christians, is an impossible fantasy. It could come about only at the end of some horrible, probably nuclear, war, which would leave few Arabs, Jews, and Christians to create such a Palestine. Still, in spite of the politics of this paragraph, there was something fundamentally hopeful in Hanafi's tone, and in his general approach. Hanafi told a number of us later that he was giving a seminar in contemporary Islam at the United Nations University in Tokyo, and that he would be eager to have one of the Jewish scholars join him in discussions on the relationship between Judaism and Islam.

Another hopeful moment was the report by Vitaly Naumkin on the study of Maimonides in the Soviet Union. It was somewhat startling to hear that Igor Medvedev, an associate in the Institute of Oriental Studies of the Academy of Sciences in Russia, was working on a translation into Russian of parts of Maimonides' legal code, and that he was giving considerable attention to the rabbinic commentaries on this work, and even to the sources of Maimonides in the seldom-studied Talmud of Jerusalem. Still, this news had to be interpreted with some caution. Even during Stalin's murderous persecution of Yiddish culture during the 1950s, several scholars of classic Jewish texts, and even of modern Hebrew, continued to work in major libraries, and especially in the library in Leningrad, which houses the great Guinzberg collection of Jewish books and manuscripts.

The most unexpected participant among those who spoke during the conference was Huseyin Atay, a Turk by nationality, who is a professor at the University of Petroleum and Minerals in Dárán, Saudi Arabia. Of all the Arab states, the Saudis have been among the most careful through the years to avoid all contact with Israel and with Judaism. Atay's presence suggested that something had changed. Atay is the editor of a critical edition of the Arabic text of *The Guide of the Perplexed*. In his remarks he took issue with Pines' translation of the *Guide* into English on a number of specific points. Pines answered in detail—and the result was a learned discussion about the meaning of medieval Arabic philosophical terms conducted by two scholars whose countries have remained at war since 1948.

The least likely of all the participants was Professor Pourjawadi, of the department of philosophy of the University of Teheran. Pourjawadi said not a word in the public discussion, and he read no paper, but he did not miss a single minute of the sessions. Pourjawadi is reputed to be a senior adviser of the Iranian government. Nonetheless, he had come, and he could not help but take back with him the dominant mood of the conference: elation that such a meeting had taken place and that the discussions had, on the whole, been so civil.

As I have reread the papers and thought back on the discussions, I have found myself, if anything, a bit further away from the historical Maimonides than closer to him. I left Paris with the feeling, which has only deepened afterward, that Maimonides would have been amused by the sight of an intellectual victory over the Islamic fanatics who had chased him out of his native land in Córdoba and over the Jewish fundamentalists who had so often excommunicated him. Indeed, I suspect that my own reaction to the conference might have something to do with my own life as a Jew who grew up in the Hitler era and whose religious commitments are not those of the ultra-Orthodox. Distinguishing between what we learn from Maimonides as he would have wanted us to learn from him, and what we make of him because that is what we want to hear, remains an insoluble problem. So it is with the Bible, and with all other great texts. Polite but intense intellectual conflicts took place in Paris, but, even as some of us were inventing some new Maimonides for ourselves, we were united by a reverence for the texts and for the man who wrote them, mainly in Arabic, at a high point in the history of the relations between Islamic and Hebrew cultures.

1986

25. *The Emancipation: A Reassessment After Two Centuries*

The emancipation of Jews is now two centuries old. The war of the American Revolution was effectively over by 1781 and everyone knew that in the new country Jews would be equal in the law. In that very year Moses Mendelssohn persuaded a Prussian official, Christian Wilhelm Dohm, to write a book pleading for "the improvement of the civil estate of the Jews." Dohm argued, in part, that Jews could become good and useful citizens in a Western state, for were not those in North America an admirable example of what the inhabitants of the ghetto could become in freedom?[30]

A century later, in 1881, large-scale pogroms in Tsarist Russia brought those hopes of the emancipation into question. Leon Pinsker and Yehuda Leib Lilienblum contemplated those horrors and concluded that the only emancipation that was possible for Jews required that they reconstitute their own nation. After 1881 some handfuls went to Palestine in the first modern *aliyah*. The masses of Jews, two million or more, chose to go westward, mostly to the United States, in search of economic advancement and personal freedom.

In these last two centuries, the Jewish world has, thus, been reordered much more radically and fundamentally than anyone imagined at the dawn of the era of emancipation. A European and Middle Eastern people of two centuries ago is now an Israeli-Western people. A once totally unemancipated people now lives everywhere under conditions of equality in law: perhaps three-quarters of Jewry, almost all except those in the Soviet Union, are actually emancipated. To be sure, that equality both for the nation that is Israel and for the Diaspora has to be protected and fought for again and again. A convincing case can be made for the proposition that even in the floodtide of emancipation, both national and individual, Israel is not a state like any other state, and that even the most powerful of the Diasporas, the Jewish community in the United States, is not quite like all other groups in America. Nonetheless, to the degree to which emancipation was conceivable, it has now arrived.

A century after the effective beginnings of Zionism and two centuries after the first signs of the dawning of the new age, it is fair and important that a number of questions be asked: In a world far more turbulent than was imagined a century or two ago, how is the emancipation to be defended? In the next century, who will be our friends—and our enemies?

There is another order of question which I think is more fateful. The era of the emancipation has brought Jews out of the ghetto so that their being Jewish, even in Israel, is totally voluntaristic. Even the Sabra can choose quite freely to leave for other shores and to forget both his Israeli and his Jewish identity. That process is even more available in the Diaspora, where the open society presents the individual Jew with insistent opportunities and temptations simply to leave his Jewishness without even willing a decision for assimilation. The majority of the Jewish people now lives, in Israel and in the Diaspora, outside the Halacha, the structure of religious law. The religious tradition has been translated either into national memory and group experience or to sentiment, or sentimentality, of individuals. Under these conditions, now that the emancipation has succeeded, the question needs to be asked: can the Jewish people survive?

Despite the cliché that no lessons can be drawn from history, some lessons can indeed be learned, for there are several recurrent patterns in the response of Jews to the emancipation. History has repeated itself, and it continues to do so. In 1840, the grandchildren of the handful of Jews who had been present in the American colonies were reaching marital age, and the rate of intermarriage was one in three.[31] This pattern was to recur again in the United States in the 1920s and the 1930s, when the grandchildren of the Central European immigrants reached adulthood. It exists today in a much vaster Jewish community, now that the grandchildren and the great-grandchildren of the hundreds of thousands who came at the turn of the century are marrying.[32]

There are places in the Diaspora where this pattern of evaporation seems reversed. In contemporary France the Jewish temperature has been rising because of the recent arrival of the North African Jews from the last intensely Jewish ghettos in Algeria and Morocco. In several of the big cities of the North American continent, the post–World War II immigration of survivors of the death camps represents an increase in Jewish intensity. More than ever before, self-ghettoized ultra-Orthodox communities exist in contemporary America. This phenomenon is also to be found in places as far-flung as London and Melbourne. This relatively small group, with its high birthrate and its struggle to remain apart from the Gentile and even from most of Jewish society, may outlast the attritions of the Diaspora. My own guess—and here I offer only a guess—is that it will not go quite as well as some of those who romanticize this phenomenon think. Even in the original home of Lithuanian and Hassidic orthodoxies, the continuing losses to the surrounding world were large. In Western Europe before 1933, Orthodoxy of the brand of Samson Raphael Hirsch had a continuity of five or six generations, but its numbers were maintained more by migrants to the West from Eastern Europe than by the descendants of its own German-Jewish founders.

It is too early to tell what the destiny of the last stand of Orthodox Jewish separatism, now transplanted to the West, and especially to America, will be. It is, however, not too early to know that the vast majority of the Jews in the Diaspora who came from Lemberg or Vilna, or the villages round about, three or four generations ago are everywhere opting out of the Jewish community at an alarming rate. What makes this phenomenon frightening is that it is happening in the aftermath of the Holocaust, in the very sight of the existence of Israel and the worldwide passion for it, and at a time when there are no East European ghettos or North African mellahs left. The few Jews who wear caftans in a couple of Romanian villages, or the defiant synagogues in Soviet Georgia, are now remnants and museum pieces.

The first lesson therefore to be learned from two centuries of experience with the emancipation is that a generational clock has ticked over and over again in the open society. Whether in New York and Philadelphia in 1840, in Paris and Bordeaux in the 1850s, in Budapest around the turn of the century, in Berlin and Vienna in the 1920s, and now in the United States in the 1970s, it tells the same frightening time. The third generation in the open society intermarries and erodes out of Jewry at a rate of one in three. Some of the intermarried remain within Jewry and some not intermarried become indifferent. The rate of erosion thus remains of the order of one in three.[33]

There is a second pattern now, more than two centuries old, of Jewish spiritual response to the emancipation. Here the issue is not the era of legal equality, but rather the era of religious doubt, which began even earlier than the 1780s. Here we go back, at the very least, to the middle of the seventeenth century, to the shaking of the Halachic structure from within by Shabtai Zvi, and from without by Spinoza. These attacks were resisted by halachists and believers, some of whom even understood that the open society was not a boon but a danger. Did not a number of Hassidic leaders oppose Napoleon, because they made a conscious choice between the freedom of the Jewish individual and the dangers that emancipation would bring to the inherited Jewish religion?[34] Nonetheless, by the twentieth century the bulk of world Jewry is, by choice or by economic necessity, living outside the religious tradition.

For the post-Orthodox mass of Jews, the recurrent pattern has been to imagine some substitute ideal sufficiently attractive and compelling so that Jews by their allegiance to it would choose to remain Jews. Early Reform Judaism posited the Jews as the supreme bearers of universal ethical ideals. In the nineteenth century, some Jewish Saint Simonians, and even an early Socialist like Moses Hess, imagined for Jews a priestly role in the ushering in of the new era of universal brotherhood.[35] In due course, this notion was reiterated by a staggering variety of revolutionaries. They have argued that, since Abraham broke the idols, marginality, protest, and being protagonists of the new is what being a Jew means. To compile a catalog of the Jewish motifs in these movements is beyond the capacity of an individual scholar. He would have to range across the whole spectrum of Western culture—in music, art, history, law—to produce such a list.

In the Zionist phase, despite a minority that pleaded for "normalcy," most Zionists have hoped that the reconstituted nation would represent, one way or another, "a light unto the nations." In the Diaspora, the rationale for the Jewish philanthropic establishment has been that Jews ought to lead the rest of society toward compassion. Succeeding generations of Jews will then be inspired to associate themselves with so noble a Jewish community. Not so long ago, in America in the 1950s and 1960s, the Jewish community was being told by its leaders that its most important function was to fight for the right of blacks, and that, impressed by such nobility, the young would want to remain with their elders as Jews.

There is no need in this context to deal with an intellectual analysis of any of these ideologies and to answer the question of whether they were indeed validly Jewish and adequate heirs of the *gravitas*, the weight and seriousness, of the inherited tradition. This is in itself an important subject that requires special treatment. It is enough, here, to make a point about social history: none of these doctrines, not even those that looked within, like the varieties of Jewish nationalism, and certainly not those that looked without, such as the various revolutionary doctrines, has really provided the bulk of world Jewry with an ideal that has effectively replaced the older religious vision. Moral passion has not provided the reason for Jews to remain within the fold. Felix Adler, the founder in America of Ethical Culture, a sect in which Jews and Gentiles intermingled and intermarried in the name of ethical ideals, was the son of Rabbi Samuel Adler, the rabbi of Temple Emanuel, the cathedral synagogue of Reform Judaism in New York in the middle of the nineteenth century. Moral universalism did not persuade Felix Adler to be in his turn a rabbi. Zionism is not a total success. Before our eyes in Israel, there is now a great and pained outcry about *yeridah* (emigration). Whatever may be the truth about the numbers involved, one thing is clear: the most intense Jewish nationalism available, the glory and travail of Israel, has not stopped several hundred thousand Sabras from opting out.

It is particularly important that we come to terms, more than a century after the effective beginnings of modern Zionism, with the major Zionist analyses of and prescriptions for Jewish modernity. Let it be stated flatly: both Theodor Herzl and Ahad Ha'am have been proved wrong by life. Herzl presumed that anti-Semitism would persuade the bulk of the Jews to prefer to live in their own nation. In fact, except for a short decade between the late 1930s and the late 1940s, when almost all the other doors of the world were closed, the bulk of Jewish migration during the whole of the past century has gone to destinations other than Israel. Ahad Ha'am presumed that the existence of a modern Jewish culture in a national center would preserve the Diaspora. That center has now been in existence for several generations. It has not stopped the clock of assimilation in the Diaspora, or even radically affected it.

What is to be done? It is, of course, possible to maintain that large-scale destruction of our physical being has happened before, and so have ages of doubt and indifference. A minority of Jews is intensely Jewish in the Diaspora, and especially in Israel. It is the "saving remnant." The commandment of this day would then be simple: do what you have already been doing as Jews with as great passion as you can muster, and hope that in the long run, in half a century or so, out of the ten million Jews now present in the world, there will still be half or more who care as Jews.

Such a judgment asserts that the problems with which we are wrestling, are really no different, except perhaps in degree, than those of past ages—*but they are*. The era of the emancipation, the last two centuries, is the first time in Jewish history that Jewish existence, both in politics and faith, has become voluntary. This age is the first time in which secular conversion, rather than the traumatic choice of a change of religion, is the possibility open to Jews—and it is a possibility that is widely used. This is the first age in which, effectively, the Jewish people is in its majority postreligious, at least with respect to obedience to norms enforced by some authority. It is this unprecedented community, which has ever less of even the anchor of memory in an earlier, more orderly Jewish existence, that we are charged with preserving and inspiring. The problem before the Jewish world is not the minority that cares very much, but the majority that cares impressionistically, or not at all. It is for that majority that modern Jewish thought was invented, and modern Jewish politics and, yes, Zionism. It is this majority that, especially in the Diaspora, is ever less certain of its values.

The fundamental problem of world Jewry is not anti-Semitism. It was not in 1860, and it is not in 1981. On the contrary, a certain level of anti-Semitism, provided it is not murderous, has acted in the modern era as a preservative, artificially, of the Jewish community, even as it has been losing its inner content. The problem is loss of faith, of commitment, of raison d'être. The Diaspora offers the individual Jew many possibilities. He can find his reason for being at the smorgasbord of the West—in art, music, politics, or, most often, simply in the service of the bitch goddess, Success. It is the Jewish people that has no role of its own in the Diaspora, unless one wants to define raising money and political lobbying for the state of Israel as the content for centuries to come of Jewish existence. This, and only this, do Jews now do in the Diaspora, to a degree remarkably different than conventional actions of the best-educated elements of the Western bourgeoisie.

At the end of two centuries of the era of emancipation, we are thus at a tragic and fateful paradox which can no longer be escaped.

Those who rejected the emancipation, that small minority that opted out of it from the very beginning, seem safe as Jews in the new age. Those who accepted the emancipation are, in all their varieties, in far more substantial danger. Precisely because they care less about the Jewish component in their existence than do the self-ghettoized, the majority of Jews are today, as before, the ones more in need of radical solutions to their Jewish problem.

There is an answer to the question, Is Jewish continuity safe in the open society? The answer is, No.

This pessimism does not, of course, apply to the State of Israel, though Israeli society has not yet assumed stable form. Nonetheless, after more than a generation of statehood, despite its manifold problems, the prospect for the future of Israel as home for Jewishness in many varieties is bright. The problem area is the Diaspora, where Jews are by any index, whether economic or cultural, very successful as individuals, but where the continuity of the Jewish community is seriously in doubt.

There still remains the question, as yet unsolved and seemingly insoluble, of why? Why want to survive as a discrete people? In the name of what?

Two centuries of intellectual modernity in all its varieties prove one simple conclusion: universalist ideas such as democracy and socialism have not provided those Jews who have been their proponents with any long-range reason for remaining within a distinctly Jewish community. Ultimately, even if disguised in secular rhetoric, the reason for continuing a distinctly Jewish community has been religious.

I suspect that many more Jews believe in the God Who chose them than are willing to affirm that He also commanded them to be obedient to every stricture of the Halacha. Jewish disbelief is not of the variety that asserts "let us be like all the other nations." It wants to assert the divinely ordained mystery of Jewish existence without quite knowing what to do with the inherited Law.

The true watershed in Jewish life in the modern age is between those who share in awe at this otherness and those who would abandon it or forget about it. It is only to the degree to which such a conviction is alive that Jewish existence continues. Those for whom it has died remain at best, or at worst (there is no difference), Jews by situation.

Such a Jew has been described, at Auschwitz, by Jean Améry in a set of moving biographical essays. Améry's Jewishness amounted, even at the end, to the numbers tattooed on his wrist.[36] Sartre knew such Jews in the Resistance in the 1940s; they were people without a Jewish past or future, trapped in a tragic Jewish present.[37]

The Jewish people will not survive in the open society either in memory of the tragedy of the Holocaust or in contemplation from a distance of the glory of Israel. Of course, those who will choose *aliyah* to live in Israel will be secure in their destiny as Jews, but it is clear on present evidence that their numbers, especially those in relatively free and open societies, will not be overwhelming. Even with the help of Israel, to a far greater degree than obtains at the moment, the question remains open: is there enough positive energy in the postemancipation Jewish community for it finally to solve the problem of continuing as a discrete entity?

The problem exists today before world Jewry in all its gravity because now at last the momentum of the preemancipation Jewish ghetto is completely spent. The issues of "Judaism and modernity" and of "Jews in an open society" are even more open today than they were at the beginning of the era of the Emancipation.

1981

NINE

The Holocaust: In Debate with Man and God

Everyone who lived through the years when the Nazis dominated Europe, and made it their chief aim to murder Jews, cannot help but carry a large burden of guilt. Even those who spent no time in the death camps ask themselves (I know that I do), why did I survive, while so many Jews were murdered? Could the Jews in the free world have behaved differently, then, and would they have succeeded in saving some from death? Why were the powers of the world so largely indifferent? Why did they pretend not to know that these horrors were taking place? Most archives are open now. It is beyond doubt that the British and American governments knew. The German codes had been broken, and the Allies had day-by-day reports of the horrors being carried out in Nazi Europe. The Pope, Pius XII, was as well informed, from his own sources. The local bishops and other papal representatives in Central and Eastern Europe informed the Vatican in detail of the "actions" against the Jews, as they were taking place. Men failed in those years. But where was God?

These questions have continued to upset me all my adult life. Yet in the last forty years I have given perhaps five speeches on the Holocaust, and I have written only three essays. One was published in a magazine in 1970 and reprinted in 1979 in a previous book of mine, *Being Jewish in America*, under the title "A Generation Later." The other two appear in this chapter. I do not believe that I shall ever have the emotional strength to write about this subject again.

26. Who Looked Away?

The evidence is now incontrovertible that American Jewish leadership did know what was happening in Nazi Europe and that the Allied governments to which they were appealing knew even more precisely than the Jewish leaders the details of the horror. In England, the now famous decoding operation in Bletchley produced daily lists of the transports to the slaughter, and in Washington American intelligence sources were hardly less well informed. Certainly everybody knew what was going on *before* the war, in the 1930s, openly and in front of the eyes of the world. Why, then, was so little done?

The simplest answer, and the one that has been given over and over again, is to indict the Western governments for callousness and to castigate the Jewish leaders of that generation for conducting interorganizational feuds rather than uniting for rescue. There is just enough in both charges, and especially in the first, to obscure other factors that complete the picture and make moral judgment not an exercise in black and white but rather one in shades of gray. It is true that, despite Churchill's oft-proclaimed Zionism, he had his mind on other things during the war and that he essentially allowed the Jewish question to be dealt with by subordinates who preferred not to have a problem of more Jewish refugees, especially if they needed to be placed in Palestine. Roosevelt, despite a number of Jewish advisers in his entourage, did not have the instinctive concern for Jews in danger that was very much one of the passions of his wife Eleanor. His overriding interest was to win the war. He chose not to make the Jewish aspect of the war a central issue because he feared that to do so would lose domestic support. He was thus able, in good conscience, to send supplies across enemy lines through the Mediterranean in 1942 to alleviate hunger in Nazi-occupied Greece, but he drew no parallel from this action to the plight of Jews in Auschwitz and Majdenek.

Roosevelt and Churchill were the central figures whom Jewish leaders in the free world had to persuade to act. On the record, repeated approaches were made to both, and especially to Roosevelt, by delegation after delegation. The questions are, therefore, whether these delegations pressed hard enough and whether they mounted sufficient public outcry to lend force to their demands. The answer to both questions is that they did not, certainly not by the standards of today, when the Jewish community in America is much freer and more powerful than it was before and during World War II. Jews were afraid that the isolationists and the American Nazis would succeed in persuading the country that this was "Rosenfeld's War" and not a battle against the most evil tyranny that the world had ever seen. Jews, too, worried that Gold Star mothers would be persuaded that their sons had fallen in a narrow cause. The more "American" the Jewish leaders were, the more they worried about the future of the Jews in America itself and the more they tended to take the route of private persuasion rather than public outcry. But, in fairness, it must also be remembered that the Jewish community forty years ago, emerging from immigrant status, lacked the political muscle, financial means, and security that it now possesses.

To these considerations one must add the Zionist issue. Both before and during the war, international Zionist leaders, notably Chaim Weizmann and David Ben-Gurion, and American ones like Abba Hillel Silver, believed that the major hope for the future of the Jewish people was to put an end to its own powerlessness, its dependency on the goodwill of others, through the creation of a Jewish state. These men did intervene repeatedly with the Allied governments on behalf of the Jews being murdered in Europe, but their interventions were usually heard as being related to their desire to bring more Jews to Palestine, and thus, to break the policy that Great Britain had announced in 1939 effectively ending immigration to the "Jewish national home." For that matter, the Jewish community in Palestine in the war years, despite a few heroic incidents (a handful of parachutists were dropped in Hungary and Italy in 1944 but they were soon discovered), was not any more effective in the struggle to stop the Nazi murders than the Jews of America. In 1942, Palestine itself was in imminent danger, because Rommel was then at the gates of Cairo. The Jewish community was preparing itself for a last-ditch defense against the Nazi advance. A considerable number of Palestinian Jews, however, served with the Allied forces. Later in the war, several attempts were made through pressure on the British to open doors for those who might be saved from Hungary, Romania, and the Balkans. All failed, just as all attempts in America failed to elicit action, until 1944, when the War Refugee Board was created.

The core of the issue of responsibility can thus be clearly defined. The British and the American governments were essentially immovable. They did not want to deal with a specifically Jewish issue during the war even though at least some leaders in both governments knew all the facts about the slaughters. So, for example, the conference on refugees called by both governments in April 1943 in Bermuda was an elaborate charade designed to appear to express concern but not to do anything. In the face of all of this, even if the American Jewish organizations had not been factionalized, under-financed and too cautious, could they have done better?

Our answer is: they should have but they could not. Of course, world Jewry and, especially, the American Jews, the only major community relatively untouched by the war, should have cried out, day after day, to pierce the prevailing indifference. Certainly it was the moral obligation of this community not to continue with "business as usual." The silence was not caused by the immediate, all too usual, failures of organizations, which sometimes protected their turf or reflected their fears more than they kept their eye on the issue of rescue. This tragic failure cannot be blamed on these leaders alone. Most Jews were afraid to stand apart during the war and raise a separate Jewish issue. This was the attitude of a number of Jewish figures who were high on the councils of the Roosevelt administration, and were informed through government sources about the Jewish tragedy. With the exception of Henry Morgenthau, these men did not insist on bringing the issue of the rescue of Jews to the center of the political stage, or even to the center of Roosevelt's attention.

American Jewry was thus in a double trap, made up of its fears for itself, in a still anti-Semitic America, and of its cautious political attitudes, fashioned by many centuries of powerlessness in the Diaspora.

For centuries, the Jewish response to a time of danger had been to keep one's head down, to plead with the powerful of the earth: not to push them so far as to enrage them, and to hope that even the most devastating pogroms would destroy only a minority of the Jewish people. In fact, these attitudes worked relatively well in the first phase of Hitlerism, before the onset of the war. Quietly, without frontally assaulting American opinion to change quota restrictions against immigrants, and despite unfriendliness in some American consulates in Europe, many tens of thousands were admitted to the United States.

The policy of working even with anti-Semites, where a Jewish cause might be served, led the World Zionist Organization in 1934 to make an arrangement with the Nazis for the orderly transfer of some Jewish property to Palestine. Attitudes toward the Nazis were thus defined by casting them for the role, which they played in the first years of their rule, of old-line anti-Semites who could be dealt with by using conventional, time-honored Jewish defensive tactics.

The war years, when the mass killings took place, were hard times in which to change attitudes. It was only in 1944, when the war was clearly won, that Jews dared to mount enough concentrated pressure, both inside the Roosevelt administration and outside it, in Congress and public opinion, to bring about the creation of the War Refugee Board in January 1944. It was too late to save the millions already murdered, but many thousands were saved through the appointment of energetic WRB representatives with broad powers and ample funds. In Hungary, Raoul Wallenberg's heroic efforts, in cooperation with Charles Lutz of Switzerland and the valiant Zionist youth leaders, saved tens of thousands of Hungarian Jews from death camps. In Turkey, Ira Hirschman was instrumental in the rescue of large numbers of Jews from Romanian ships in Istanbul harbor and for an arrangement with the future Pope John XXIII (he was then the papal nuncio in Turkey) in which the Catholic church provided baptismal certificates to many thousands of Jews in Budapest. Also, despite certain political risks, Roosevelt authorized a secret deal by Hirschman to exchange four U.S. visas issued to the Romanian ambassador in

Ankara for the breakup of the death camp in Transdnistria and the release therefrom of many thousands of Jews.

The record of rescue after 1944 is, thus, far better than the record between 1942 and 1943 precisely because the fortunes of war had changed. Even in the last months of the war, much more could have been done; for example, the Allies still obdurately refused to bomb Auschwitz or the railroad lines leading to it. But there was far greater willingness by Jews to push hard. General John Dill, the British military liaison in Washington, found even the usually diplomatic Nahum Goldmann intolerably rude and pushy when he fought for such action.

Immediately after the surrender of Germany, in the years between 1945 and 1948, the very Jewish leadership that had been fearful and largely ineffective during the war was remarkably outspoken and courageous in confronting both the American and British governments in the cause of the creation of the State of Israel. Now confrontation and moral demand were the daily stuff of Jewish public action. In part, the motivation was guilt for having been ineffective in the cause of rescue during the war years. In largest measure, however, it was the change of situation. American Jewry, as part of a triumphant world power, was less afraid after 1945 to fight in public for specifically Jewish objectives.

Those who have kept calling for rethinking and reevaluating the Jewish response to the Holocaust have often said there is a lesson to be learned for the present. There is no point in pretending that there could be unanimity or consensus about such lessons. The ultra-Zionists among Jews argue that the Holocaust proves that, as a minority, Jews are ultimately safe nowhere; only in the Jewish state can they protect themselves through the use of power that is not dependent on the goodwill of others. Universalists assert that the lesson of the Holocaust is that no group in humanity is safe without some general assent everywhere to moral principles; one must work in a world ruled by humane international law. Neoconservatives in America have been saying in recent years that Jews must unabashedly protect their interests, even the least of them, whenever they are threatened, and not allow anyone to diminish their rights, for any slight attrition that goes unanswered is the preamble to tragedy. Liberals derive from the

Holocaust a contrary lesson—that only in nondogmatic pluralistic societies, in which communities relate to each other in such ways so as to preserve the social peace, is any group, including the Jews, ultimately safe.

There is only one conclusion that is beyond doubt: no matter how able the leadership of a besieged minority, or of a small people, may be in calling attention to its danger, there has to be someone out there willing to listen, who has the power to act. The human tragedy in the twentieth century, and in those centuries before, is that moral altruism is rare among the wielders of power. Yes, Jewish leaders during the war years did not cry out with sufficient effectiveness. They concluded from a long and bitter history that there were not many who would listen and that the masters of power would be angered by their importunity.

1984

27. A Lifelong Quarrel with God

Fifteen years ago, I took part in a large conference on the "lessons of the Holocaust." The meeting was held in New York but organized from Jerusalem by the Hebrew University. The participants included almost everyone, in Israel and America, who was then engaged in research or reflection about the murder of the Jews during the Nazi years. The conferees talked mostly about history, but they could not avoid—and they did not want to avoid—moral judgment. Ten years earlier, Hannah Arendt, in her account of *Eichmann in Jerusalem* (1963), had raised a new, most painful question: had the Jews, and especially their leaders, done enough to save themselves? Arendt had maintained that the Jewish organizations in Europe should have dissolved and burned their records. Some kept registers which the Nazi authorities used, and others were even forced to choose whom to send to "labor camps." It would have been better, so Arendt had argued, that the Jews had been left with no leaders: "There would have been chaos and plenty of misery," but more Jews could have escaped identification and more would have survived.

When Hannah Arendt had first announced these views, she was bitterly attacked by old friends, such as Gershom Scholem, and by an almost univocal Jewish establishment. How could anyone dare to suggest that the victims of the Nazis bore any share of the guilt for their own destruction?

Despite the passage of a decade, the question that Arendt had posed was still at the center of a painful debate. Tempers had cooled. Some of the participants at the New York conference were now willing to admit that, under the Nazis, the Jewish communities could have behaved differently—but almost everyone agreed that Arendt had made an unfair and demeaning demand of the dead. She asked Jews to have acted as if they knew that the Nazis intended to murder them all. But how could most of the victims bring themselves to believe this unprecedented horror, before—and even after—they reached the railroad siding in Auschwitz?

"The lessons of the Holocaust" have been discussed in many meetings since the first one that I attended, but that early conference remains vivid in my memory because of a passionate confrontation at its closing session. One of the participants challenged his colleagues to tell him what advice they could give the leaders of today, if Jews were again under attack from vicious anti-Semites. Would armed resistance be possible in an American suburb, if the police and the army were in the hands of Nazis and the surrounding population were hostile or passive? Could the organized Jewish community really be disbanded, if the Nazis put a gun at the head of all those who resisted office? Under this challenge, two Israeli historians, Saul Friedlander and Jacob Katz, responded that there were no "lessons," as such, to be learned from the Holocaust. One dare not demand that if Jews were ever again under serious attack, they should disband their communities, or that they should arm themselves to fight hopelessly, as had the heroes of the Warsaw Ghetto on Passover Week in April 1943. These had not been the only alternatives, even under the Nazis. Some of those who survived the Holocaust fought as partisans, but most had hidden. And yet those who were looking for "lessons" were, essentially, right. The study of the Holocaust may offer no answers, no clear guidance for conduct in the future, but the questions remain, and they are always the same.

Everyone who has been touched by the Holocaust—and what decent person has not?—has his own, personal quarrel with God, with men, and with himself.

I have never found a way to absolve God of the crime of Auschwitz. I reached bar-mitzvah in 1934, the year after Hitler came to power. Even as I participated in the ritual of the Hasidic synagogue in Baltimore, of which my father was the rabbi, I knew that I had come to doubt God. How could He let the Nazis win? My troubles with God have inevitably increased year after year. I find no help in those who say that He is a limited Power who encourages humanity to do good but is not responsible for the pain and evil in the world. Naturalist, "this-worldly" theologians, such as Mordecai Kaplan, were talking of a "limited God" long before the Nazis appeared, as an answer to the problem of evil. But such a God is essentially created in the image of a fashionable preacher in a bourgeois synagogue or church; He has the power to exhort but not to command and, therefore, He has no responsibility for what is happening in life.

The most elegant version of this idea—that God is not responsible for evil, and especially not for the ultimate evil of the Holocaust—was fashioned by Martin Buber in his *Eclipse of God* (1952). He invoked the cabalistic image that God sometimes "hides his face," that He absents Himself from the world and so darkness rules. Buber turned this notion around, to suggest not that God had chosen to go away, but that some dark power eclipsed Him for a time. But, as I once screamed at Buber himself in his home in Jerusalem, what right had God to go away, or to permit Himself to be eclipsed, while my grandfather and all of my mother's brothers and sisters and their children were being murdered?

I have always been even angrier with those who find reasons with which to justify the ways of God, as He acted in the 1930s and 1940s. These theologies seem rooted in Scripture. In the historical books of the Bible, the usual explanation for the suffering of the Jews is that they had disobeyed the will of God and, thus, they deserved to be punished. So, an ultra-Orthodox Jewish theologian, Rabbi Joel Teitelbaum, the Rebbe of Satmar, insisted in a book in Hebrew, entitled *On Salvation and Redemption* (1967) that the Jews were punished by God for the sin of Zionism, for refusing, as they had been commanded, to wait passively for the Messiah; the Zionists had rebelled against God by creating the State of Israel by their own hand. Many Zionists, including even David Ben-Gurion, argued the opposite, that the Holocaust was the punishment of history on those Jews who refused to leave Europe in time, long before 1933, for their own national home. That God, or His secular avatar "history," would let a million and a quarter small children, and five million of their parents and grandparents, die horribly because they were either too Zionist, or not Zionist enough, has always seemed to me to be an obscene idea. In my angrier moments, I have said, and not only to myself, that a God with such motives deserves to be defied.

A number of my friends, who were firmly Orthodox before 1933, became fierce atheists. I have not joined them because I keep re-reading the Book of Job. Every conceivable woe happens to this righteous man, Job. He rejects all the explanations that his solicitous friends try to offer him. Ultimately he summons God to give him an answer. Replying out of the whirlwind, God offers Job no explanation, but He does not disclaim responsibility. "Where were you," God asks Job, "when I founded the world?" His powers are indeed un-limited, and He is never absent from the world, either by choice or because He is in eclipse. God simply asserts that there is meaning to the world, and even to Job's suffering, but it is beyond man's un-derstanding. And yet, even as I read these verses over and over again, I keep asking the question: what about Job's children? Job survived the tragedy of their death, but could he ever forgive God?

Why God was silent from 1939 to 1945 will forever be a mystery. The disbeliever will insist that this silence proves God's irrelevance or his nonexistence; the believer will hold on to the faith that the world adds up, but only in the mind of God.

The conversation about the Holocaust that lives with me—and haunts me—was one that never took place. Rabbi Aaron Rokeach, the rebbe of Belz in southeastern Poland, lost his entire family—his wife and all his children and their children—in the Holocaust. He never again mentioned them, or even said prayers in any visible ritual in their memory. I was in his presence in Tel Aviv in the summer of 1949. I tried to get the rebbe to talk to me about my grandfather and my uncles who had been his disciples and friends, but he simply did not respond, not even with a gesture. The dead were too holy, so his closest associates explained, to need words. The rebbe of Belz had accepted the tragedy, his and everyone else's, in silence—and he was rebuilding his Hasidic court in the Holy Land. Silence and rebuilding—that was how he spoke for his faith in God.

I have had even more trouble believing in man. Throughout the thirties, as I was growing up, I continued to believe that decent people would ultimately band together and make a stand against the Nazis. This hope was shattered, for me, in the darkest days of the Second World War in June 1940, when France was falling. It was the week of my graduation from Johns Hopkins, and so I went to say farewell to the professors who had taught me. In the office of one of the younger instructors, I mentioned the fear that the Nazis might come to America, and I asked this teacher what he would do. He answered that he knew that I had no escape, but, as a Gentile, he had choices. If a Gauleiter would ever be sent to the university, this professor would stay on, to protect the library as best he could, and to keep some humanist values alive. He added that he would do nothing to endanger himself by protesting or resisting the expulsion of the Jews. He would certainly not risk hiding me in his cellar.

And so I had encountered the American version of a "good German," one who might ultimately persuade himself not just to look away but even to collaborate in order to defend his "values." I was, thus, prepared early for the prelate whom I met at an interfaith conference in Europe in the 1970s. He wanted me to think well of him, so he told that as a parish priest in 1943 in a city under Nazi occupation, he had hidden a Scroll of the Torah, which a Jew had brought to his rectory. I could not stop myself from asking him: "Why did you not hand the Nazis the Torah and hide the Jew?"

In 1950 a massive study of the Nazis, and of anti-Semitism in general, was published by the American Jewish Committee. This series of five books made famous the title of its largest volume, *The Authoritarian Personality*. The essential thesis of the study was that Nazis and other Jew-haters were skewed, sick people. If "authoritarian personalities" were cured of their disease, anti-Semitism would end. This study was done by Freudians, many of whom were also Marxists. They suggested that authoritarian personalities are bred, most often, by the discontinuities of capitalism and that they would disappear in a communist society. This study was, of course, nonsense. One did not have to cite Joseph Stalin, the ultimate Communist, who was clearly an "authoritarian personality," or to wait until 1963 for Hannah Arendt to describe Eichmann as a banal bureaucrat, to disprove the argument. At the Nuremberg trials in 1946, four years before these volumes appeared, it was clear that the Nazi generals, and the architect Albert Speer and the banker Hjalmar Schacht, were not lunatics. They were practical men, clearheaded leaders of the Nazi regime to whom the fate of the Jews, or of the Gypsies, simply did not matter.

The knowledge that most of the world looks away from the pain and murder of the weak is no personal monopoly of mine—but is there a clear lesson to be derived from this bitter wisdom? Menachem Begin spoke for one attitude among Jews, when he proclaimed, over and over, "never again." This slogan is used, most often, by those who feel that Jews can ultimately trust only other Jews, and that those whose relatives once went quietly to the slaughter must now be tough in their own interest.

But what about the million or more who did survive the Holocaust in Europe? Most owed their lives to "righteous Gentiles" who took mortal risks, often for strangers. In the memorial of the Holocaust in Jerusalem, Yad Vashem, there is a growing alley of trees planted in honor of these friends.

In the mid-1980s, I took part in a Jewish tribute to the people of Denmark. In October 1943 the Danes had hidden 7,200 Jews, and 800 of their non-Jewish relatives, and had ferried them to Sweden. Forty years later this heroism was remembered in New York by speeches of praise and by the gift of educational scholarships. One of the speakers shattered the warm and glowing mood. He insisted that praising the Danes was too easy; they needed to be emulated. He asked: For whom were we, who were now comfortable in New York, willing to man the boats on dark nights? Were we willing to be less well off, to help the homeless and the growing underclass? Were we, as Jews who care passionately about Israel, willing to let ourselves feel the pain and the sense of loss of Palestinians?

The most painful of all debates among Jews about the Holocaust is the question of their own responsibility—witness the reaction to

Hannah Arendt. In the United States, there is by now a large literature of self-criticism. It has been established that American Jewish leaders knew of the mass murders almost as they were happening. Everyone else could have known from a careful reading of newspaper accounts during the war. Haskell Lookstein in *Were We Our Brother's Keepers?* (1985) and Deborah Lipstadt in *Beyond Belief* (1986) have proved this point. In the spring of 1943, Hayim Greenberg, writing in Yiddish, said Kaddish, the memorial prayer, not for the Jews of Europe but for the moral demise of the Jews in America who were not doing enough to save their brethren. That spring three seminary students, led by Jerome Lipnick, published a manifesto demanding that Nazis be pushed by the Allies to stop murdering Jews and treat them all as "prisoners of war." Even earlier, in the fall of 1941, my father, Rabbi Zvi Elimelech Hertzberg, pleaded in the *Jewish Daily Forward* that all the Jews of America should converge on Washington. He hoped that hundreds of thousands in the streets would persuade our government to intervene, to save the lives of the Jews in Hitler's Europe. He was not heeded; the Jews did not converge on Washington then, and the Nazis did not desist. The murders continued in occupied Europe to the very end of the war. Franklin Delano Roosevelt certainly knew, both from his own intelligence sources and from what Jewish delegates were telling him, as David Wyman proved in *The Abandonment of the Jews* (1984). Some have attributed the failure of the American Jewish community to move Roosevelt to its weakness; the Jews did not want the domestic anti-Semites, who abounded in the 1930s and 1940s, to attack them for supposedly having dragged America into the war with the Nazis. Others have argued that the Jewish community did the maximum within its power to influence policy, but most Jews were still poor and powerless, then, and many were still immigrants. The Jewish lobby of those days was not even a pale shadow of today.

And so, in expiation of the sins of the fathers, whose quiet interventions in Washington did little good, this generation of American Jewish leaders is largely confrontationist with enemies and critics. Holocaust consciousness has created a sense of Jews as an embattled bastion in the very America of today, which is free and open enough for Jews to enshrine their most painful memory in museums in very public places. But there is a deep truth to this paradox. Somewhere within men and women of my generation remains the question I ask myself in my darkest thoughts about each of those friends who are not Jews: who among them would risk his life, if Hitler ever came again, to hide my grandchildren? But that fearful doubt is always accompanied by another: how would I behave inside Auschwitz if it were ever built in Scarsdale, or in Idaho, or near Camp David? I cannot answer either of these questions with certainty. I must hope—and work to increase the hope—that these questions will never be asked again.

And so, after a half century of thinking about the Holocaust, of hearing many stories, and of reading many books, I am left with a lifelong quarrel with God, and ambivalent relationships with the Gentile world, with Jews—and with myself. Even though I was once overwhelmed by the silence of the rebbe of Belz, I cannot join him. I must light candles in memory of my family, and I continue to grieve over the horror of their deaths—but it is their lives that I want to remember. Let the barracks remain in Auschwitz, untouched, as a warning to the world, that humanity should never again pollute the earth with such buildings. The Jew within me cannot forget the gas chambers, but what I most want to remember are the children who published a daily newspaper in Theresienstadt, the inmates of Auschwitz who held forbidden prayer services, and the heroes of the Warsaw Ghetto, in the years before the revolt, who conducted schools in defiance of Nazi edicts. This is what I have learned from rereading the Book of Job on the aftermath of the Holocaust. After his disaster Job begat a new family, re-created his flocks and herds, and did good again to all who came into his sight. Job remembered what he had lost, but he did not simply continue to scream; he lived on.

During Passover week Jews remember the revolt in the Warsaw Ghetto. The rising began on April 19, 1943, on the eve of Passover, that year, and the last of the resistance was not crushed by the Nazis until May 16. This hopeless revolt has become a great symbol; these were Jews who died fighting. In recent years, the passive Jews, those who supposedly went too quietly to their deaths, are being "pardoned." The gruesomeness of the tortures are now at the center of concern, "lest we forget." One cannot be like the rebbe of Belz and be silent. One must remember—but what are we to remember? Only how six million Jews died, or how they lived?

Very recently two new collections about the history of the Holocaust have been published. One is *The Encyclopedia of the Holocaust,* in four volumes, edited by Israel Gutman, a survivor who is head of research at Yad Vashem and professor at the Hebrew University; the other is thirty-two reels of microfilm, which have just been made available by the YIVO Institute for Jewish Research, containing a hundred and fifty periodicals published in the displaced persons camps immediately after the liberation in 1945. The *Encyclopedia* contains definitive accounts of the woes that happened during the Nazi years, but these volumes are most important for their collection of innumerable stories of men, women, and, above all, children whom the Nazis could kill but could not break. The periodicals that YIVO has collected and is now making available contain horrifying stories of the immediate past, but the main purpose of these survivor journals was to announce, in the Yiddish phrase that they used over and over again, "mir zeinen doh" (we are here).

The survivors did not dwell on death; they rebuilt life. This was the lesson they were teaching: a people must remember, but it cannot live on by making a cult of its woes. The faith of the Jews is not simply remembering the Holocaust; it is the Jewish religion, which—before and after the Nazis—reasserts the verse in Psalms, "I will not die, for I will live." Those who remained after the Holocaust, and their children and grandchildren, must live all the harder, and all the more decently, to carry on for every one of the unfinished lives.

1990

TEN

Concluding Reflections

The most powerful of all biblical visions is the dream of the end of days. The Messiah will come. All wrongs will be righted. Human life will henceforth be lived in bliss in the sight of the Lord. The specific woe of the Jews, their exile from the land that God gave them, will come to an end.

Through the centuries this dream has provided hope, but it has also been the source of disaster. The greatest danger of all has been to imagine, in critical times, that messianic days are at hand, and that men can therefore act as if they know what time it is on God's clock. The "armed zealots" who revolted against Rome in the year 66 were certain that the "end of days" was near. Most of the rabbis of that day were opposed to revolt. They did not believe that anyone could know the will of God; pretending to know the date of the coming of the Messiah was a dangerous, and even heretical, exercise. The rabbis have never abandoned the dream of the Messiah but, through the centuries, they have kept insisting that Jews dare not ever bet their lives, in war or politics, on the hope that he would appear, now, to save them. A fundamental, and continuing, tension exists in Jewish history between those who pant for the Messiah and plunge into danger to "force him to appear," and those who wait and act in this world with tact and pragmatism.

This tension exists not only within the religious tradition; it cuts across the secular ideologies that many Jews have adopted in recent times. In the modern era, the most contemporary minds among Jews in the nineteenth century have been eager believers in the inevitability of progress. The Enlightenment in the eighteenth century offered the dream of a heaven on earth, if only men and women would free themselves of the chains of the existing society. Many responded to this vision by being willing to assimilate, to abandon their Jewish separateness so that they might fit into a new society. Karl Marx translated the dream of the Enlightenment into economic terms: a society of equal individuals could be created, but only in a world order that had abolished class distinctions. All the hatreds that came from economic inequities would be gone. Marx was certain that a classless society was inevitable, for the dialectic of history would produce it. This assurance of a new heaven on earth enticed many Jews, because, as Marx himself had insisted in 1843 in an early essay "On the Jewish Question," anti-Semitism would disappear if its economic roots in class struggle were cut.

As I have noted in these essays, the certainty of progress was challenged among Jews by the persistence of anti-Semitism. Several central figures of the Enlightenment, such as Voltaire, had regarded the Jews as very nearly hopeless, as incapable of "regeneration." During the French Revolution, some Jacobin radicals wanted to exclude Jews from the new order of equality. A generation later, the socialist Pierre Joseph Proudhon regarded Jews as the archcapitalists who needed to be destroyed; they could not be transformed even by a new socialist society. More painful than these theories was the continuing reality of anti-Semitism. One could explain away its continued virulence in benighted Tsarist Russia, but not the renewed strength of this disease in the 1890s in centers of advanced culture such as Vienna, where Wilhelm Marr was elected mayor on an anti-Jewish platform, and in Paris, where Captain Alfred Dreyfus was judged to be a traitor on fabricated evidence because he was a Jew. By the end of the nineteenth century many people, and especially Jews, found it harder to believe that the day of a just and peaceful society was near. Even if the non-Jewish majorities were to sort out their problems and move into a golden dawn, some feared that the Jews were likely to be left behind.

At this bleak moment Theodor Herzl reinvented Zionism as utopia, as a messianic movement. He asserted that heaven on earth for Jews could be achieved, and it was indeed inevitable, through political Zionism. The unique power of Theodor Herzl's pamphlet, *The Jewish State* (1896), was not in any appeal to Jewish national emotions, for he himself was so totally estranged from the inherited practices of Jews that he did not even circumcise his children. There was almost nothing in Herzl's original vision of restoring ancient Jewish glories in the Holy Land, for he was willing to consider a Jewish state in empty land in Argentina, if that were more easily available. Herzl's vision of the culture that would prevail in the future Jewish state was nebulous; he seemed to have imagined some version of Vienna or Paris, without anti-Semites to trouble the Jews. Nonetheless, this Jewish "goy" almost instantly became the leader of the Zionists, most of whom were deeply rooted in Jewish culture and history.

Herzl offered them something more than an imposing presence and a gift for staging diplomatic theater. He suggested a solution to the "Jewish problem": Jews should choose between living in a state of their own or total assimilation everywhere else; thus the situation of the Jewish people would be "normalized." By creating a state, and making such choice possible, the "Jewish problem," the anomaly of Jewish existence everywhere as an embattled minority, would be brought to an end, once and for all.

The state of Israel did not arise according to Herzl's blueprint. Even in his lifetime the Zionist movement refused to follow his detachment from Jewish culture. But Herzl's Zionist vision has remained dominant, to this day. The Jewish state thinks of itself not just as a refuge for Jews in trouble, or as a place in which Judaism can define itself in a home of its own, but as the climactic achievement of Jewish history. The Zionist movement continues to insist, in its official platform, that Jews who dwell outside the state of Israel are in a "state of sin," because they are obstructing the normalization of the Jewish people. The leaders of Israel, almost without exception, from right to left, have no doubt that Israel's purposes must predominate in setting the agenda in the Jewish world, and not simply because the state is embattled. The deepest undercurrent is the conviction that the Zionist state is the transforming event of Jewish history and that it is, at the very least, a preamble to the end of days, in this world.

But even within Zionism itself, a countertradition has existed. Ahad Ha'am, the central figure of cultural Zionism, did not believe that the Messiah, in either secular or religious garb, was around the corner. The problems of the Jewish people would remain, for no resolution of the tensions between Jews and the world could be found through progress, or socialism, or nationalism. A homeland was necessary, so that Jews could reinvigorate their spiritual energies in a place where they would, at last, be the majority culture. Ahad Ha'am's Zionism was thus a holding operation; he was devising a new tool through which the Jewish people could maintain its morale, while continuing to make again the myriad of pragmatic accommodations through which the Jews had survived the centuries of their exile. In this attitude Ahad Ha'am was followed by Martin Buber and Judah Leon Magnes and, more recently, by Gershom Scholem and Isaiah Leibovits. Their hopes for the Zionist state have ranged from casting it as a place of refuge to hoping that it would be a model community for all the world, but all these thinkers, and many more besides, have agreed on a fundamental premise: to concentrate part of the Jewish people into a nation of its own is necessary, for Jews need some national power in their own hands, but achieving the Zionist state does not represent the ultimate redemption of the Jews. The business of the Jewish people as a whole, and especially of that part that has settled in the state, is to be conducted prudently, and without grandiose pretensions.

Messianic believers and pragmatists have also been quarreling about religion. Some elements within the Orthodox community insist that the Messiah is near at hand. The Temple is about to be restored, and the Holy Land, in Jewish hands, will be the permanent spiritual center for all humanity. In the name of this certainty, not one inch of the soil of the land of Israel can be surrendered, even if political reasons are advanced, for such action would betray God's will. This Orthodox religious messianism has gone to war not only over "foreign policy"; these believers have also broken the tissue of pragmatic ac-commodations among the factions within the Jewish community. The very idea that Jews have become a plural people which harbors many versions of belief, or disbelief, has been dismissed as concession to heresy. The arrangements that make it possible for these disparate groups to exist together as Jews are not to be fostered, repaired, or renegotiated; they are simply to be swept away.

Both secular and religious messianists have been self-centered. The ultra-Orthodox regard other Jews as a disturbing periphery. Their senses of hurt, if such there be, are irrelevant to those who regard themselves as the true bearers of Judaism. The ultranationalists, whether secular or religious, look at the world of the non-Jews as a source of help to be used, or of obstruction to be removed. The moderates have opposed such self-centeredness in all its forms. They have worked for peace within the Jewish community; they have insisted on justice and equality in the behavior of Jews toward Arabs. The moderates remain convinced that ethnocentrism and self-righteousness are self-defeating. They are sure that, though ultra-Orthodoxy has recently been creating turmoil within the Jewish community, it cannot win unless the Messiah really appears on the side of these believers. The moderates point out that ultranationalism has embittered the Arabs, but it cannot cow them into submission. It cannot win a permanent victory unless the war of Gog and Magog soon commences, and the Messiah, with sword, subdues the Arabs.

I do not belong to the messianic believers. I do not believe that the Jews will soon become a "normal people" by being gathered into Zion. On the contrary, the State of Israel is profoundly important because it has added contemporary energy to the Jewishness of all Jews, wherever they might continue to live. I am even less persuaded that the Messiah of religious belief will soon appear. I continue to ask the nagging question: if he did not appear at Auschwitz, why is he more likely to come to earth to save the West Bank for Jewish sovereignty?

The Jewish people cannot survive among the nations in an attitude of defiance. What echoes within me—and in these essays—is an attitude that was once defined in the Talmud: if you are planting a sapling and hear that the Messiah is coming, finish the planting before you leave to look for him. And I continue to remember a more pointed remark by one of the rabbis in the Talmud: if the Messiah will appear only amidst suffering and injustice, let him come but I will not receive him. We are commanded to cultivate decency in a world that only God can redeem, in His own time. This faith is the true utopian vision of the Jews.

ENDNOTES

1. See Edward Tivnan, *The Lobby: Jewish Political Power and American Foreign Policy* (New York: Simon and Schuster, 1987), which gives a careful account of AIPAC's influence and activities.

2. Shimon Peres recently said on Israeli television's prime news show (*Mabat*, December 30, 1987) that King Hussein was ready to accept control of Gaza—but Peres has more than once reported that King Hussein was ready to act decisively when the king was, at most, floating a trial balloon. Peres' interview was ignored by the government in Amman.

3. A new and important book, published in Hebrew, by Yosef Salmon, *Religion and Zionism: First Encounters* (Jerusalem: Ha-Sifriyah ha-Tsiyonit, 1990) makes it clear that the founders of religious Zionism were not apocalyptic believers who wanted the "end of days." In Salmon's account "they put off a personal messiah to later history which no longer depends on human effort." Even today, when many of their heirs have become hard-liners, these moderate views still have adherents among religious Zionists.

4. Gershom Scholem, *Mi-Berlin li-Yerushalayim* (Tel Aviv: Am Oved, 1982), p. 53.

5. Gershom Scholem, *Devarim be-Go* (Tel Aviv: 1975) Am Oved, pp. 385–403. The essay first appeared in *Luach Ha'aretz* (Tel Aviv: Haim Publishing, 1945). It is entitled "Mi-Toch Hirhurim al Hochmat Yisrael."

6. Scholem, *Mi-Berlin li-Yerushalayim*, p. 213.

7. This was said in the first of two letters to Walter Benjamin from Jerusalem, dated February 20, 1930, reprinted in Hebrew translation in Scholem, *Devarim be-Go*, pp. 146–147.

8. Scholem, *Mi-Berlin li-Yerushalayim*, p. 81.

9. Scholem, *Devarim be-Go*, p. 46. Scholem told, in the course of a long interview in 1974, that Alan Ginsburg, the American poet, had visited him and that his wife, "as was her wont," had asked Ginsburg why he did not move to Israel. Scholem then added: "I never ask anybody. . . . A person knows whether to go or not. To behave this way is for me a matter of basic principle. . . . I do not find within myself the strength to say to anyone that he must come to the land of Israel—but my wife is different." This was the opinion of Scholem in his latter years, for the young Scholem, as his letters to Benjamin and many passages in his autobiography attest, was a passionate preacher of *aliyah*.

10. Scholem, *Devarim be-Go*, p. 219.

11. Ibid., pp. 534 and 537.

12. Ibid., p. 220.

13. Ibid., pp. 385–403; on Abraham Geiger, see pp. 392–93.

14. Scholem, "Hirhurim al Afsherut shel Mistikah Yehudit be-Yameinu," in *Devarim be-Go*, p. 79.

15. Ibid., p. 81.

16. Scholem, "The Holiness of Sin" (Mitzvah Haba be-Averah), in J. P. Lachover, ed., *Knesset*, (Tel Aviv: DVIR, 1937), 374–92.

17. Scholem, "Hirhurim al Afsherut shel Mistikah Yehudit be-Yameinu," in *Devarim be-Go*, p. 82.

18. Ibid.

19. Scholem, "Hagigim al Teologiah Yehudit," in *Devarim be-Go*, pp. 587–88.

20. Ibid., pp. 589–90.

21. Scholem, *Mi-Berlin li-Yerushalayim*, p. 60.

22. Harold Bloom, *Agon: Towards a Theory of Revisionism* (New York: Oxford University Press, 1982), p. 325, in an essay entitled "Free and Broken Tablets: The Cultural Prospects of American Jewry."

23. Scholem, "Hagigim al Teologiah Yehudit," in *Devarim be-Go*, p. 588. See also *Mi-Berlin li-Yerushalayim*, pp. 212–13.

24. The *Ma'ariv* interviews have been translated from the Hebrew text.

25. My thanks to Malcolm Hoenlein, the executive director of the Jewish Community Relations Council, and to Henry Siegman, executive vice president of the American Jewish Congress, for making the data for these studies available to me. The interpretation in this article is my own.

26. In keeping with Shamir's decision at the beginning of March, AIPAC has tried to cover some of its tracks. Several of its officials have been making speeches at Jewish meetings in which they have deplored the letter of the thirty senators. However, the most recent fund-raising letter circulated by AIPAC simply asserts the hope that some solution will be found for the continuing crisis in the territories; and the letter mentions Senators Edward Kennedy and Daniel Patrick Moynihan, who were among the principal signers of the letter of the thirty, as admiring AIPAC's activities. It is worth recalling that in 1984 the pro-Israel Political Action Committees, which are under AIPAC's influence, made intense and successful efforts to defeat Senator Charles Percy of Illinois because he said that while Israel's existence and security must be insured, the Palestinians should be allowed national expression. The

Israel lobby is doing no such thing now in any of the campaigns for reelection by the signers of the recent letter.

27. Franz Rosenthal, *Knowledge Triumphant* (Leiden: E. J. Brill, 1970), p. 96.

28. Moses Maimonides, *The Guide of the Perplexed*, translated with an introduction by Shlomo Pines and an introductory essay by Leo Strauss (Chicago: University of Chicago Press, 1963), p. cxviii.

29. These quotations are from the preface and introductory essay by Isadore Twersky to his *A Maimonides Reader* (New York: Behrman House, 1972); see especially pp. xiv and 26. It was revealing that later, in his magnum opus on Maimonides as a legalist, entitled *Introduction to the Code of Maimonides* (New Haven: Yale University Press, 1980), Twersky twice denies that Maimonides was very much influenced by Arabic models. But he also admits (pp. 77 and 259) that even Maimonides "was generally aware of the surrounding tendencies" in the Islamic world to write codes of law, and that this could have provided a stimulus for him. It is intriguing that in a long and definitive volume on the *Mishneh Torah*, the subject of Islamic models is dismissed in a few lines, with the assertion, in the second passage, that the subject cannot really be investigated.

30. Arthur Hertzberg, *The French Enlightenment and the Jews* (New York: Columbia University Press, 1968), pp. 185, 272–7, 292.

31. Malcolm Stern, *Americans of Jewish Descent* (Cincinnati Hebrew College Press, passim).

32. *American Jewish Yearbook* (Philadelphia: Jewish Publication Society, 1973) pp. 292–93.

33. Arthur Hertzberg, *Being Jewish in America* (New York: Schocken, 1979), pp. 82–83.

34. Martin Buber, *For the Sake of Heaven* (Philadelphia: Jewish Publication Society, 2nd ed., 1953), pp. 96, 258ff.

35. J. L. Talmon, *Political Messianism: The Romantic Phase* (London: Secker and Warburg 1960), pp. 77–81.

36. Jean Améry, *At the Mind's Limits* (Bloomington: Indiana University Press, 1980).

37. Jean Paul Sartre, *Anti-Semite and Jew* (New York: Schocken, 1948), p. 96.